Queers Online

This book is number six in the series *Gender and Sexuality in Information Studies*, Emily Drabinski, series editor.

Also in the series:

Ephemeral Material: Queering the Archive, by Alana Kumbier

Feminist and Queer Information Studies Reader, edited by Patrick Keilty and Rebecca Dean

Feminist Pedagogy for Library Instruction, by Maria T. Accardi

Make Your Own History: Documenting Feminist and Queer Activism in the 21st Century, edited by Lyz Bly and Kelly Wooten

Out Behind the Desk: Workplace Issues for LGBTQ Librarians, edited by Tracy Nectoux.

Queers Online

LGBT Digital Practices in Libraries, Archives, and Museums

Edited by Rachel Wexelbaum

Litwin Books
Sacramento, CA

Copyright respective authors, 2014

Published in 2015 by Litwin Books

Litwin Books
PO Box 188784
Sacramento, CA 95818

This book is printed on acid-free, sustainably-sourced paper.

Library of Congress Cataloging-in-Publication Data

Queers online : LGBT digital practices in libraries, archives, and museums / edited by Rachel Wexelbaum.
    pages cm. -- (Gender and sexuality in information studies ; no. 6)
  Includes bibliographical references and index.
  ISBN 978-1-936117-79-6 (alk. paper)
  1. Libraries--Special collections--Sexual minorities. 2. Sexual minorities--Computer network resources. 3. Library materials--Digitization. 4. Libraries and sexual minorities. 5. Sexual minorities--Archives. 6. Archival materials--Digitization. 7. Museums and minorities. 8. Museum conservation methods. 9. Digital preservation. I. Wexelbaum, Rachel.
  Z688.S47Q44 2015
  025.2730776--dc23
                              2014047417

Table of Contents

Acknowledgements vii

Introduction. 1

A Note on Language and Acronyms 3

Section One 5

    Introduction to Section One: Queering the Online Realm. 7

    Preserving the "Nexus of Publics":
    A Case for Collecting LGBT Digital Spaces
    Kevin Powell 9

    Pornographic Website as Public History Archive: A Case Study
    Sine Nomine 19

    Organizing the Transgender Internet: Web Directories
    and Envisioning Inclusive Digital Spaces
    Jane Sandberg. 43

    Queering Wikipedia
    Rachel Wexelbaum, Katie Herzog, and Lane Rasberry 61

Section Two 81

    Introduction to Section Two: Transitioning from Print to
    Digital in LGBT Archives 83

    Tape-by-Tape: Digital Practices and Cataloguing
    Rituals at the Lesbian Herstory Archives
    Shawn(ta) D. Smith-Cruz 85

Privacy, Context & Pride: The Management of Digital
Photographs in a Queer Archives
Rebecka Sheffield and Kate Zieman 111

Copyright, Copywrong, and Ethics: Digitising Records
of the Australian Gay and Lesbian Movements from 1973
Graham Willett and Steve Wright 129

Section Three **145**

Introduction to Section Three: Nuts and Bolts of Queer
Digitization Projects 147

Open Up! LGBT History Coming Out of the Closet
Sally Johnson and Michel Otten 149

Documenting an Aftermath:
The Matthew Shepard Web Archive
Laura Uglean Jackson 165

Lesbian Gay Bisexual Transgender Religious
Archives Network 181

Section Four **201**

Introduction to Section Four: Still Not Totally Out: Continuing
Obstacles to Queer Resource Access 203

Censorship of Online LGBTIQ Content in Libraries
Rachel Wexelbaum 205

The Quest for LGBTIQ EBooks
Rachel Wexelbaum 215

Afterword **229**

Author Bios **231**

Acknowledgements

It is not easy writing a book chapter. For some contributors, this was their first time ever writing for publication. I would like to recognize their courage, patience during the editing process, and willingness to dig deeper if I asked. I would also like to recognize the time that harried graduate students and overworked librarians and archivists took out of their busy schedules to write in the first place. It is worth it, believe me.

I would like to thank series editor Emily Drabinski for her patience and support during the creation of this book. I would like to thank her for believing in me, and believing in this project.

I would like to thank Lambda Literary Foundation for supporting and promoting my international LGBTIQ reading study, which provided important information for my chapter on LGBTIQ EBooks.

A posthumous thank you goes to Wikipedan Adrianne Wadewitz for her detailed responses to my interview questions for the Wikipedia chapter. I am honored that she thought it was important enough to do in the middle of working on nearly 40,000 Wikipedia entries and providing Wikipedia education across the country.

A special thank you goes to Lonneke von den Hoonaard of IHLIA, who helped Sally Johnson and Michael Otten bring the story of the "Open Up!" Project forward. I also would like to thank her for her hospitality during the 2012 LGBTI conference at IHLIA LGBT heritage in the Open Bare Bibliotheek in Amsterdam.

I am grateful to St. Cloud State University for approving my sabbatical to complete this book. Thank you to my staff and colleagues at Learning Resources Services for juggling my duties during that time. Thank you Judith Thrush and Kathleen Smith, who always supported my ambition for writing and research before, during, and after library school. It was in library school where I encountered the pioneer Ellen Greenblatt, who gave me an example to follow. Last but not least, thank you so much Ping Lew for twenty years of love and acceptance.

Our writers would like to thank the following people and organizations that helped make their work possible:

Dr. Ciaran B. Trace for her encouragement and help with the draft, and Jennifer Hecker for being an excellent mentor and professional role model (Kevin Powell);

Becca Songert for her editing help and friendship (Jane Sandberg);

Tom of Finland Foundation as well as Jay R. Lawton (Katie Herzog);

Maxine Wolfe for her careful editing, Saskia Scheffer for her openness, and Rachel Corbman for her willingness—thanks to all of them for their contributions to the chapter (Shawn(ta) Smith-Cruz).

Introduction

Preservation versus access. For centuries, librarians, archivists, and museum curators have walked a tightrope in their attempt to define the mission and activities of their institutions. On one hand, we collect treasures and wish to protect them from harm. On the other hand, we want to open the doors and share the resources so that current and future generations can appreciate them.

In or out of the closet, stealth or not stealth. As individuals, lesbians, gay men, bisexuals, transgender, intersex and queer (LGBTIQ) individuals around the world have each grappled with this decision. Each person, and each community, has an identity and history that they may or may not want the heterosexual or cisgender worlds to know. To this day, LGBTIQ people in most countries—including the United States—still do not have the same personal protections and civil rights as cisgender heterosexual people. For this reason, LGBTIQ spaces have existed in secret. This need for safe spaces and protection has had a major effect on how LGBTIQ communities have decided to record and preserve their histories and cultures. It has also made LGBTIQ individuals and communities become early adopters of online communications and digital spaces.

As physical LGBTIQ spaces—bookstores, cafes, bars—yield to online ones, librarians, archivists, and museum curators handling LGBTIQ books, photographs, and other artifacts walk the preservation versus access tightrope. In the age of Google and Wikipedia, people can easily find "good enough" information on any subject—including LGBTIQ people. Most of that information, however, is recycled from secondary and tertiary sources. Libraries, archives, and museums with LGBTIQ collections are often slow to digitize their collections due to lack of funding, trained staff, copyright restrictions, lack of permissions for photographs, or the wishes of donors to keep their materials in the hands of their community.

Those LGBTIQ individuals, communities, libraries, archives, and museums that increase access to valuable LGBTIQ information while preserving the anonymity and dignity of individuals and communities deserve recognition for their efforts. This small book in your hands or your Kindle right now—*Queers Online: LGBT Digital Practices in Libraries, Archives, and Museums*—explores the significance of queer online space and ownership of queer history, provides a mere snapshot of existing projects, and a hint of what could come in the future. The book itself is a repository of queer history, as this may be the only place where the existence of particular LGBTIQ cultural heritage institutions have been fleshed out in detail.

A Note on Language and Acronyms

Contributors to this volume came from all over the English-speaking world and the Netherlands. While most editors force their writers to conform to standard American or British English conventions, I believe that this strips people of their identity and voice. At conferences it would be highly inappropriate to ask presenters to imitate one accent and leave their dialects and regionalisms at the door—we go to conferences to meet people from different places as well as obtain information. As editor, I have simply ensured that there were no mechanical errors in the writing, and that each writer provided a well-organized narrative.

With that said, we all have different perspectives on the acronym which should include lesbian, gay, bisexual, transgender, intersex, queer, questioning, asexual, pansexual, and all other people on our rainbow spectrum. I use the acronym LGBTIQ to represent everyone, other writers have used LGBT or similar acronyms with the same intention. "Queer" is also used throughout the book to identify LGBTIQ people, ideas, or artifacts. While some people prefer the word "gay" to describe our community, this term does not include lesbians (particularly those who do not identify as "gay women"), bisexuals, heterosexual intersex people, heterosexual transgender people, or those who question or reject established sexual identities. Assume that the term "gay" in this book is used specifically to describe gay male people, ideas, or artifacts.

SECTION ONE

Queering the Online Realm

Introduction to Section One: Queering the Online Realm

Cisgender heterosexual men, for the most part, invented the Internet, programming languages, computer systems, software, and open source. They have also written the textbooks for cataloging, web design, and user experience. At the same time, women and LGBTIQ people were pioneers in exploring and developing online communities, social media, and folksonomy. They redefine intended uses of online space, recognize the information gaps in online resources, and desire equal communication and collaboration over hierarchical structures.

Before we can appreciate the digitization of LGBTIQ information, we must investigate the evolution of queer online space, revisit our preconceived notion of a cultural heritage institution, and discuss what factors influence the provision of LGBTIQ spaces and information in online spaces. Kevin Powell has the honor of beginning this conversation. In his chapter "Preserving the 'Nexus of Publics': A Case for Collecting LGBT Digital Spaces," Powell will share his personal chronology of visiting online communities during his coming out process to connect with other queer people. He will demonstrate how these spaces are the equivalent to physical brick-and-mortar gay neighborhoods, and will make the case for their historical value and preservation. With that said, we are ready to take the next step—challenging our heteronormative colonialist ideas of archiving. In the scholarly analysis "Pornographic Website as Public History Archive: A Case Study," author Sine Nomine will prove how a particular porn site functions as a public history archive, exhibit, and safe space for a particular community. The transgender community still struggles to locate information and support in both physical and online spaces; Jane Sandberg explains how the transgender community works around these challenges to build directories connecting people with support in "Organizing the Transgender Internet: Web Directories and

Envisioning Inclusive Digital Spaces." Last but not least, librarians Rachel Wexelbaum and Katie Herzog and Wikipedian Lane Rasberry will address the successes and challenges of recruiting LGBTIQ Wikipedians and creating and improving LGBTIQ information on Wikipedia in their chapter "Queering Wikipedia." We hope that the chapters in Section One provide some theoretical groundwork for the rest of the book.

Preserving the "Nexus of Publics": A Case for Collecting LGBT Digital Spaces

Kevin Powell

Introduction

As LGBT people have fought for visibility and acceptance, the spaces in which they learn about themselves have changed. Before the Internet, gay and lesbian neighborhoods helped disseminate LGBT stories, mores, and ideologies. Physical spaces like San Francisco's Castro and New York's Christopher Street neighborhoods accepted the LGBT community unlike many other parts of the country. Even outside of these neighborhoods, meeting places like gay and lesbian cafes, bookstores, and bars served similar purposes. In recent years, these physical spaces have moved online, and the storytelling of "coming out" has changed shape. While today we see digital spaces influencing physical spaces, LGBT collections focus primarily on the records of physical rather than digital spaces. This is largely because the preservation of digital spaces presents a litany of challenges for archivists. Even so, this work of preserving those digital spaces is important for preserving an important era in the LGBT community's history.

Queer People and Space

The "physical" queer neighborhood is declining in importance. In the past, physical spaces such as bars, clubs, coffee shops, and bookstores were useful as channels of communication between LGBT people. This was especially true among young people who had only recently come out. In "Demise of The Gay Enclave," Nikki Usher and Eleanor Morrison describe these tolerant neighborhoods' importance for young LGBT people as places "to find out how to dress, how to date, how to 'be' gay, and to shed his or her sense of isolation" (2010, 274). In the digital age, these physical gay and lesbian spaces are moving online.

Bars, clubs, and bookstores are no longer the only places to meet other LGBT people. Online spaces allow a level of anonymity that may appeal to LGBT people who are early in the coming out process. According to Usher and Morrison, the neighborhoods as a whole have changed character as well. Due to growing acceptance of LGBT people by mainstream society, The Castro has changed drastically from a "seedy underground" of non-normative sexualities to an area filled with large commercial interests (Usher and Morrison 2010). Although they note gay activism has transitioned into online spaces, "...it is unclear how local and national community organizations can work together to harness energy online. The translation from online community to offline activism is still uncharted territory, developing terrain which the gay community should take note of with particular interest" (283).

Larry Gross discusses the move from physical to online spaces with more detail in his chapter "The Gay Global Village in Cyberspace":

> Typically, the first alternative [communication] channels to appear were those with low entry barriers, minimal technological needs, and relatively low operating costs. Indeed, newspapers and magazines have long been the principal media created and consumed by minority groups... But the problem of distribution remains a major hurdle... The balance of power shifted somewhat with the emergence of the Internet, which utilizes a relatively cheap technology to provide Web-based news and magazine sites, chat lines, bulletin boards, and mail networks. For the first time, it seems, the control over the means of reproduction has been placed in the hands of ordinary citizens – the residents of cyberspace (2003, 259).

For the reasons that Gross addresses, queer people were some of the first to utilize the Internet as a space to meet others and exchange experiences. While he notes that magazines and political organizations such as Parents and Friends of Lesbians and Gays (PFLAG) and the Gay & Lesbian Alliance Against Defamation (GLAAD) took to the Internet to disseminate information, Gross also highlights the importance of digital space, especially for queer youth. An entire subsection of his chapter is devoted to a discussion of teens who used chat rooms, bulletin boards, and forums to meet other queer people (Gross 260). To be sure, queer digital spaces present problems that physical spaces do not, but they are also making it easier to be queer in the "real world."

Mary Gray demonstrates this blurring of space in her ethnographic study of rural queer populations. After seeing LGBT youth use new media spaces to "simultaneously confound and blur boundaries among experience of online/offline, rural/urban, and private/public," Gray made some conclusions about how LGBT youth are using online spaces to influence their physical lives:

> New media are experienced as social engagements that enhance young people's sense of inclusion to broader, imagined queer communities beyond their hometowns. In other words, new media came to be understood as one among several interlocked, ephemeral moments of queer visibility and public belonging. They effectively — though not without cost — suture the queer social worlds they find in their hometowns and online. (2007, 290).

The queer youth she observed used social media to create a "nexus of publics," where online spaces influence how they express themselves in the physical world.

Literature on LGBT uses of social networks such as Myspace and Facebook illuminate this nexus by discussing how teenagers use the Internet to develop identity and manage their coming out process (Macintosh and Bryson 2007; Cooper and Dzara 2010). Macintosh and Bryson, for example, refer to a 21-year-old Muslim who used MySpace to "come out." (137). Cooper and Dzara's article eloquently articulates how LGBT youth use social media (specifically Facebook) for connections with the larger community:

> The young gay person can gain a sense of not being alone and of belonging to a community larger than oneself. Through online communities and through the social and political events and activities they promote, cultural markers of community can be learned by the individual. These may include the knowledge of the rainbow flag, the pink triangle, and other symbols and customs of a community. (107).

Coming Out Over the Internet

My own relationship with online resources mirrors the research done by these authors. As an adolescent, the Internet became a safe place for me. My conservative hometown was not the ideal location for a closeted gay teenager, and I heard pretty clearly through eight years at Christian school and eighteen years of church attendance that homosexuality is undeniably wrong. Online resources provided a different narrative. In 2003, I became an active member of the BloopDiary.com community where I blogged anonymously. Knowing the whole time I am primarily attracted to men, I wrote cryptic diary entries about "my friend" who said he was gay but clearly misinformed about the inherent sin of it all. Through these blog entries I met other LGBT people who gave me advice in the form of blog comments, and they helped reformulate my perspective. I befriended people who understood what it felt like to be a small fish in a big pond; they heard and appreciated my unique methods of self-expression. I used the space to voice thoughts I didn't think anyone else would understand, and I was surprised by others' genuinely valuable feedback. The anonymity gave me permission to be vulnerable without fearing rejection.

I switched to a public school in 2004 where it was much easier to be inquisitive. With a new group of friends that enjoyed interacting online, my social Internet activity switched to venues like Xanga, Livejournal, MySpace, and Facebook where I no longer interacted anonymously with others. During this period I started to actively (though privately) identify as a gay person. As a mode of discovery, I used search engines to find photography collections of gay pride parades, I joined forums like EmptyClosets.com, and I started questioning what the Bible says about homosexuality. While the Internet is definitely not always a safe place for minors, I felt it was my only resource for this knowledge. Too fearful to check out books from the library in case my parents discovered them, I turned once again to the Internet as a means of identity development. This period very much reflects the research done by Mary Gray as the spaces I found online influenced how I viewed myself and interacted with others. During my first year in college these interactions led me to self-identifying as a feminist who supported gay rights. My newfound empowerment eventually facilitated honest conversations with conservative people like my parents, who, to their credit, have always been (and continue to be) loving and compassionate role models.

My activism was largely influenced by weekly involvement in a YouTube vlogging (video-blogging) community that discussed feminism, queer rights, and the intersections between them. This particular activity reflected the "nexus of publics" from Gray's research as I participated in this community with someone I met at school. By the end of my sophomore year in college, I formally came out on Myspace and Facebook. Social networks made the coming out process easier by cutting out many uncomfortable individual coming-out conversations with acquaintances like co-workers and classmates. In this way, I used the Internet to "confound and blur" the boundaries of my public life. Digital spaces armed me with the knowledge and subsequent confidence to discuss my sexuality in heteronormative environments.

Preserving Spaces

The work of scholars like Cooper, Macintosh, Usher, Gray, and others state that, in the Internet age, online communal spaces are important in the coming out process for many gay people. Much in the way that Jim Kepner, ONE National Gay & Lesbian Archives founding donor, found his voice as a gay activist through literature, many LGBT people are visiting online spaces to find *their* voices (1998, 176). The added benefit of anonymity constructs a space for people who may not be comfortable enough to use analog information retrieval methods (checking out library books, consulting with reference librarians/archivists, etc.) What if these online spaces, which proved so critical for gay people in the early 2000s, are not being saved?

This is a troubling thought since, in the past, queer activist archivists fought for the preservation of LGBT history as a way to preserve the community itself. Scholarship on LGBT archives explores and validates these activists' passion for preservation. Brittany Bennett Parris, in "Creating, Reconstructing, and Protecting Historical Narratives: Archives and the LBGT Community," succinctly describes the mission of preserving queer material:

> In the end, queer archives are primarily concerned with the future instead of the past. They concern themselves with protecting LBGT materials for current users and for posterity by accurately and adequately presenting the many narratives that run throughout this community. (2005, 17).

Indeed, early LGBT activist archivists like Harry Weintraub, Joan Nestle, Jim Monahan, and Jim Kepner (among others) recognized this truth and acted upon it. Even so, there are still endangered sections of LGBT heritage. It was only in 2005 that Los Angeles's Gay and Lesbian film festival, Outfest, recognized a crisis in LGBT film preservation. Disintegrating prints called for immediate attention, and soon the newly formed Legacy Project partnered with the UCLA Television and Film Archive to preserve works by and about LGBT people. Digital spaces, much like these films, risk exclusion from the historical record. While this risk is certainly made worse by the marginalization of LGBT people, there is another very crucial factor that may doom the preservation of digital spaces. Frequently released updates to hardware, software, applications, and file formats quickly render obsolete digital spaces like websites, forums, and chat rooms. In this way, digitally born material and spaces require immediate preservation work. Our current digital era could be known to future researchers as a "digital dark age" if left unattended.

In *Personal Information Management*, Catherine Marshall writes on the dangers of lackadaisical attitudes towards digital recordkeeping. Her chapter, "How People Manage Information over a Lifetime," outlines a common technique for managing personal papers called "benign neglect" (Marshall 2007, 59). Simply put, benign neglect involves basic preservation with zero quality control. A dusty shoebox of photographs in a drawer or a folder of love-letters in the garage may be "saved," but they may not be touched for decades. Presumably, these records can be discovered many years from now in roughly the same condition. At fifteen years old, this is the exact way I approached my digital belongings. Unfortunately due to website redesigns and hardware updates, the digital space in which I kept these belongings is no longer the same. Even though I downloaded a ZIP file of my BloopDiary before I deleted its online presence in 2006, I did not commit to migrating the file from computer system to computer system. Consequently, the BloopDiary content has been very difficult to retrieve, copy, and transfer into new locations. According to Marshall, many people struggle with this problem.

Marshall claims computer users are "optimistic" about technology; that in the future machines will be able to read obsolete formats (2007, 60). Additionally, "people tend to view disk crashes, computer viruses, and media obsolescence with a certain sense of inevitability," as if they are bound to happen and one must simply move past them (2007, 60). As she rightly points out, "From this perspective, we cannot expect to have any of our personal digital information in 50 years; it will be long gone" (60).

Archiving the Internet faces similar problems. Even though Adrian Brown states, "the history of web archiving is almost as long as that of the web itself," various transformations of popular Internet uses make its preservation problematic (2008, 8). In Simson Garfinkel and David Cox's article "Finding and Archiving the Internet Footprint," they outline some of this task's basic problems. Most importantly, website maintainers cannot be trusted to back-up files, and servers cannot be trusted to last forever. The example Garfinkel and Cox give is that of a site named Journalspace, "which was wiped out on January 2, 2009 due to an operator error and the lack of backups" (2009, 2). Services like the Internet Archive's WayBack Machine are attempting to remedy this problem with web-crawlers. While this service helps greatly, Garfinkel and Cox rightly point out that "The Internet Archive is itself another organization... which may cease operation at some point in the future" (2). Therefore, the WayBack Machine is unreliable as a permanent archive.

Literature by scholars like Adrian Brown ask some pertinent questions about how and why we should archive the Internet. Researchers like Garfinkel and Cox have investigated the problems that come with Internet archiving.

Alas, there seems to be a severe lack of theory regarding the curation of such collections. Instead of continuing to ask *how* to archive these spaces, we should start asking *whose* spaces are routinely overlooked. By scholars' own admission, websites should not be trusted to archive their own material, and archiving certain areas of the Web requires proactive work. If the act of Web archiving requires such proactive measures, then digital archivists should consider the historical and social significance of certain Web communities, specifically those communities who are already marginalized by mainstream society.

Conclusions and Future Research

The digital preservation crisis facing the LGBT community is put in perspective by scholarship that shows queer people are increasingly replacing physical gay spaces with online equivalents. If the Internet has proven so useful in the past twenty years for political activism, the coming out process, and the fight against homophobia, then gay online spaces should be the next target of archivists.

If LGBT archivists choose to avoid the digital realm and develop an attitude of benign neglect, then these spaces will certainly be lost for future generations. It would leave a hole in the historical record, just like Kepner, Nestle, and Monahan feared. Furthermore, the "digital dark age" for LGBT people would exclude a highly influential era of advancement.

Nikki Thomas and Melissa Gohlke at The University of Texas at San Antonio (UTSA) are on a team of archivists and librarians who are doing such work. Through the Internet Archive's service, Archive-It, UTSA has collected over 500 LGBT related web sites (Archive-It – The University of Texas, San Antonio). In an interview with Gohlke, she stated "the primary reason we started collecting LGBTQ websites through Archive-It is because **no one else was doing this**" (2013). Indeed, a quick search of Archive-It shows very few curated collections of LGBT websites, and none are on the same scale as UTSA's. While their work is certainly commendable, UTSA should not have to shoulder the entire burden alone. Since these spaces are valuable, fragile, and *replicable*, it stands to reason that other institutions should collect such spaces as a means of preserving LGBT history.

Works Cited

Brown, A. (2006) *Archiving Websites: A Practical Guide for Information Management Professionals*. London, UK: Facet Publishing.

Cooper, M., and Dzara, K. (2010) The Facebook Revolution: LGBT Identity and Activism. In C. Pullen and M. Cooper (Eds.) *LGBT Identity and Online New Media*. New York, New York: Routledge. 100-112.

MacIntosh, L., & Bryson M. (2007) Queer (Re)presentation: Youth, MySpace, and the Interstitial Spaces of Becoming and Belonging. *Journal of LGBT Youth*, (1), 133-142.

Garfinkel, S., & Cox, D. (2009) Finding and Archiving the Internet Footprint. Retrieved from: http://simson.net/clips/academic/2009.BL.InternetFootprint.pdf

Glazer, G. (September 15, 2011) Cornell Library receives gay-related photo collection. *Cornell Chronicle*.

Gohlke, M. (2013, April 25). Interview by Kevin Powell.

Gray, M. L. (2007). From Websites to Wal-Mart: Youth, Identity Work, and the Queering of Boundary Publics in Small Town, USA. *American Studies* 48(2), 49-59. Mid American Studies Association.

Gross, L. (2003). The Gay Global Village in Cyberspace. In N. Couldry & J. Curran (Eds.), *Contesting Media Power: Alternative Media in a Networked World*. Lanham, Maryland: Rowman & Littlefield.

Kepner, J. (1998). An Accidental Institution: How and Why a Gay and Lesbian Archives?. In J.V. Carmichael Jr. (Ed.) *Daring to Find Our Names*. Westport, CT: Greenwood Press, 175-182.

Legacy Project. (2013). About the legacy project. Retrieved from http://www.outfest.org/about-the-legacy-project/

Marshall, C. (2007) How People Manage Personal Information Over a Lifetime. In Jones, W. & Teevan J. (Eds.) *Personal Information Management*. Seattle, WA: University of Washington Press, 57-75.

Monahan, J. (1979) Considerations in the organization of gay archives. *Gay Insurgent*, 4(5), Spring, 9.

Nestle, J. (1979) Notes on radical archiving from a lesbian feminist standpoint. *Gay Insurgent*, 4(5) Spring, 11.

Parris, B. B. (2005). Creating, reconstructing, and protecting historical narratives: Archives and the LBGT community. *Current Studies in Librarianship*, 29(1/2), 5-25.

Usher, N. & Morrison, E. (2010). The Demise of the Gay Enclave, Communication Infrastructure, Theory, and the Transformation of Gay Public Space. In C. Pullen & M. Cooper (Eds.) *LGBT Identity and Online New Media*. New York, New York: Routledge, 271-287.

Pornographic Website as Public History Archive: A Case Study

Sine Nomine

Introduction

Museums, archives, and public history repositories increase intercultural understanding and create community. Local or specialized repositories, often community-based, are a way to accurately represent minorities as well as majority populations, and provide a space for dialogue. This chapter will demonstrate that an online collection of videos and accompanying stills that could be considered pornography by the majority can serve as an online public history collection by a particular community, particularly if it is a repository created by members of that community. The online male-on-male (M/M) spanking video collection, Spanking Central (SC), exists as a living example of such a repository.

Definitions

For the purposes of this chapter, the following terms are defined.

ARCHIVE / REPOSITORY / MUSEUM. An *archive* is traditionally viewed as a location where materials of historical interest are found, "a repository for stored memories or information" ("Archive" 2007). As a repository, or "place or receptacle in which things are or may be deposited, esp. for storage or safe keeping" ("Repository, n." 2012) the *archive* serves as a place where things may be put for safekeeping; a museum" ("Repository" 2007). "A room or building in which interesting artefacts, works of art, etc., are gathered for display, a museum; an (official) institution in which documents, books, or manuscripts are deposited; an archive, a library" ("Repository, n." 2012). And, as a *museum*, the *repository* or *archive* serves as a physical location "devoted to the acquisition, conservation, study, exhibition, and educational interpretation of objects having scientific, historical, or artistic value" ("Museum" 2007), a "building or part of a building, dedicated to the pursuit of learning or the arts" ("Museum, n." 2012). A local, or community, *archive*, *museum*, or *repository* is one that documents, records, and explores that community's heritage whether formally or informally (Flinn 2007), offering artifacts that help create new knowledge by igniting responses and memories based on previously held knowledge and experience. Repositories, archives, and museums open a dialog between artifacts and consumers by drawing out new ideas and rekindling old (Carr 2011). For the purpose of this chapter, the three terms *archive, repository,* and *museum* will be used interchangeably.

ARTIFACT. An *artifact* is a human-made creation believed to have historical interest ("Artifact" 2007; "Artifact, n." 2012). It is not only a physical item, but also text, image, video, or anything else available on the Internet that future researchers and viewers can access and interpret (Williams 2008). Artifacts which are images, whether still or moving, "show how the subject had once been seen by other people ... No other kind of relic or text from the past can offer such a direct testimony about the world which surrounded other people and other times" (Berger 1977, p. 10).

COMMUNITY. As defined by Flinn (2007, 153), a *community* is "a group who define themselves on the basis of locality, culture, faith, background, or other shared identity or interest. Many communities tend to have a local focus even if they meet virtually but others have another shared focus altogether such as sexuality, occupation, ethnicity, faith, or an interest, or a combination of one or more of the above".

MARGINALIZED GROUP. A *marginalized*, ostracized, stigmatized, or underdocumented *group* is not part of the dominant, majority, or center, group. It lacks the privilege and power of the majority, mainstream or dominant group. Based on the context and level of analysis, a group viewed as marginalized in one context can be perceived as the dominant group in another (Greene 2003-2004). For example, gays or those into BDSM are often seen as *marginalized groups*. In this chapter, gays will be considered the majority and the BDSM community, particularly those into non-sexual adult male on male spanking will be the minority, or *marginalized group* (Daniel and Fletcher Linder 2002).

PORNOGRAPHY. *Pornography*, according to the *Oxford English Dictionary* is "[T]he explicit description or exhibition of sexual subjects or activity in literature, painting, films, etc., in a manner intended to stimulate erotic rather than aesthetic feelings; printed or visual materials containing this" (2012). It is traditionally defined as obscene materials that have no artistic merit and are "intended only to arouse sexual desire" ("Pornography" 2010). Kristol (2001) clearly differentiates *pornography* from erotic art, indicating the whole purpose of pornography "is to treat human beings obscenely, to deprive human beings of their specifically human dimension" it is not considered artwork. McGowan (2005, 23) indicated that "pornography means so many different things to so many different people". Unlike Barthes' (2010) definition of *pornography* as "without intention and without calculations ... completely constituted by the presentation of only one thing: sex" (41), this chapter defines *pornography* as visual materials that raise sexual arousal in viewers whether or not the materials contain sexually explicit content. In this chapter, the pornographic materials in the repository under study are adult videos and still images intended to "arouse sexual desire; [they have] artistic ... historical or other social value ... not patently offensive under community standards ... because the work taken as a whole does not appeal exclusively to a prurient interest in sex" (Mazur and Bertin 2001).

MARGINALIZED GROUPS AND THEIR ARTIFACTS IN TRADITIONAL MUSEUMS, ARCHIVES, AND REPOSITORIES

Marginal groups are often ignored, ostracized, or misrepresented in the field of museum and archive studies, as the majority group traditionally creates and maintains museums, archives and repositories (Greene 2003-2004; Hay, Hughes, and Tutton 2004; McKemmish, Gilliland-Swetland, and Ketelaar 2005). J. M. Donaldson, Vice President of the Detroit Museum of Art, insists that museums "are in a position to diffuse that kind of culture that indicates appreciation of whatever is inherently noble and beautiful" (Zeller 1989, 19), no matter the source or size of the culture. This applies not only to the majority; people visit museums to see representations of all groups (Ambrose and Paine 2006). The histories of all cultures are important to show, in order to show how each community develops and influences the others (Flinn 2007).

Opinions of minority groups, often cursory, are based mostly on "popular culture rather than academically elaborated sources" (Stainton 2002, 216). Those in power "use ... discourse of normalization to make the achieved order of the world to be a fact of nature, because then their dominant position in this order is also a fact of nature, and hence cannot be changed" (Linde 1993, 195). This power play causes some groups, particularly minority or underrepresented groups, to challenge what the museums are doing and to demand equal representation of their own histories and artifacts (Dubin 1999).

Museum exhibitions representing minorities, particularly in the United States, are often governed by members of the majority. Representation of subjects and presentations of materials held in the repository may reflect the bias and prejudice of the majority, hiding or altering the originally intended message and true history, whether intentionally or unintentionally (Christopher 2007; Gable and Handler 2007). The curators, as selectors of artifacts for inclusion or exclusion, interpret the public history of the represented group, tell the life stories of members of the represented group, describe these artifacts, and determine how to exhibit the artifacts to help guide visitors in their own interpretations (Hay et al. 2004). In the process of representing and chronicling the past, deciding to remain true to the represented group or to bend to the desires and interpretations of the majority, museums become controversial sites (Dubin 1999; Greene 2002).

The first museums were "curio cabinets": collections of "stories, personalities, experiences, and artifacts" housed in the homes of the wealthy and open to a select few (Alexander 1960; Skramstad 2010, ix). Almost every collection housed in a museum or other location originated from one person's eclectic interest, which grew to encompass and engage the enthusiasm and interest of others, and made the maintenance and expansion of the collection viable and worthwhile (Coleman 1927). Eventually these collections became open to the public, to provide an educational experience also intended to entertain. With the growth of the Internet, the "curio cabinet" – owned by an individual or group, open to registered members or the general public – has become popular once again, keeping all in one place, curated by a member of the community, owning and controlling this group's, or his own, history and providing a safe place to explore the community (Brown 2011; Gordon 2010).

Traditional vs Online Museums, Archives, and Repositories

One often thinks of a museum as a building that houses three-dimensional artworks or two-dimensional paintings. A digital archive may or may not serve as a "traditional" museum, where artifacts are simply stored (Brown 2011). By virtue of their collections, museums are considered primary sources for visual education (Zeller 1989). With the growth of online repositories, the digital representation of these works becomes a second norm, requiring a "second step of translation, beyond the text, into space and design, using objects, images and text in another form" (Bouquet 2004, 194). The images, or visual representations, can reflect the creator's way of seeing (Berger 1977).

The surge in Web 2.0 has influenced how people create, exchange, and use information. It has also influenced how communities form and preserve their histories and memories (Flinn 2007). A website or digital repository containing videos, still images, and narratives created and recorded by an individual or a group within the represented community is a museum, offering personal "gifts of memory and fabrication" (Carr 2011, xxiii) to the general public (Gordon 2010). This repository or museum can offer interviews which often document experiences and life stories that tend to be missing from mainstream sources (Perks and Thomson 2006). An online repository is often one person's "curio cabinet", opened for others to view through a new media, the Internet (Ellenboger 2002).

Learning occurs in physical and online environments. Visitors must familiarize themselves with the environment before they are comfortable in beginning or extending their experience (Bourdon Caston 1989). Museums, archives, and repositories provide a place to see the history of the represented group from a variety of perspectives: the represented group, the minority group, and museum visitors themselves. Visitors will use their own knowledge and ideas, in conjunction with information they have acquired during their visit, to come to a new knowledge of the represented community (Carr 2011). This section explores the similarities and differences of traditional and online museums, archives, and repositories, and how environment affects the learning experience.

The value of an online archive, and presentation of artifacts online, arises through sharing—when the creator evokes pleasure and similar emotions in others through the sharing of artifacts, and two-way communication about the artifacts or the subject takes place (Paris and Mercer 2002). For marginalized, isolated communities, the virtual repository can also provide a place of support and advocacy (Greenblatt 2011; Woodward 2013). The minority group repository helps members of the community, as well as outsiders, to understand the community itself and its influence (Carr 2011).

In online spaces, the private becomes public, partially because there is a perceived sense of anonymity, the ability to not be 'seen' while seeing. Those who fear being 'outed' if they were just seen visiting a physical repository or community meeting place can now, via the virtual archive, check out the archive in the privacy of their own homes. In the virtual archive, one can visit the space and view the contents in anonymity. The virtual repository offers a way to reach others and gather information without fear of reprisal or repercussions (Holt

2011). As Hogan (2011, 113) noted, "Just because someone has an information need, does not always mean they feel safe enough to ask in person". This sense of anonymity exists for both the viewer and the artifact creator; both become members of a diverse, potentially subversive community (Flinn 2007).

How Online Spaces Encourage Marginalized Groups To Record Their Culture And History

The Internet has changed how communities communicate, connect and mobilize. Small community-based organizations who construct repositories have radically expanded their visibility and outreach through Web 2.0 (Greenblatt 2011). Archivists, particularly those from marginalized groups, use the Internet to connect the community to their oral histories and public history artifacts. Community members often share common memories, having grown up in the same time, lived in the same area, or otherwise experienced similar situations that present a shared nostalgia and collective memory (Flinn 2007). The ideas and artifacts added to a digital archive expand the range of ideas, common memories, and artifacts that can be preserved to present a collective memory (Windon 2012).

Museums, including digital projects, are repositories of a selected public or population. Due to generational and internal cultural differences, the presented collective memory still might not be an accurate memory for all visitors or members of the represented community (Lehman 2007). Museums serve not only those who wish to visit the represented community, but also those community members who wish to build on their currently held knowledge and information (Gough and Greenblatt 2011). Both groups are served; the artifacts speak for themselves, and others speak about the artifacts. Members of each group gain an understanding of the roots of a population, and how others see the roots of this group represented. This process allows both groups to gain additional information about the culture, ignite memories, and see how others view and interpret the culture and history (Perks and Thomson 2006).

Expansion of Web 2.0, ecommerce, and online communication has led to the growth of online communities devoted to minority sexual practices, including the creation and exchange of erotica and pornography (Ashford 2006; Kruger 2010). As the number of sites devoted to sexual and erotic activities has increased, the variety of depicted acts has also expanded (Hagelin 2006). The ability to connect with others who are similar in identity, concerns and interests helps individuals engaged in such practices abandon their former, isolated, stigmatized status (Hooper-Greenhill 2007). The visible distinction between groups and ideologies disappears as one moves from real, face-to-face activities to simulated online environments and representations (Kellner, n.d.).

Pornographic digital repositories can provide a sense of anonymity for the viewer, the visitor, and the artifact creators. The models may use pseudonyms, and may not share any identifying information in the final products or pornographic artifacts, as they may fear repercussions of 'outing' such as losing jobs, housing, and more (Brown 2011). The artifacts about those performing the act of pornography, or creating the pornographic materials themselves, may also require anonymity. Even if the curator shares viewer feedback and comments with others, he or she must respect that need for anonymity.

How Online Spaces Redefine What Is Pornography

The definition of "representations of sex or sexuality" as obscene or pornographic in the nineteenth and early twentieth century museums, leading to censorship, segregation in 'secret museums' or simply ignoring them, has changed (Frost 2010). With the ability to share personal materials online, curio-cabinet style repositories are made open to the public via the Internet and Web 2.0, bringing marginalized groups into the mainstream popular media medium (Weiss 2006). This expands the visibility and accessibility of marginalized group repositories, including those repositories that present pornographic and 'kinky' materials (Nichols 2006).

Pornographers have been innovative driving forces in using new technologies to bring their work into the home consumer market (Lehman 2007). Web 2.0 such as blogs, wikis and the growth of personal sites allows for faster dissemination of information without outside mediation. Professional, semiprofessional, and amateur pornography creators and distributors are now able to share their materials through similar venues (Flinn 2008).

Increased awareness and openness towards the habitually troublesome concept of 'pornography' has grown with the accessibility and anonymity that the Internet provides (Kendrick 1996). Pornography has long existed in a plethora of forms (Woodward 2007). Increased publicity of such artifacts and collections has helped to expand awareness of the subtleties and nuances in the broad field of pornography. The definition of pornography has been expanded or redefined to include subgenres such as BDSM, male/male spanking discipline, and others.

Visitors come to museums often for enlightened entertainment, personal enrichment and art (Stebbins 2013) in a safe place where one is encouraged to think, build personal knowledge, and engage. The number of visitors searching for a "rich fantasy life in an age of corporate sterility" (Slade 1997, 1) is growing. The Internet and Web 2.0 remove class and sex distinctions for visitors, and provide spaces that can accommodate an infinite range of fetishes and fixations (Ashford 2006; Kendrick 1996; Kruger 2010). With the growth of the Internet, the range of pornographic materials and the scope of the genre has grown. Plante (2006, 75) noted in particular the growing distinction between sexual spanking and BDSM "borne out in multiple publications, Internet interest groups, videos, and toys focused on this sexual practice", illustrating how the Internet has helped define not only what is pornography, but to delineate types of pornography. This has impacted the definition of pornography, and thus the field of pornography, moving it from solely obscene materials to works of varying purposes and raising senses of aesthetic, erotic, and/or obscene pleasure to people with differing needs, desires, and definitions, such as male-on-male (M/M) discipline scenarios.

Museums and collections, including those hosted on the Internet and through Web 2.0, provide a permanent symbol of the community's existence and representation over time. Repositories that collect artifacts from sexual minority groups—including those engaged in pornographic activities—raise awareness and hopefully acceptance. One such repository is SC, a repository of non-sexual male on male (M/M) discipline scenarios that include erotic videos, still images, and personal stories presented through text and video blogging. This repository is unique because it provides a sense of community and a glimpse of what truly goes into making these artifacts and the life stories of these participants. Unlike other pornographic websites, SC builds visitor empathy for the human subjects engaged in the creation of these artifacts and performance of these acts. SC treats the community members' interests and concerns respectfully by constructing a public history repository to build a broader social acceptance of those who participate in the act of creating M/M spanking videos (Greenblatt 2011).

Case Study: Spanking Central

The digital repository SC was started in October 2003 as a paid access site by a male-on-male (M/M) spanking enthusiast. Through SC, the creator provides access to a personal collection of primary source artifacts serving a small, marginal group within the lesbian, gay, bisexual, and transgender (LGBT) and Bondage/Discipline/SadoMasochistic (BDSM) communities: those who eroticize the pain of physical discipline performed through rituals of dominance and submission as observed in fantasy scenarios involving relationships between parent and child, teacher and student, and other authoritative/subservient pairs (Weinberg 2006). The creator hoped that his website, or curio-cabinet, would bring recognition to those interested in M/M spanking fetish audiovisual and still image materials.

The creator saw a gap in M/M spanking content; he had not seen any non-sexual M/M spanking videos and found a need to create and share artifacts for those isolated from the dominant sexually-focused M/M spanking community. SC serves as an archive that preserves M/M spanking participants' life stories and their process of creating videos, primarily to provide access for members of the community, and to ensure visibility of M/M spanking fetish and workers in the field.

While other archives such as the Leather Archives & Museum (http://www.leatherarchives.org) are devoted to sexual subgroups, these archives do not address the non-pornographic aspect of those working in the field of M/M spanking pornographic videos.

SC collects ephemera, consisting of still photographs and videos that reenact and recreate the act of M/M spanking and the rituals associated with the act of discipline (Weinberg 2006). These artifacts create and present actualizations of M/M discipline fantasies visitors might have, as well as informal interviews and discussions between the creator and those involved in the creation of these artifacts. This collection serves as a digital repository of local public history for the community interested in M/M spanking (Gordon 2010).

As a community-based archive, SC follows an activist tradition for M/M spanking aficionados (spankos) and provides a safe gathering place (Brown 2011) for this group where guilt is assuaged (Weinberg 2006). The creator has built a collective memory, raised nostalgia, and provided male pornographic entertainment for an adult audience. Through this repository, he has also educated others about the creation of these still image and video artifacts. SC provides pornographers and sex workers with a public history repository. Those working in this field may not be spankos themselves; they are doing this simply to earn a living. SC offers a space for the M/M spanking community to exchange stories about its 'models' (Albin 2011).

SC shows the actual filming of the video artifacts through behind-the-scenes (BTS) or "bonus" videos. They appear through video blogs of the lives of those who engage in M/M spanking, and the creator's textual blog. By serving as a public history repository, SC demonstrates that workers in this field and other sex fields are real people from all walks of life who do what they must in order to earn a living, not doing what one wants as in sexual play and fantasy (Coleman 1927; Maurer 1994). These videos are "communal stories that for too long have been lost or devalued in the larger canon of film pornography history" (Albin 2011, 137-38). The creator, through his behind the scenes videos, video blog and textual blog, demonstrates that not all sex workers do this work because they "like that sort of thing" but rather do it out of necessity and succeed because they are good at it. The discipline that occurs in the videos is real – real sounds, real impacts, real visual effects, and real reactions. There is no make-up used, no theatrics on the part of the recipient of the discipline, and only rarely are sounds amplified or visuals enhanced to make the strokes' lead-up appear harsher than what truly happens during the filming. At the same time, these artifacts are created without causing permanent injury to the recipient, taking special care to meet any indicated requirements of the individual model. A secondary, unintended value offered by commentary videos is to fill a gap in the purview of most making-of documentaries, offering "discussion about the cinematic logistics of creating a [sex] scene – how, when, and with what resources" (Hankin 2004, 39).

The creator's work enables others to independently determine whether the reasons presented by the workers as to why they perform or partake in M/M spanking are justifiable based on the interpreter's own individual beliefs and ideas (Linde 1993). Those who come to SC for erotic entertainment believe that those who engage in M/M spanking discipline enjoy it. The BTS materials help to disprove this myth by adding facts about each model's history. These life stories are products of members of this culture, demonstrating that their "identity is not defined by their work circumstances ... for those who are in circumstances where having any job or any job with a sufficient wage to survive, the identity of the specific job does not require an account in their life story" (Linde 1993, 4). At the same time, these behind the scenes materials lead to a sense of betrayal, of finding out facts that one would rather not believe, taking away the myth of erotic fantasy being enjoyed by the participants as the viewer is having (Capino 2007).

The videos often have nothing to do with the model's sexuality; in fact, the model's sexual passion is minimized, enabling the viewer to obtain the only sexual pleasure in the making and viewing of the video (Berger 1977). The models are there to feed an erotic appetite of the audience member, not to have any of their own. SC provides a place for those who remember spanking in their past (or present) and wish to have this memory revived, reinforced, or seen through the eyes of others. SC serves to share these memories, and to evoke them, through non-sexual M/M spanking videos and still images that depict how people remember their spankings. It also serves to create new memories and revive or reinforce old ones.

SC's main purpose is to reenact spankings and other corporal punishments occurring between a dominant male figure and a submissive male figure, such as father/son, coach/student athlete, dean or teacher/student, and so on. These reenactments are real, meant to portray what really happened, which is not sexual in nature. The videos produced as the original mission of SC, the Prime Videos, provide a basic story, but are often surreal enough for the viewer to fill in the details from their past or fantasy or other prior knowledge such as books or family stories. The creator also provides discipline scenarios on occasion with dungeonesque and judicial ambiance, including the use of restraints and chains, which are not true realistic memories of corporal punishment in the domestic sense. Through providing these fantasy videos, the creator is appealing to a slightly wider audience, drawing additional viewers to ensure the fiscal viability of the repository as a whole. For members of the sadomasochism (S&M) subgroup, this type of discipline fantasy enactment does occur at SC.

SC exists for several groups – those actively seeking M/M spanking videos for the erotic aspect, those curious about the act of M/M spanking, those who wish to learn more about the production of spanking and discipline videos, and those who want to know more about pornographers and sex workers involved in M/M spanking pornographic video creation. Unlike most other spanking video sites, SC also serves the academic and scholarly needs of those studying the population represented in the artifacts (Gordon 2010; Stebbins 2013). "Researchers" may be looking for reactions of diverse body types and personalities during different types of corporal punishments, or looking for insights as to why some get into performing in such videos and what their 'other' lives are like. Those researchers may also want to learn more about pornographic video production and how to start such a business operation. Some visitors to SC come to have an erotic experience then leave, while others come for the erotic experience and stay to watch the "behind the scenes" videos and become part of the community whether actively or passively.

SC was originally created to entertain rather than educate, but it also presents M/M spanking pornography in a way that was never provided before, re-enactments of authentic encounters without sexual content. Sharing behind the scenes videos and videos about the models all came later. To the surprise of the creator, these behind the scenes videos and videos about the models and the life of SC as a whole quickly became the most popular aspect of the repository, rather than the erotic experience itself (Stebbins 2013). These behind the scenes materials offer "Mise-en-scene analysis's attention to cinematic staging [which] benefits from appreciating the pornographer's expertise in choreography" (Capino 2007, 122).

The homepage of SC (http://www.spankingcentral.com) presents the image of red buttocks and the option to see free videos and photos (stills). The main navigation menu is on the left side of the screen, enabling the viewer to access the Site Map and Login to the (paid) Premium Site. One can also access contents of the site— Spanking Central Free, Spanking Central Premium, and Website Help— through the main page by clicking on an unlabeled logo of red buttocks.

29

Due to the nature of the content, the site is limited in two ways. First, the homepage states that one must agree they are 18 or of the legal age to view such materials in their country. Second, to access most of the materials, paid membership is required. A visitor can view previews or 'advertising samples' for free, but must pay for the full versions of prime content or behind the scenes materials.

The site map is organized in tables. The left column of each table focuses on materials geared for the "typical" visitor – stills and videos of the final products of M/M spanking, along with terms of use, polls, and access to the Advanced Search for the free and paid materials. The right columns include information for the research-oriented visitor who wants to learn more about the practice through other resources. The right columns include resources for the "research-oriented" visitor such as help areas, tutorials, contact information for the owner/curator, a privacy policy, legal statements, Viewer Mail, and behind the scenes materials. The top table is for the free site, while the bottom table is for the paid site. The labeling of the two tables, Spanking Central Free and Spanking Central Premium, clarifies for each visitor which navigation menu he should use.

The advanced searches enable quick location of desired materials through pre-determined characteristics, similar to indexes. There is no ability to browse the indexes easily; one must select a single characteristic for one or more of the indexes provided in the Advanced Search: model, implement type, position, scenario type, scenario setting, severity level, clothing type, target type; and then select whether one wants, does not want, or does not care about the following characteristics of the video: restraints used, dialog, mouth soaping, 2 or more models per video, HD (high definition), and miscellaneous videos. Though not clearly stated, when a visitor retrieves their results, they have access to both the videos and still photos.

Curators strive to stimulate interest and the desire to learn, drawing on the intellectual, sensory and emotional faculties of the viewer to engage the viewer's feelings and leading to a tacit learning experience. The goal of the curator of any collection is to have the visitor elicit nostalgic recognition or to learn historical narrative or research methods (Hooper-Greenhill 2007). When the visitor feels like a part of the exhibit for a moment, it is a success. By acknowledging these similarities or bonds across cultures represented in public history exhibits, visitors are having the desired experience – that of learning about the history of themselves and others. At SC the visitor experiences integration into the exhibit, standing in the room where the discipline takes place, empathizing with one or more of the participants in the scene, engaging the visitors' imagination, and making the material come alive (Weglein Kraus 2008). In the BTS footage, the visitor gets a sense of the people as people, not just recipients of discipline for the erotic pleasure of others. The visitor feels a sense of connection through life experiences and shared stories, whether facing jail time, graduating, medical problems, homelessness, marriage, job searching, death and more (Capino 2007). These stories help viewers to come to terms with their identities by seeing the identities of others in the community (Weglein Kraus 2008).

DISCUSSION

Any online collection of artifacts can be defined as a digital repository for educational learning experiences. One can apply such a justification even to the most unlikely collections, as demonstrated in the case study of SC. Several theories exist on how to determine the effectiveness of the educational purpose of a public history exhibit or repository.

Two theoretical approaches from the late 1960s for evaluating the success of the educational purpose of a public history exhibit, particularly one hosted in a local museum, were posited by Joseph Schwak and Dwayne Huebner (Vallance 2007, 41). Schwak's four elements, or commonplaces, are: (1) schools are created to address specific grade levels and subjects; (2) progression is tracked by tests; (3) teachers with specified qualifications; and (4) know who students are. These commonplaces are applicable to public history exhibits. SC was created to address a specific topic: M/M spanking as demonstrated through stories and videos. SC traces the "success" of these portrayals through audience size and retention. The curator and "teacher" of this public history repository is a M/M spanking aficionado who creates what he feels he would enjoy. As others share his interest, some of whom make themselves known through email feedback and paid memberships, the creator knows how to reach the M/M spanking community and invite them into his curio cabinet.

Another way to evaluate success of a public history repository was posited by Dwayne Huebner, who identified five rationales: (1) the technical – did the student respond as hoped, did they learn; (2) the scientific – what did the curator learn about teaching from this lesson; (3) the political – what is the value of this curriculum for the power structure of the community or the political weight of the school; (4) the aesthetic – was this lesson artfully done, did it hold together in its own terms; and (5) the ethical – was the relationship between viewer and curator a respectful one, did the lesson respect the integrity of the visitor.

At SC, the visitor's mind is engaged when viewing the Prime videos, taking in all of the visual and auditory narrative being portrayed, whether for an academic or pornographic/entertainment purpose. For those drawn to the videos for nostalgic reasons, as many viewers are drawn according to the creator, there is remembering and going back in time within one's head while viewing the videos (Carr 2011). The creator intentionally uses a surreal approach in creating his final, Prime videos, encouraging if not requiring viewers to draw connections between one's prior knowledge or desires with the new knowledge presented in the video. By creating various scenarios using a variety of implements, positions, and dress, and having a range of model types, the creator is encouraging viewers to open their minds to additional views and thoughts that might not have otherwise been encountered, seeing new experiences, coming to enjoy looking at new body types, and experience new scenarios or types of implements for corporal punishment. For the scholar of film, the creator offers records and other information about the production, distribution, exhibition, and reception of the M/M spanking videos he presents, materials that are rare to find and which offer insights into social conditions that might not otherwise be available, particularly as primary source documents (Schaefer 2005).

Silverman (2010, 16-17) noted that there is agreement among theorists "that museums offer an environment in which people can meet specific, predictable human needs" as organized into three experiences: "educational; associational, or opportunities to connect and share with others; and reverential, a connection with something bigger than oneself and/or awe-inspiring". Hein (1998, 16) proposed a need for three theories in order to obtain a clear theory of education in a museum setting: a theory of knowledge (do museum exhibitions show the world as it really is,' do they represent convenient social conventions, or do they provide phenomena for the visitors to interpret as they will?), a theory of learning (do we believe that learning consists of the incremental addition of individual 'bits' of information into the mind or do we think that learning is an active process that transforms the mind of the learner?), and a theory of pedagogy (how should we teach?).

SC is a place that enables viewers to see artifacts in new ways, ways that can offer a different interpretation or meaning (Vallance 2007). Visitors come to SC to see pornography and are sometimes enticed to stay to view the additional materials that document the creation of these pornographic artifacts and the lives of those who take part in the creation of these artifacts. The artifacts at SC, both intentionally and unintentionally, serve to educate viewers and visitors about the experiences of the range of people involved in the creation of M/M non-sexual spanking pornography, offering a way to reduce the stigma and bias associated with this work (Silverman 2011). This indicates that the purpose of educating outsiders about the represented group is met. The BTS offers knowledge through sharing not only the artifacts themselves and how the artifacts were made, but also how the artifacts were received by other visitors through text and video blog entries and Viewer Feedback posted on the website (Schaefer 2005).

Schaefer (2005) found a lack of information regarding the production, distribution, exhibition and reception of adult films, although these videos, as any artifacts, deserve proper recordkeeping and archiving. SC provides these records, these archives, in textual and audiovisual format, as primary sources not only from the curator but from those involved in the field, to aid the scholars of this field. SC was originally intended as a pornographic site. What turned SC from being a solely entertainment-oriented site to a public repository was a happenstance. The creator discovered that the extra footage from videotaping the prime, or final, videos might be of interest to viewers as behind-the-scenes, or bonus, video. The feedback on the first behind-the-scenes video was so positive that the creator proceeded to include such footage as an extra video with each 'prime' or final version of the pornographic video, for viewers to enjoy as they wished. This led to also having a videolog, where the creator keeps a camera running while doing things both related to the site and not, related to work with his co-creators of the artifacts demonstrating their being 'real people,' not solely entities that receive the corporal punishment. The prime videos serve the main, and original, purpose of the site, to offer pornographic entertainment, yet the real value of the repository is in the behind the scenes materials which serve as a public history repository of the creation of such artifacts and a subsection of those working in the sex video creation field (Brown 2011).

The curator and creator of SC is a self-proclaimed amateur, yet his extensive knowledge and skill, gained through years of hands-on experience as a spanking fetishist, a viewer of spanking pornography on VHS, DVD, and other websites, and a spanking video producer, has led him to create works of a professional level (Linde 1993). This has enabled the creator's exhibits to be seen as professional and high quality by a majority of the visitors who provide feedback, evidenced in part in the Viewer Mail section of the repository (http://www.spankingcentral.com/pages/comments.php), a place where the creator posts anonymous excerpts of feedback received (Gordon 2010). The creator's lack of professionalism, according to Barthes (2010), indicates that the creator's work is professional. In the field of photography, the creator is an amateur, one who "stands closer to the noeme of Photography" (98-99).

SC is an extraordinary place, offering an incredible range of experience of not only the pornographic experience but also, for the visitor who goes further, the experience of the creation of these pornographic materials, and the lives of those who participation in the creation of these artifacts (Hein 1998). SC removes a distinction between us and them, normal and freak, showing there are others interested in, and men willing to work in the production of such materials for the enjoyment of others, despite the men's non-interest in the spanking fetish (Gomoll 2007). The creator enables the visitor to not only have the pornographic experience, but to become a part of the pornographic experience, raising one's own memories and nostalgia, igniting fantasies to come to life in a visual manner, exposing one to additional ways or methods of corporal punishment.

Conclusion

Museums, archives and public history repositories often build community and intercultural understanding. This occurs not only in the traditional museum, archive, and public history repository, but also in any collection of artifacts that is shared with others. In particular, minorities are often underrepresented in the traditional, larger museums, archives, and repositories but have found a place for community building in the smaller, local repositories, particularly those that are available on the Internet. This chapter has demonstrated that an online collection of videos and accompanying stills that could be considered pornography by the majority can serve as an online public history collection by a particular community, particularly if it is a repository created by members of that community through one such example.

REFERENCES

Albin, T. (2011). 'It was only supposed to be twenty interviews': GLBTQ oral history as librarianship – the Under the Rainbow Collection. In E. Greenblatt (Ed.). *Serving LGBTIQ library and archives users: Essays on outreach, service, collections and access.* (pp. 136-145). Jefferson, NC: McFarland.

Alexander, E. P. (1960). "History museums: From Curio cabinets to cultural centers." *The Wisconsin Magazine of History, 43*(3), 173-180.

Ambrose, T. and Paine, C. (2006). *Museum basics.* 2nd ed. NY: Routledge.

Archive. (2007). In The American heritage dictionary of the English language. Retrieved from http://www.credoreference.com.library.esc.edu/entry/hmdictenglang/archive

Artifact. (2007). In The American heritage dictionary of the English language. Retrieved from http://www.credoreference.com.library.esc.edu/entry/hmdictenglang/artifact

Artifact, n. (2012). In *Oxford English dictionary online.* Retrieved from http://www.oed.com/view/Entry/10416?isAdvanced=false&result=1&rskey=6FQu0w&

Ashford, C. (2006). "The only Gay in the village: Sexuality and the net." *Information & Communications Technology Law, 15*(3), 275-289.

Barthes, R. (2010). *Camera lucinda: Reflections on photography.* Trans. R. Howard. NY: Hill and Wang.

Berger, J. (1977). *Ways of seeing.* NY: Penguin Books.

Bourdon Caston, E. (1989). A model for teaching in a museum setting. In N. Berry and S. Mayer (Eds.), *Museum education: History, theory, and practice* (pp. 90-108). Reston, VA: The National Art Education Association.

Bouquet, M. (2004). Thinking and doing otherwise: Anthropological theory in exhibitionary practice. In B. M. Carbonell (Ed.). *Museum studies: An anthology of contexts* (pp. 193-207). Malden, MA: Blackwell Publishing.

Brown, A. (2011). How queer 'pack rats' and activist archivists saved our history: An overview of lesbian, gay, bisexual, transgender, and queer (LGBTQ) archives, 1970-2008. In E. Greenblatt (Ed.). *Serving LGBTIQ*

Library and Archives Users: Essays on Outreach, Service, Collections and Access. (pp. 121-135). Jefferson, NC: McFarland.

Calder, T. L. (2011). *Curating cultures: An empirical history.* MA Thesis, Stony Brook University.

Capino, J. B. (2007). Seizing moving image pornography." *Cinema Journal, 46*(4), 121-126.

Carr, D. (2011). *Open conversations: Public learning in libraries and museums.* Santa Barbara, CA: Libraries Unlimited.

Christopher, T. (2007). The house of the seven gables: A house museum's adaptation to changing societal expectations since 1990. In A. K. Levin (Ed.). *Defining memory: Local museums and the construction of history in America's changing Communities.* (pp. 63-76). Lanham: Alta Mira Press.

Coleman, L. V. (1927). *Manual for small museums.* NY: G. P. Putnam's Sons.

Daniel, M., & Fletcher Linder, G. (2002). Marginal people. In L. Breslow (Ed.). *Encyclopedia of Public Health.* Vol. 3. (pp. 712-714). NY: Macmillan.

Dearstyne, B. W. (July / Aug 2007). "Blogs, mashups, & wikis: Oh my!" *The Information Management Journal,* 24-33.

Dubin, S. C. (1999). *Displays of power: Memory and amnesia in the American museum.* NY: NYU Press.

Ellenboger, K. M. (2002). Museums in family life: An ethnographic case study. In G. Leinhardt, K. Crowley, & K. Knutson (Eds.). *Learning Conversations in Museums.* (pp. 81-101). Mahwah, NJ: Erlbaum.

Flinn, A. (2007). Community histories, community archives: Some opportunities and challenges. *Journal of the Society of Archivists, 28*(2), 151-176.

Flinn, A. (2008). Other ways of thinking, other ways of being: Documenting the margins and the transitory: What to preserve, how to collect. In L. Craven (Ed.) *What are archives? Cultural and theoretical perspectives: A Reader* (pp. 109-128). Abingdon, UK: Ashgate Publishing.

Frost, S. (2010). The Warren Cup: Secret museums, sexuality and society. In A. K. Levin (Ed.). *Gender, sexuality, and museums: A Routledge reader.* (pp. 138-150). New York: Routledge.

Gable, E., & Handler, R. (2007). Public history, private memory: Notes from the ethnography of Colonial Williamsburg, Virginia, U.S.A. In A. K. Levin (Ed.). *Defining memory: Local museums and the construction of history in America's changing communities.* (pp. 47-62). Lanham: Alta Mira Press.

Gabriel, P. (2010). Why grapple with queer when you can fondle it? Embracing our erotic intelligence. In A. K. Levin (Ed.). *Gender, sexuality, and museums: A Routledge reader.* (pp. 71-79). New York: Routledge.

Gomoll, L. (2007). Objects of dis/order: Articulating curiosities and engaging people at the Freakatorium. In A. K. Levin (Ed.). *Defining memory: Local museums and the construction of history in America's changing communities.* (pp. 201-216). Lanham: Alta Mira Press.

Gordon, T. S. (2010). *Private history in public: Exhibition and the settings of everyday life.* Lanham: Alta Mira Press.

Gough, C., & Greenblatt, E. (2011). Barriers to selecting materials about sexual and gender diversity. In E. Greenblatt (Ed.). *Serving LGBTIQ library and archives users: Essays on outreach, service, collections and access.* (pp. 165-173). Jefferson, NC: McFarland.

Greenblatt, E. (2011). The internet and LGBTIQ communities. In E. Greenblatt (Ed.). *Serving LGBTIQ library and archives users: Essays on outreach, service, collections and access.* (pp. 42-50). Jefferson, NC: McFarland.

Greene, M. A. (2002). The power of meaning: The Archival mission in the postmodern age. *The American Archivist 65,* 42-55.

Greene, M. A. (2003-2004). The messy business of remembering: History, memory and archives. *Archival Issues: Journal of the Midwest Archives Conference, 28*(2), 95-103.

Hagelin, R. (2006). Pornography is harmful, in M. E. Williams (Ed.). *Sex.* Greenhaven Press. Opposing Viewpoints Database.

Hankin, K. (2004). "Lesbian 'making-of' documentaries and the production of lesbian sex." *The Velvet Light Trap, 53,* 26-39.

Hay, I., Hughes, A. and Tutton, M. (2004). Monuments, memory and marginalization in Adelaide's Prince Henry Gardens. *Geografiska Annaler. Series B, Human Geography 86*(3), 201-216.

Hein, G. E. (1998). *Learning in the museum*. London, UK: Routledge.

Hein, H. (2010). Looking at museums from a feminist perspective. In A. K. Levin (ed.). *Gender, sexuality and museums: A Routledge reader*. (pp. 53-64). New York: Routledge.

Hogan, K. P. (2011). Quatrefoil Library: The next generation. In E. Greenblatt (Ed.). *Serving LGBTIQ Library and Archives Users: Essays on Outreach, Service, Collections and Access*. (pp. 113-119). Jefferson, NC: McFarland.

Holt, D. B. (2011). LGBTIQ teens – plugged in and unfiltered: How Internet filtering impairs construction of online communities, identity formation, and access to health information. In E. Greenblatt (Ed.). *Serving LGBTIQ Library and Archives Users: Essays on Outreach, Service, Collections and Access*. (pp. 266-277). Jefferson, NC: McFarland.

Hooper-Greenhill, E. (2007). *Museums and education: Purpose, pedagogy, performance*. NY: Routledge.

Kellner, D. (n.d.). Jean Baudrillard. Retrieved from http://www.gseis.cla.edu/faculty/kellner/essays/baudrillard.pdf

Kendrick, W. (1996). *The secret museum: Pornography in modern culture*. Berkeley: University of California Press.

Kristol, I. (2001). Pornography should be censored. In L. K. Egendorf (Ed.). *Censorship*. Greenhaven Press. Retrieved from Opposing Viewpoints Database.

Kruger, S. F. Gay internet medievalism: Erotic story archives, the Middle Ages, and contemporary gay identity. *American Literary History, 22*(4), 913-944.

Lehman, P. (2007). You and voyeurweb: Illustrating the shifting representation of the penis on the internet with user-generated content. *Cinema Journal, 46*(4), 108-116.

Levin, A. (2007). No business like show business. In A. K. Levin (Ed.), *Defining memory: Local museums and the construction of history in America's changing communities* (pp. 231-234). Lanham: Alta Mira Press.

Linde, C. (1993). *Life stories: The creation of coherence*. NY: Oxford University Press.

Maurer, H. (1994). *Sex: An oral history*. NY: Viking.

Mazur, M. C., & Bertin, J. E. (2001). Sexual material is too wisely censored. In L. K. Egendorf (Ed.), *Censorship*. Greenhaven. Retrieved from Opposing Viewpoints Online.

McGowan, M. K. (2005). On pornography: MacKinnon, speech acts, and 'false' construction. *Hypatia, 20*(3), 23-49.

McKemmish, S., Gililland-Swtland, A., & Ketelaar, E. (2005). Communities of memory & pluralising archival research and education agendas. *Archives & Manuscripts, 33*(1), 146-174.

Museum. (2007). In The American heritage dictionary of the English language. Retrieved from http://www.credoreference.com.library.esc.edu/entry/hmdictenglang/museum

Museum, n. (2012). In *Oxford English dictionary online*. Retrieved from http://www.oed.com/view/Entry/124079?rskey-A0EDKT&result=1&isAdvanced=false

Nichols, M. (2006). Psychotherapeutic issues with 'kinky' clients: Clinical problems, yours and theirs. *Journal of Homosexuality, 50*(2/3), 281-300.

Paris, S. G., & Mercer, M. J. (2002). Finding self in objects: Identity exploration in museums. In G. Leinhardt, K. Crowley, & K. Knutson (Eds.), *Learning conversations in museums* (pp. 401-423). Mahwah, NJ: Laurence Erlbaum Associates.

Perks, R., & Thomson, A. (2006). Introduction to second edition. In R. Perks and A. Thomson (Eds.), *The Oral history reader* (pp. ix-xiv). NY: Routledge.

Plante, R. F. (2006). Sexual spanking, the self, and the construction of deviance. *Journal of Homosexuality 50*(2/3), 59-79.

Pornography. (2010). In The Hutchinson unabridged encyclopedia with atlas and weather guide. Retrieved from http://www.credoreference.com.library.esc.edu/entry/heliconhe/pornography

Pornography, n. (2012). In *Oxford English dictionary online*. Retrieved from http://www.oed.com/view/Entry/148012?isAdvanced=false&result=1&rskey=14v74u&

Repository. (2007). In The American heritage dictionary of the English language. Retrieved from http://www.credoreference.com.library.esc.edu/entry/hmdictenglang/repository

Repository, n. (2012). In *Oxford English dictionary online*. Retrieved from http://www.oed.com/view/Entry/162955?rskey=SCrzDT&result=1&isAdvanced=false

Schaefer, E. (2005). "Dirty little secrets: Scholars, archivists, and dirty movies." *The Moving Image, 5*(2), 79-105.

Silverman, L. H. *The social work of museums*. New York: Routledge, 2010.

Skramstad, H. (2010). Foreword. In T. S. Gordon, *Private history in public: Exhibition and the settings of everyday life*. Lanham: Alta Mira Press.

Slade, J. W. (1997). Pornography in the late nineties. *Wide Angle, 19*(3), 1-12.

Stainton, C. (2002). Voices and images: Making connections between identity and art. In G. Leinhardt, K. Crowley, & K. Knutson (Eds.), *Learning conversations in museums* (pp. 213-257). Mahwah, NJ: Erlbaum.

Stanton, C. (2007). Performing the post industrial: The limits of radical history in Lowell, Massachusetts. *Radical History Review, 98*, 81-96.

Stebbins, R. A. (2013). *The committed reader: Reading for utility, pleasure, and fulfillment in the 21st century*. Lanham: Scarecrow Press.

Vallance, E. (2007). Local history, "old things to look at," and a sculptor's vision: Exploring local museums through curriculum theory. In A. K. Levin (Ed.), *Defining memory: Local museums and the construction of history in America's changing communities* (pp. 27-42). Lanham: Alta Mira Press.

Weglein Kraus, J. (2008). Petticoats and primary sources: Lessons learned through public history. *Journal of Archival Organization, 6*(3), 141-150.

Weinberg, T. S. (2006). Sadomasochism and the social sciences: A review of the sociological and social psychology literature. *Journal of Homosexuality 50*(2/3), 17-40.

Weiss, M. D. (2006). Mainstreaming kink: The politics of BDSM representation in U.S. popular media. *Journal of Homosexuality 50*(2/3), 103-132.

Williams, C. (2008). Personal papers: Perceptions and practices. In L. Craven (Ed.), *What are archives?: Cultural and theoretical perspectives: A reader* (pp. 45-67). Abingdon, UK: Ashgate.

Windon, K. (2012). The right to decay with dignity: Documentation and the negotiation between an artist's sanction and the cultural interest. *Art Documentation 31*(2), 142-157.

Woodward, I. (2007). *Understanding material culture*. Los Angeles: Sage.

Woodward, J. (2013). *Transformed library: E-books, expertise, and evolution*. Chicago: ALA Editions.

Zeller, T. (1989). The historical and philosophical foundations of art museum education in America. In N. Berry and S. Mayer (Eds.), *Museum education: History, theory, and practice* (pp. 10-89). Reston, VA: The National Art Education Association.

Organizing the Transgender Internet: Web Directories and Envisioning Inclusive Digital Spaces

Jane Sandberg
Linn-Benton Community College

Abstract

Problematic features of the Internet have complicated transgender people's information seeking. Transgender people have historically created Web directories to counteract these limitations and to guide others toward resources that are accurate, relevant, and respectful. These directories offer valuable insights for librarians and others interested in designing positive online environments that address transgender people's needs.

Keywords: transgender, information needs, Web directories, hostile online environments, search engines

Introduction

The Internet has had transformative effects on the transgender community. Its anonymity allows individuals to participate in frank information exchanges and to enact identities that they may be unable to express in real life, while its vast scale facilitates community building across long distances. The Internet also presents challenges to the transgender community, including hostile online environments, search engine exclusions, and a dearth of authoritative sources relevant to transgender people's information needs. Members of the transgender community have historically attempted to address such limitations by selecting and organizing accurate, relevant, and respectful resources in projects such as Web directories.

This chapter will use several of these directories as case studies that reveal digital practices that successfully meet the information needs of transgender people. These cases will be situated within a critical examination of the online information landscape for transgender people. The chapter will close with a set of recommendations for designing transgender-inclusive digital spaces.

Transgender People's Information Needs

An information need is a "gap in a person's knowledge that, when experienced at the conscious level as a question, gives rise to a search for an answer" (Reitz, n.d., para. 1). There are a number of information needs unique to trans[1] individuals; these needs have been met with varying degrees of success by digital and print resources. A survey of the literature reveals a diverse set of information needs that individuals may face because of their transgender identity, many of which can be classified as medical, legal, or emotional support needs.

People who choose to undergo a medical transition often face information needs surrounding surgeries and/or hormone replacement therapy (HRT). Surgery questions may concern the different types of surgeries, their costs and how to fund them, aftercare and the recovery process, and the work of particular surgeons. HRT questions may pertain to hormone types and regimens, methods of administration (e.g. how to self-administer hormone shots), and potential side effects and interactions with the hormones. Regardless of whether an individual chooses to medically transition, they still face questions about whether their medical providers will be supportive and how much information about their transgender status they can safely share. Trans people of any gender identity may face these information needs, but individuals with non-binary identities face the additional challenge of navigating resources that assume that these concerns are specific to transsexuals with binary identities.

Transgender individuals also face a number of legal issues. One key area is legal recourse in response to situations of anti-transgender prejudice, such as employment discrimination or hate crimes. Another area of concern is the often complex process of changing one's name and sex designation on official documents, for individuals seeking such changes. Family law questions are not uncommon. Questions about Selective Service registration in the United States also fall into this category.

---

1 In this chapter, the terms transgender and trans will be ussed interchangeably.

Emotional support needs are also important due to the stress of facing antitransgender prejudice, particularly when a transgender identity intersects with other marginalized identities. Several studies have indicated the importance of locating support groups, trans-friendly counselors, and narratives that document other trans people's personal experiences. Other common emotional information needs include learning how to accept one's self as transgender, navigate a cisgender-centric society, and develop romantic and sexual relationships.

A number of needs do not fit neatly within these categories. Many transgender people seek information that helps them cultivate an appearance or style that better matches their gender identity. Trans people may wish to research chosen names or find information about pronouns or titles. Individuals may also wish to locate social spaces in which they can enjoy themselves while not having to worry about how others will react to their trans identity.

Taylor's (2002) survey was the first to focus on transgender people's information needs. This survey asked respondents both to express their current information needs and to recall the questions they had when first coming to terms with their trans identities. Early information needs tended to involve emotional support, leading participants to search for local support groups, counseling services, and the personal experiences of other trans individuals. By the time of Taylor's study, 83% of the participants reported still having information needs related to their transgender identity, although the knowledge gaps had changed somewhat. These new questions tended to focus more on legal issues, particularly employment discrimination, hate crimes, and family law. While the study identified several important information needs, Taylor noted that the results are "unlikely [to be] representative of the transgender population" (Taylor 2002, 89). Respondents were disproportionately White and well-educated, and most of the respondents were known to be transsexual women and male-to-female crossdresser individuals. Taylor's survey questions also assumed that respondents were interested in presenting themselves in feminine ways, asking only about traditionally feminine gender presentation techniques such as makeup and hair removal.

Otto (2005) identified information needs specific to transsexual men, based on "literature review and Internet search." Otto's paper was the first to classify transgender people's information needs into medical, legal, and emotional support needs. The needs listed were similar to those revealed by Taylor's study, but with a strong emphasis on HRT and document changes, both of which were absent from Taylor's survey. In the same article, Otto noted that information literacy skills are vitally important for transgender individuals, since transspecific information needs are unlikely to be met through mainstream channels

(Otto 2005). In a subsequent presentation for the American Library Association, Otto (2007) reiterated and refined these three basic categories. The presentation also emphasized that respect and confidentiality by librarians are central to positive transgender information-seeking experiences.

Beiriger and Jackson (2008) conducted a survey to determine the information needs of transgender communities in Portland, Oregon. Unlike previous papers, which focused primarily on transsexual identities, the Portland study intentionally included a large number of identities that fall under the transgender umbrella. The survey instrument included 61 terms participants could use to describe their gender identity, and each option was selected at least once. While the major information needs expressed in this study fit into the three established categories, respondents were also interested in locating trans fiction, information about queer politics and theory, trans-friendly employers, medical journals, and non-English materials.

Finally, Fisher's (2011) piece about Second Life, an online virtual world, offers a compelling exploratory way to meet identity-related information needs. In the piece, Fisher described using a female avatar in Second Life because of the author's "lifelong urge to be female" (Fisher 2011, 52). Using the avatar provided opportunities to explore a female identity and experience a sense of authenticity that were not then available to Fisher in real life. After being able to transition virtually through Second Life, Fisher decided to transition in real life as well. The piece also referred to a number of other individuals who likewise "enjoy[ed], often for the first time, their authentic selves in a sincere way [through Second Life]" (Fisher 2011, 53). In the online space provided by Second Life, Fisher was able to fill a personal knowledge gap about experiencing the world as female in an inclusive, supportive, anonymous environment.

Information Seeking Environments

When an individual is seeking an answer to fill their information need, the quality of their search experience depends greatly upon the environment in which they are searching. If the tools they use do not contain answers to their questions or make these answers difficult to find, the individual is unlikely to have a positive experience. Furthermore, if the tools offend or marginalize an individual because of their identity or perceived identity, their experience is also unlikely to be a good one.

The Limitations of Physical Library Spaces

Traditional librarianship has often failed to create supportive environments in which transgender people feel safe searching for answers to their questions. A report issued by the Oak Park Public Library (OPPL) identified barriers to access in its catalog, collections, customer services, facilities, official communications, policies, and procedures (*Service focus committee: Transgender people report*, 2007). Specific issues included the absence of an easily accessible non-gendered bathroom, gender-specific greetings on official communications, and library card applications that required applicants to identify themselves as either male or female. OPPL addressed these issues, creating a well-respected collection of trans materials in the process, but trans-exclusionary library practices are too often left unquestioned. As a result, libraries are "grossly underutilized as an information resource" by transgender communities (Beiriger and Jackson 2008, 52).[2]

Creating Online Spaces

While physical library spaces are grossly underutilized, Internet spaces have seen heavy use by transgender people. The transgender community has leveraged many of the Internet's features to effectively address several of its unique information needs. Numerous surveys (Taylor 2002; Adams and Peirce 2006; Beiriger and Jackson 2008) have confirmed the importance of Internet resources to transgender individuals. In Taylor's (2002, 90) survey, 82.2% of respondents consulted online resources to learn about "transgender identity and issues" at a time when only 53.9% of Americans used the Internet ("Computer and Internet use" 2002, Table 2-2).

Several features make the Internet a compelling medium for transgender information seeking and sharing. The Internet provides a level of anonymity that allows trans individuals to participate in frank information exchanges and to express identities that they cannot in real life. The Internet's vast scale also facilitates community building and ally education across long distances. Trans Internet pioneer Gwen Smith positioned the transgender community as "one of the first communities[...] to take full advantage of the cyber world, using it as a way of educating both each other and those outside of [the transgender] experience" (Highleyman 2002, 68).

Taylor (2002) attributed the popularity of the World Wide Web to its convenience and the relative unlikeliness that an individual will be outed by their information seeking. Shapiro (2004) discusses the Internet as a tool that facilitates transgender organizing and activism. A respondent to Adams

---

2 See Thompson (2012) for a comprehensive bibliographic essay on issues of transgender information access in physical library spaces.

and Pierce's (2006, 5) study also emphasized the technology's potential for community building and self-empowerment, saying:

"[T]he development of the internet is the single-most important tool fueling the development of the transgender community, and in fostering empowerment within it. When we realize that we're *not* alone, that there *is* hope for a fulfilling life, that others have already walked this path and have shared their experiences – that's an incredibly powerful thing."

Hostile Environments: Web Services and Barriers to Access

The Internet, for all the benefits it has provided the transgender community, has problematic features that complicate information seeking. These features include the normative biases of search engines, naming practices that render online environments hostile, Web filters, and a lack of authoritative information. This section will address each of these issues in turn.

Search Engines, Trans-Misogyny, and Racism

The abundance of information available on the Internet leads to limited user attention and a high reliance on gate-keeping discovery tools, particularly search engines. These gate-keeping tools capitalize on users' limited attention by channeling that attention toward certain resources and away from others (Hargittai 2000). While search engines present this process as neutral and mechanical, search algorithms and their designers are in fact responsible for highly subjective decisions: which Web sites are most "relevant" or "important" to a user's query? In their classic article, Shaping the Web: Why the Politics of Search Engines Matter," Nissenbaum and Introna (2002) critiqued the assumptions inherent in modern search engine algorithms. According to the article, these algorithms operate by promoting wealthy, popular, and otherwise powerful interests, undermining the apparent democratic nature of the Internet. This leads to a systematic exclusion of Web sites that espouse non-normative interests; this exclusion has ramifications for the transgender community.

The intersection of several prejudices can be painfully apparent when using search engines to locate trans-specific information. The intersection between *trans-misogyny* (the marginalization of trans people with feminine and/or female gender identities) and racism is particularly evident. Serano (2012) explained in the "Trans-misogyny Primer" that all trans people potentially face social stigma, but "those on the male-to-female or trans female/feminine spectrum generally receive the overwhelming majority of societal fascination, consternation and demonization" (Serano 2012, para. 1). Serano pointed to "the way in which trans women and others on the trans female/feminine spectrum are routinely sexualized in the media" (Serano 2012, para. 3) as a particularly visible example of trans-misogyny.

This routine sexualization of transgender bodies, particularly those of trans women of color, leads to search engine results dominated by pornography intended for White cisgender men, lacking both authentic portrayals and reliable information. Google search results for queries that include terms like "transgender" and "transsexual" typically include a fair amount of pornography, particularly if the query includes a term denoting a racial identity such as "Asian", "Black", "Latina", or "Latino."[3,4] Even though Google has taken steps to offer a more diverse portrayal of women of color, it supposedly "targeted" advertisements are also often dominated by pornography and dating services. Google's search result pages reduce trans people to their bodies, and then tell trans people that their bodies are only valuable as sexual objects for White cisgender men.

Search engines trivialize entire trans communities of color. In 2012, the first result for the query *African American transsexuals* was a site asking why African American transsexuals do not exist. Prominent results like these, in conjunction with the fetishization mentioned above, trivialize a community with a rich history of contributions to the African American, transgender, and LGBTQ communities (Roberts 2012). Black trans women such as Marsha P. Johnson and Miss Major have played pivotal roles throughout 20th and 21st century LGBT activism, and the erasure of their contributions and community does a great disservice to trans information seekers.

Naming Practices

According to the Gay & Lesbian Alliance Against Defamation, transgender people "should be afforded the same respect for their chosen name as anyone else who lives by a name other than their birth name," even if they have not changed their name legally (2010, Names, Pronoun Usage & Descriptions section, para. 1). It is imperative that Web resources respect the chosen names of their users and the people described within the resource.

Many Web sites, such as Facebook and Google have implemented "real name" policies. These policies can be difficult to navigate for transgender people

---

3   See Noble (2012a, 2012b) for a discussion of the problematic treatment of women, particularly women of color, in search engine results.

4   See Sweeney (2013) for a study of the racial bias exhibited by Google's advertisement services.

who use a name other than their birth name, or who go by multiple names. For example, Google+'s policy required users to identify themselves with "the name your friends, family, or co-workers usually call you," (York 2011, para. 4) which excludes transgender people who have not yet come out to these groups, or who wish to use a pseudonym to avoid harassment or cyberbullying. Google+ has moved away from its real name policy, but Facebook has recently drawn attention for enforcing its own real name policy by suspending several drag queens' accounts (Holpuch 2014).

These policies do not only affect trans people on an individual level. When an online resource misnames a trans person, or when its policy requires a trans user to use a name they don't identify with, "an entire group of people sees a part of themselves erased and devalued" (Gay & Lesbian Alliance Against Defamation 2013, para. 1).

Identity Terms

Information systems that refer to transgender identities using inaccurate, outdated, or offensive terms can also exclude transgender users. Online Public Access Catalogs (OPACs), for instance, are offered by many libraries. The classification systems used by the vast majority of these catalogs – Library of Congress Subject Headings (LCSH) and Dewey Decimal Classification (DDC) – have frequently been critiqued for their problematic treatment of LGBTQ identities, particularly transgender identities (Adler 2009; Johnson 2010; Greenblatt 2011; Roberto 2011). According to Roberto (2011), "[t]hrough the use of inaccurate language in the [LCSH] and problematic classification schemes, catalogers often unwittingly contribute to the creation of library environments that are passively hostile to transgender users." LCSH excludes and conflates transgender identities, hindering access to resources that discuss such identities.

Adler (2009) systematically compared library-assigned LCSH with user-generated LibraryThing tags for twenty works containing transgender themes. Adler's work suggested that a combination of LCSH and user-generated terminology effectively provides users with the findability and precision of controlled vocabularies as well as the currency and responsiveness to self-identification provided by the tagging approach.

Libraries sometimes publish their authority file within their OPAC. The RDA cataloging code allows catalogers to add information about a person's gender to an authority record, but restrictions placed by the Library of Congress limit catalogers to three options (female, male, not known). This simplistic approach to describing gender results in inaccurate descriptions and a marginalization of trans authors and contributors (Billey, Drabinski, and Roberto 2014).

None of these problems unique to library descriptive practices. Many Web sites restrict gender options and include inaccurate terminology, which contribute to an environment that is hostile toward transgender users.

Access Restrictions

Even if a tool works to overcome transphobic, trans-misogynist, and racist prejudices and respects trans people's chosen names and identities, its utility may be negated by limitations on users' access to the tool. Users who rely on public Internet access may feel uncomfortable searching for sensitive information in a public space. Users, particularly trans youth and low-income trans people, may also face Internet filtering. While there is compelling evidence that unfiltered Internet access allows LGBTQ youth to make informed decisions about their health and feel more comfortable with their identities, regulations such as the Children's Internet Protection Act make it financially difficult for libraries and schools to offer patrons this type of access (Holt 2011).

Medical Information Needs

Some specific information needs are harder to meet online than others. As noted previously, many information needs specific to the transgender community are medical in nature. However, popular health information sites typically have no formal peer review process. Even if an information seeker finds information online that does not fetishize their body, trivialize their community, or disrespect their identity, there is no guarantee that the information they find will be trustworthy or intelligible (Cline and Haynes 2001).

Trans Web Directories

Because of limitations such as those discussed above, the transgender community has historically felt a strong need to guide community members toward reliable Internet sources. Many of these initiatives have involved the construction of *Web directories*, which are categorized collections of links to other Web sites, typically arranged hierarchically by subject. Transgender people have curated such directories since at least 1994, only a year after the release of the first widely used Web browser, NCSA Mosaic. Successful Web directories address several of the problems explored above: search engine exclusions, hostile environments, disrespectful naming practices, and the difficulties of locating authoritative information.

Table 1

Transgender Web Directories, 1994-2013		
Directory	URL	Years Active
GenderWeb	http://web.archive.org/web/*/ http://genderweb.org	1994 – 2004
IFGE Web Links	http://web.archive.org/web/*/ http://ifge.org	1998 – 2010
Open Directory Project "Transgendered" Category	http://dmoz.org/Society/Transgendered	1998 –
Rachel's Web	http://web.archive.org/web/*/ http://www.rachels-web.com	2000 – 2008
Susana Marques TV/ CD/TS/TG Directory	http://web.archive.org/web/*/http://tgirls. liplock.org/tvcddirectory/menu.htm	2002 – 2005
Susan's Place	http://susans.org	2002 –
trans411	http://web.archive.org/web/*/ http://www.trans411.net/	2007 – 2012
Trans Mentors International, Inc. Resource Directory	http://web.archive.org/web/*/http:// transmentors.org/resource-directory.html	2010 – 2014

The earliest of these resource, *GenderWeb,* was created in 1994 by Julia Case, the owner of a small Long Island computer company, "so that we could all share some knowledge and educate those around us[...]" (Case n.d., What's not so new section, para. 1). This participatory rhetoric is not necessarily shared by later, more closely curated directories. However, most directories do encourage some type of user participation – all but one of the directories mentioned in this chapter have chosen to include a mechanism for users to submit sites they find useful.

The next directory, maintained by the International Foundation for Gender Education (IFGE), represented a more institutionalized initiative than *GenderWeb.* The IFGE is one of the most established trans organizations in the United States, and as of 1996, it was the only national transgender organization to have paid staff members, according to a study of national organizations carried out by Dallas Denny (as cited in Shapiro 2004). The resource's connection to a structured nonprofit organization allowed it to enjoy a remarkably long 12-year lifespan. This longevity is also a testament to the resource's value to its users; respondents to Taylor's survey identified the site as the "best source on the internet," (2002 102) preferring the site to Google and Yahoo for trans-related information seeking.

The next directory is the "Society: Transgendered" category of the general *Open Directory Project* (ODP, also known as *dmoz*). All links collected on the site are submitted, reviewed, and maintained by a community of volunteer editors. By 1999, only a year after the directory's 1998 launch, the "Society: Transgendered" category had become a very active resource with a distinct personality. The category then contained links to 788 resources, divided into whimsical subcategories such as "Hangouts", "Fun", and "Our Sweeties". The "Transgendered" category still exists, but its subcategories use generic labels and the number of linked resources has dropped substantially. Between 2004 and 2012, though the size of the ODP as a whole increased from four to five million links, the number of resources listed in its Transgendered category dropped from 1,362 to 689.

Susan's Place began not as a directory, but as a chatroom (Larson 1999). The site currently includes the original chatroom, forums, news specific to trans communities, and a directory of community-submitted Web sites. The directory is very loosely curated, including many listings for commercial sites. *Trans411*, a directory active between 2007-2012, also included a number of commercial sites in its roughly 1,000 links. This was partly the result of *Trans411's freemium* model, in which a basic resource listing was free, but a commercial site could pay for additional metadata elements to be included in their listing.

Several directories intentionally define more specialized scopes for themselves. One early resource, *Rachel's Web*, collected links to personal Web sites of trans individuals. *Susana Marques' TV/CD/TS/TG Directory* provided a comprehensive guide to the many personal transgender Web sites hosted on the now defunct Geocities, primarily in the LGBT-specific West Hollywood Geocities neighborhood. Trans Mentors International Inc. (TMII), a nonprofit in Arizona, also operated a database of online resources focusing on support resources within specific local communities, rather than general Web resources.

Web Directory Curation

Each directory has taken a different approach to curation and editorial policy. While all sites except IFGE's have encouraged trans people to submit links they found valuable, some sites include a careful review process or detailed selection policies, while others adopt a more flexible process.

Selection policies varied widely across Web directories. *Rachel's Web* explicitly excluded pornographic sites, but would include any other type of personal site. TMII's directory listed no requirements except that the submitted resources be "trans-friendly." Most directories included a form with which users could anonymously submit resources for inclusion, but *Rachel's Web* and *Susana Marques' TV/CD/TS/TG Directory* asked users to email the directory's curator directly with link suggestions.

Directories also varied in the types of commercial sites they chose to include – an important decision as commercial interests begin to recognize transgender people as a marketing demographic and may or may not have an interest in providing accurate or helpful information. None of the trans-specific directories discussed here exclude commercial sites outright, but some have chosen to exclude specific types of commercial sites. Others place no restrictions on such sites, and have been filled with advertisements for clothing, services, makeup, prosthetics, and online pharmacies.

The *ODP*'s editorial practice provides an interesting counterpoint to those of trans-specific directories. It has far more extensive editorial policies than any of the trans-specific directories; these policies specifically exclude product listings from the directory. *ODP* editors also have a mandate to represent "all topics and points of view" (Open Directory Project n.d., Overview section, para. 1) in the directory. As a result, the "Society: Transgendered" category includes resources both *for* and *about* trans people, and resources written from points of view that transgender information seekers may find unhelpful or offensive.

The directories listed here also take different approaches to who does the work of curation. Some directories solicit suggestions from the community at large but remain under the curatorial control of a single individual. Other directories have a strong volunteer base responsible for selecting, moderating, and revising directory entries.

Limitations of Web Directories

While all of these directories has approached their work in different ways, some overall trends regarding the resources' target audiences can be noted. Most of the directories show a decided bias toward resources for trans women rather than trans men. With the exception of *Susana Marques' TV/CD/TS/TG Directory*, these directories focus on transition resources for transsexuals. Information needs unrelated to physical and legal transition are more difficult to meet using these directories. Resources for trans people of color or people with non-binary identities are often completely absent.

Contemporary directories have had difficulties providing access to new forms of Web based media. Despite the current explosion of trans expression on Web 2.0 platforms like YouTube, tumblr, and reddit, current directories are not equipped to provide access to the vast amounts of trans-specific information these resources provide. Because of these limitations, and because of a general trend away from rigidly structured information access, more informal ways of organizing and collocating trans bodies of knowledge are gaining in prominence. Chen (2010) discusses YouTube's popularity within the trans community. The article points to Asian transmasculinities as identities historically excluded from official archives, and notes that this exclusion is reproduced by search engines and their quantity-driven logics. According to Chen, it is only through "everyday archives" such as those facilitated by YouTube that trans Asian men are able to express their personal narratives in archivable ways and to position Asian transmasculinity as an archivable subject.

One of Chen's case studies provides a particularly illuminating example of organizing trans-related information on YouTube. The video was made by "Zach, an early 20s pre-transition FTM-identified transsexual of Asian provenance who[...] proposes a revisory approach to tags, language and the YouTube archive." Zach expresses frustration with the difficulty of searching for YouTube videos made by FTM individuals, noting that "a lot of FTM tags actually are weird things like *fear the mullet*," and proposes that channel owners collocate their videos within YouTube by using the tag "FTMTrans" (Chen 2010). Another vlogger started a similar collocation project by requesting that channel owners respond to a single video with their username and a brief description of their channel. This video had 319 comments at the time of writing, most of which are concise descriptions of trans-related Youtube channels (Elias 2011).

Informing a New Digital Practice

The successes and limitations of these web directories suggest a number of practices that improve information seeking experiences for transgender people. This chapter concludes with a list of recommendations for librarians, Web designers, information architects, and other information workers who wish to create safe, informative environments in which transgender people can find answers to their questions. This author hopes that these recommendations will serve as a step toward a digital practice that successfully addresses the information needs of transgender people.

Counteract Systemic Exclusions

Actively incorporate resources that users cannot easily discover using other tools. The normative biases of search engines marginalize information relevant to certain communities, particularly transgender women of color. To counter this marginalization, Web services should emphasize resources relevant to these communities.

Evaluate Tools for Biases

Be aware of the biases of the tools that you use. For example, if a project uses Google products to provide search access or advertising revenue, be aware that the advertisements and rankings produced by this tool may be racist, transmisogynist, or otherwise hostile to users.

Respect Chosen Names

If names play a prominent role in a tool's design, make sure that the names it displays match individuals' actual identities. A "real" name policy is rarely necessary, but if it is a firm requirement, the policy should explicitly recognize transgender people's chosen names as real names.

Use Respectful Terminology

Make sure that any controlled vocabularies are held accountable to terminology preferred by the transgender community. Base your controlled vocabularies on folksonomies and controlled vocabularies from within the trans community, such as tags listed on a group blog.

Allow Non-Binary Gender Identities

Web applications should not require gender identification at all for use of a service. If gender identification is absolutely necessary, allow users to describe their identities using free-form strings rather than selecting an identity from a limited list.[5]

Don't Assume Access

Before publicly releasing a digital tool, experiment with common Internet filters to discover whether or not the tool's target audience will be able to access the resource. Note that some content filters, such as McAfee's *SiteAdvisor* service,

---

5 If you are trying to identify transgender populations statistically, the recommendations provided by the GenIUSS Group (2014) may be helpful.

allow Web site administrators to dispute ratings and categorizations that cause their sites to be blocked.[6]

Recognize the Impact of the Interface

When designing a tool's interface, recognize that some users may be outed by interfaces that attract the attention of others, and therefore require a discreet interface. At the same time, other users may prefer an interface that proudly reaffirms their identity. If possible, tools should offer users an opportunity to indicate which type of interface they prefer, and to switch between these interfaces as they feel necessary. An "escape" button – a common feature of Web sites designed for survivors of sexual violence that will immediately redirect a user to a different website – is another element that may be included.

Consider Curatorial Roles

Some projects benefit from a strong volunteer base, while others are better served by a more restrictive editorial process. Consider your project's scope and establish curatorial roles accordingly.

Conclusion

While the Internet has offered the transgender community opportunities to create information resources without the limitations of physical spaces and traditional librarianship, it also presents many new challenges. Information workers interested in offering digital information to transgender people must confront issues such as search engine exclusions, hostile naming practices, identity regulation, and a lack of authoritative information.

However, a number of tools, such as Web directories, have originated within the transgender community itself to address these and other issues. A critical examination of these tools offers invaluable insights for librarians and other information workers who wish to create inclusive digital spaces for transgender people. It is hoped that the recommendations and experiences offered in this article can serve as a starting point for information workers interested in digital outreach to transgender information seekers.

---

6 http://www.siteadvisor.com/webmasters/index.htm

REFERENCES

Adams, S., & Peirce, K. (2006, June). Is there a transgender canon?: Information seeking and use in the transgender community. In H. Moukdad (Ed.), *Information science revisited: Approaches to innovation*. Toronto: Canadian Association for Information Science. Retrieved from http://www.cais-acsi.ca/proceedings/2006/adams 2006.pdf

Adler, M. (2009). Transcending library catalogs: a comparative study of controlled terms in Library of Congress Subject Headings and user-generated tags in LibraryThing for transgender books. *Journal of Web Librarianship*, 3 , 309–331.

Beiriger, A., & Jackson, R. M. (2008). An assessment of the information needs of transgender communities in Portland, Oregon. *Public Library Quarterly*, 26 , 45–60.

Billey, A., Drabinski, E., & Roberto, K. R. (2014). What's gender got to do with it? A critique of RDA 9.7. *Cataloging & Classification Quarterly*, 52 , 1–10.

Case, J. (n.d.). *Julia's page*. Retrieved from http://web.archive.org/web/20000819003830/http://www.genderweb.org/julie/

Chen, M. Y. (2010, June). Everywhere archives: Transgendering, trans Asians, and the Internet. *Australian Feminist Studies*, 25 (64), 199–208.

Cline, R. J., & Haynes, K. M. (2001). Consumer health information seeking on the Internet: the state of the art. *Health Education Research*, 16 (6), 671–692.

Computer and Internet use. (2002, February). In *A nation online: How Americans are expanding their use of the Internet*. [Washington, DC]: [National Telecommunications & Information Administration]. Retrieved from http://www.ntia.doc.gov/legacy/ntiahome/dn/nationonline 020502.htm

Elias, M. (2011, February). *Transgender channel directory*. https://www.youtube.com/watch?v=3EvyNgEQI3s.

Fisher, K. (2011). It's not Monopoly: Gender role explorations in online environments. In E. Greenblatt (Ed.), *Serving LGBTIQ library and archives users: Essays on outreach, service, collections and access* (pp. 51–53). Jefferson, NC: McFarland & Company.

Gay & Lesbian Alliance Against Defamation. (2010). *GLAAD media reference guide*. Retrieved from http://www.glaad.org/reference/transgender

Gay & Lesbian Alliance Against Defamation. (2013). *When journalists mis-identify a trans person*. Retrieved from http://www.glaad.org/blog/when-journalists-mis-identify-trans-person

GenIUSS Group. (2014). Best Practices for Asking Questions to Identify Transgender and Other Gender Minority Respondents on Population-Based Surveys. J.L. Herman (ed.). Los Angeles, CA: The Williams Institute.

Greenblatt, E. (2011). The treatment of LGBTIQ concepts in the Library of Congress Subject Headings. In E. Greenblatt (Ed.), *Serving LGBTIQ library and archives users: Essays on outreach, service, collections and access* (pp. 212–228). Jefferson, NC: McFarland & Company.

Hargittai, E. (2000). Open portals or closed gates? Channeling content on the World Wide Web. *Poetics*, 27 (4), 233–253.

Highleyman, L. (2002). Interview: Gwendolyn Ann Smith. In A. Ellis, L. Highleyman, K. Schaub, & M. White (Eds.), *The Harvey Milk Institute guide to lesbian, gay, bisexual, transgender, and queer Internet research* (p. 66-70). New York: Harrington Park Press.

Holpuch, A. (2014, October). Victory for drag queens as Facebook apologises for "real-name" policy. *The Guardian*. Retrieved from http://www.theguardian.com/technology/2014/oct/01/victory-drag-queens-facebook-apologises-real-name-policy

Holt, D. (2011). LGBTIQ teens – plugged in and unfiltered: How internet filtering impairs construction of online communities, identity formation, and access to health information. In E. Greenblatt (Ed.), *Serving LGBTIQ library and archives users: Essays on outreach, service, collections and access* (pp. 266–277). Jefferson, NC: McFarland & Company.

Johnson, M. (2010). Transgender subject access: history and current practice. *Cataloging & Classification Quarterly*, 48 , 661–683.

Larson, S. ([1999]). *My biography*. Retrieved from http://www.susans.org/susan/index.html

Nissenbaum, H., & Introna, L. D. (2002). Shaping the Web: Why the politics of search engines matter. In V. V. Gehring (Ed.), *The Internet in public life* (pp. 7–27). Lanham, MD.: Rowman & Littlefield Publishers, Inc.

Noble, S. U. (2012a). Missed connections. *Bitch Magazine: Feminist Response to Pop Culture*(54), 36–41.

Noble, S. U. (2012b). *Searching for black girls: old traditions in new media*. Unpublished doctoral dissertation, University of Illinois at Urbana-Champaign, Urbana, IL. Retrieved from http://hdl.handle.net/2142/42315

Open Directory Project. (n.d.). *Open directory editing guidelines*. Retrieved from http://www.dmoz.org/guidelines/

Otto, J. (2005). *Information instruction for female-to-male transsexuals* [PDF document]. Retrieved from http://www.jotto.info/FTM/info %20 for ftm.pdf

Otto, J. (2007). *Addressing the information needs of female-to-male transsexuals* [PDF document]. Retrieved from http://www.jotto.info/FTM/GLBT ALMS 4.1.pdf

Reitz, J. M. (n.d.). Information need. In *ODLIS: Online dictionary for library and information science*. ABCCLIO. Retrieved from http://www.abc-clio.com/ODLIS/odlis i.aspx#infoneed

Roberto, K. R. (2011). Inflexible bodies: Metadata for transgender identities. *Journal of Information Ethics*, 20 (2), 56–64.

Roberts, M. (2012, March). A look at African-American trans trailblazers. *Ebony*. Retrieved from http://www.ebony.com/news-views/trans-trailblazers

Serano, J. (2012). A trans-misogyny primer [PDF document]. Retrieved from http://www.juliaserano.com/av/TransmisogynyPrimer-Serano.pdf

Service focus committee: Transgender people report (Committee report). (2007, May). Oak Park, IL: Oak Park Public Library. Retrieved from http://oppl.org/sites/default/files/trc report.pdf

Shapiro, E. (2004). 'trans' cending barriers'. *Journal of Gay & Lesbian Social Services*, 14 (3-4), 165-179. doi: 10.1300/J041v16n03_11

Sweeney, L. (2013). *Discrimination in online ad delivery*. Retrieved from http://arxiv.org/abs/1301.6822

Taylor, J. (2002). Targeting the information needs of transgender individuals. *Current Studies in Librarianship*, 26 , 85–109.

York, J. C. (2011). A case for pseudonyms. *Electronic Frontier Foundation*. Retrieved from https://www.eff.org/deeplinks/2011/07/case-pseudonyms

Queering Wikipedia

Rachel Wexelbaum, Katie Herzog, and Lane Rasberry
(With acknowledgments to Fae, Allison Schulte, Srs Sharp, Toni Rodriguez, Charles Stewart, and Adrianne Wadewitz)

Photographs by Jay R. Lawton

Introduction

Wikipedia has become the ubiquitous, often maligned, free global online reference resource. In certain countries, it may be the *only* available LGBTIQ reference resource. To increase the diversity of voices, genders, and cultures among its contributors and editors, the Wikimedia Foundation has made it a strategic goal to recruit and foster more women, people of color, and other underrepresented individuals—including LGBTIQ populations (Wikimedia Foundation, 2011). While critics question the authority, accuracy, and objectivity of Wikipedia entries, "Wikipedians" (active contributors and editors) from a wide variety of subject specialization communities interact in the creation, maintenance, and expansion of each entry, thus making the content more comprehensive and robust.

There are multiple types of LGBTIQ information available through Wikipedia, and the Wikimedia Foundation has different structures and strategies in place to recruit and foster LGBTIQ Wikipedians. One initiative—"Wikipedia Loves Libraries"—encourages all cultural heritage institutions to organize "Wikipedia editathons" (also known as "Wikipedia parties") to bring people together to create and edit new entries. Ideally, libraries, archives, and museums will use these opportunities to leverage their own collections through Wikipedia and share links to their unique digitized content (if indeed this content has been digitized). The Tom of Finland Foundation has the distinction of being the first LGBT cultural heritage institution to participate in Wikipedia Loves Libraries; their brave step into Wikipedia should serve as an inspiration to others.

Basic Facts about Wikipedia

As of 2012, Wikipedia is the fifth most-visited website in the world, and the top most visited non-profit website. A Google search for any topic will retrieve at least one Wikipedia entry on the first page of search results. Each month Wikipedia receives 19 billion page views to more than 23 million articles in 285 languages. More than 80,000 volunteer editors regularly contribute content to Wikipedia (Wikimedia Foundation, 2011-2012 Annual Report).

In the *Wikimedia Strategic Plan: A collaborative vision for the movement through 2015*, the Wikimedia Foundation lists seven core beliefs. They include:

> **Information shall be accurate and unbiased**
> ...we believe that mass collaboration among a diverse set of contributors, combined with consensus building around controversial topics, are powerful tools for achieving our goals. We strive to provide information that is accurate, neutral, verifiable, comprehensive and unbiased.
>
> **We value openness and diversity**
> ...A healthy mix of demographic and cultural characteristics everywhere throughout the movement is key to Wikimedia's success.

In spite of their core beliefs, the Wikimedia Foundation recognizes that the majority of its Wikipedia contributors and editors are disproportionately male, under 22 years old, and (most likely white and straight) from "the Global North" (Wikimedia Foundation 2011). They also admit that

> Wikipedia's coverage is skewed toward the interests, expertise, and language skills of the people who created it. For example, our coverage of biographical and pop culture topics is very strong, but our coverage of Africa is quite weak. We offer much more information in German than we do in Hindi.
>
> (Wikimedia Foundation, 2011)

For these reasons, the Wikimedia Foundation is trying to do a better job in recruiting contributors and editors from a variety of communities, including LGBTIQ populations.

While LGBTIQ people are often early adopters of online spaces and new technologies, they share the same suspicions about Wikipedia as other populations. While Wikipedia has become the leading source of health information for consumers as well as professionals around the world—often the only source of health information in developing countries—Wikipedian Lane Rasberry (user:Bluerasberry) struggles to get LGBTIQ health organizations involved in contributing LGBTIQ-specific health information to entries about HIV, AIDS, and other health issues that affect LGBTIQ communities. The organizations often cite lack of time, lack of expertise, or the poor reputation of Wikipedia in medical communities for their lack of participation. Not only that, but LGBTIQ contributors have other insecurities toward editing and contributing information in an open space. Those LGBTIQ people from countries that criminalize LGBTIQ identities and monitor their behavior must take on aliases and work from various IP addresses so their LGBTIQ-related Wikipedia work cannot be traced back to them.

To increase the number of people willing to get involved in WikiProjects, the Wikimedia Foundation's most successful strategy has been to collaborate with higher education institutions, libraries, archives, and museums to create new and improve existing entries.[1] Wikipedia entries edited or created in cultural heritage institutions are more likely to include images, videos, and links to resources within those institutions' unique digital collections. Visitors to those Wikipedia entries will click on the images, videos, or other hyperlinked media within the entries and discover their origins, as well as a pathway to primary source material. Libraries, archives, and museums credited in Wikipedia entries—as well as those that have allowed Wikipedians to use primary source material from their collections—have noticed an increase in traffic to their websites and digital collections. Indeed, this has been a win-win partnership for cultural heritage institutions and the Wikimedia Foundation.

In 2011, the "Wikipedia Loves Libraries" initiative began in North America (Wikipedia: Wikipedia Loves Libraries 2014). The intent of Wikipedia Loves Libraries is to engage libraries, museums, and archives at least once a year during Open Access Week in October/November to organize wiki-workshops and

---

[1] It appears that they are having success--as the main author observed during her trip to WikiConference USA in New York City in May 2014, the number of women and LGBTIQ Wikipedians in attendance at this national conference appeared to balance out the core Wikipedian population of heterosexual men. To encourage conference attendance for women, LGBTIQ populations, and other minorities—especially those new to Wikipedia activities--the Wikimedia Foundation offered full scholarships to those who found out about the conference and scholarship opportunity.

Wikipedia editathons (also known as "parties") (2014). Wikipedia educators and ambassadors engaged fourteen institutions in the United States and Canada in their first year, including the Tom of Finland Foundation in Los Angeles.

Tom of Finland Foundation: Home of the First Queer Wikipedia Editathon

In 1984, the nonprofit Tom of Finland Foundation (ToFF) was established by the artist Tom of Finland (Touko Laaksonen, 1920 – 1991) and Durk Dehner. As Tom had established worldwide recognition as a master of homoerotic art, the Foundation's original purpose was to preserve his vast catalog of work. Several years later the scope was widened to offer a safe haven for all erotic art in response to rampant discrimination against art that portrayed sexual behavior or generated a sexual response. Today ToFF continues in its efforts of educating the public as to the cultural merits of erotic art and in promoting healthier, more tolerant attitudes about sexuality.

Historically, erotic art and texts addressing human sexuality, particularly that of a gay, lesbian, bisexual, and transgender nature, have been devalued and discarded from our cultural heritage. Because of the rampant discrimination and censorship of art that portrays sexual behavior or inspires a sexual response, The Foundation exists to educate the public about the cultural merits of erotic art, promoting a healthier, more tolerant attitude about human sexuality.

The library was always part of the Foundation, even during its earliest days. Initially the books and artwork binders consisted of Tom's work, but during the late 1980s the organization and library became inclusive of other erotic artists. This was in response to the large number of artists who had succumbed to the AIDS epidemic and the body of work they left behind, which was either regarded as shameful to family members and/or neglected by society's indifference. There are artist binders with original artwork never before seen by the public and have yet to be digitized and cataloged. The Foundation does not purchase books for the library but continuously receives donations from artists, private collectors, publishers, galleries, and estate collections.

Today the shelves are brimming with these subject areas:

- Artists (Jim French, Eric Kroll, Ken Haak, Olivia)
- Literature (Pat Califia, Larry Townsend)
- Culture (A Queer Reader)
- Models (Beefcake, Bettie Page)
- Photography (Typical Men)

- Sex (A Sexual Bill of Rights for the Erotic Minorities)
- Philosophy (Feminism & Pornography)
- Politics (Obscenity and Pornography)
- Psychology (Gay Ideas)
- Fetish (Jay Wiseman's Erotic Bondage Handbook)
- Graphic Novels (Meatmen)

There are also many other graphic novels, books, and exhibition catalogs that have been self-published and still unavailable in many places. The library also carries a vast collection of American and European gay men's magazines and newspapers, many of which have since ceased publication.

ToFF is a one room library located in a house in Echo Park, California. Like many small independent LGBTIQ collections, ToFF is slow to enter the digital age. ToFF Director Durk Dehner had conducted all communications through snail mail for a long time. ToFF Vice President Srs Sharp recognizes that connection to the Internet has not only improved and expanded promotion of ToFF, but also has improved collaboration and sharing with the Royal Academy of Turku in Finland, where the remaining Tom of Finland collections are housed. In the very near future, the library's book collection will be available for public viewing on Worldcat.org. ToFF also has plans to digitize its collection; it has applied for a grant from the Los Angeles County Arts Commission to do so. In the future, queer Wikipedia parties at ToFF will help link researchers to ToFF's unique resources when they retrieve Wikipedia entries on their subjects of interest.

In 2011, ToFF artist-librarian Katie Herzog read about "Wikipedia Loves Libraries" online through a banner over a Wikipedia entry. She proposed that the foundation should host and organize the event. With ToFF's approval, Katie did all of the organizing, public relations, invitations, and setup on a volunteer basis, putting out a call for participants on Craigslist. Charles Stewart responded to that ad, and with ToFF volunteer librarians Toni Rodriguez and Marti Pike facilitated ToFF's first editathon.

The first Queering Wikipedia editathon attracted local LGBTIQ activists, library school students, artists, and ToFF members to create and edit LGBTIQ entries. According to Katie Herzog, "the meeting inspired dialogue about gay history and generated an increased interest in activism for citizen-created content...Everyone left feeling like it was the first of many to come" (SinhaRoy 2011). ToFF's first editathon received a sizeable mention in *American Libraries*, alongside those events at mainstream public and academic libraries. Other artists in Los Angeles, inspired by Herzog's efforts, coordinated their own Wikipedia editathons to contribute and edit entries on artists from other underrepresented populations. The energy generated from this first Queering Wikipedia editathon made ToFF organize a second one in 2012.

Adrianne Wadewitz and the Second ToFF Queering Wikipedia Editathon

In 2011, Wikipedian and feminist scholar Adrianne Wadewitz worked at the Center for Digital Learning + Research at Occidental College in Los Angeles, helping students and faculty learn how to use technology and the Internet appropriately for educational purposes and research. She also worked as a campus ambassador for Wikipedia, where she would go out to visit schools and cultural heritage institutions to teach them not only how to use Wikipedia as a research tool, but also how to use Wikipedia to leverage their collections. Wadewitz performed such outreach as part of the GLAM-Wiki initiative (GLAM = "Galleries, Libraries, Archives, and Museums"), a program promoted to cultural heritage institutions to share their resources online through collaboration with experienced Wikipedians (Wikipedia:GLAM 2014).

In July 2012 Adrianne found out about the second ToFF Queering Wikipedia event through the Wikipedia event page, and contacted Katie to offer her services as an instructor for the event. It just so happened that Adrianne lived blocks away from Katie. As a Wikipedia campus ambassador, Adrianne could provide workbooks to participants and other resources that ToFF did not know about the first time around. ToFF International Liaison Allison Schulte promoted this second event through the Special Libraries Association Southern California chapter and the Art Libraries Society of North America. It also made Schulte investigate opportunities for interested parties to participate online through Skype.

According to ToFF Vice President Srs Sharp, Wikipedia is "for a non-queer audience" and "a public forum for facts." Sharp discovered that some misinformation on a queer topic of interest had been perpetuated on Wikipedia and cited by newspapers and other organizations. At this Wikipedia party, Sharp had the opportunity to correct the information using ToFF resources. Sharp hopes that more people will lose the perception that encyclopedias are published by elites and that their content is gospel—especially where LGBTIQ information is concerned.

LGBTIQA Wikipedians

No one community on Wikipedia "owns" entries. Anyone can work on an LGBTIQ entry. At the same time, a committed group of LGBTIQA

Wikipedians from around the world monitor, edit, and contribute LGBTIQ Wikipedia entries. Since 2006, they have overseen an LGBT Portal where they categorize entries, review entries for inclusion and deletion, and identify "stubs" that need further work (Portal: LGBT/WikiProjects and things you can do 2014). Some of these people have organized themselves into a group called WikiProject LGBT Studies (Wikipedia:Wikiproject LGBT Studies 2014). As of September 2014 at least 527 registered individuals have contributed to this WikiProject, with 310 identified as "active members," meaning that they have contributed entries or made edits in the past six months. Based on the number of people watching the entries, WikiProject LGBT Studies is one of the most popular WikiProjects.

In 2012, LGBT portal founders user:Bluerasberry, user:Fae, user:Tom Morris, and user:Varnent[2] wanted to develop an LGBT-specific outreach organization within the Wikimedia Foundation. In order to do this, they needed to establish channels for communication. First they created an IRC channel #wikimedia-lgbt, and requested an LGBT-specific listserv through the Wikimedia Foundation, which they received. All new and seasoned participants in LGBTIQ WikiProjects could join the listserv to share concerns, questions, and ideas. Discussion topics range from policing vandalism to current events. Jason Moore (user:Another Believer), Dorothy Howard (user:OR Drowhowa), and user:Ladsgroup took up the challenge of managing the new organization. Some individuals from this loose confederation met in person at Wikimania 2012 and decided to change their group identity from an outreach project to a "thematic organization." In August 2012, Wikimedia LGBT was born. Since then, representatives from Wikimedia LGBT have presented and facilitated discussions at the annual Wikimania conferences, the Wikimedia Diversity Conference in Berlin in 2013, and the annual WikiCon USA conferences. Wikimedia LGBT officially received its usergroup status at the 2014 Wikimania Conference in London. This is formal legal affiliation with the Wikimedia Foundation where Wikimedia LGBT has permission to use Wikimedia Foundation logos and trademarks, and otherwise represent the movement.

---

2   Some LGBTIQ Wikipedians prefer to go by their Wikipedia usernames in public spaces. The authors did their best to maintain the anonymity of those users who wished it.

Do People Use Wikipedia to Search for LGBTIQ Information?

Wikipedia provides article traffic statistics for the month of one's page visit plus the past five years of traffic to that particular page. A search on the Wikipedia site for Category: Lists of popular pages by WikiProject will show each WikiProject and its top 1000 most frequently visited pages. Each chart is sortable by rank, total number of views, views per day on average, quality assessment, and importance:

- http://en.wikipedia.org/wiki/Wikipedia:WikiProject_Feminism/Popular_pages

- http://en.wikipedia.org/wiki/Wikipedia:WikiProject_Gender_Studies/Popular_pages

- http://en.wikipedia.org/wiki/Wikipedia:WikiProject_LGBT_studies/Popular_pages

- http://en.wikipedia.org/wiki/Wikipedia:WikiProject_Sexology_and_sexuality/Popular

LGBTIQ Information on Wikipedia

Most people locate Wikipedia pages either through a direct visit to Wikipedia, or through a Google search. Most likely, an individual searching for information through Google will retrieve a Wikipedia page on their subject within the first ten search results. As of December 2012, a Google search for "gay" will retrieve the Wikipedia entry for "gay" as its first result; the same is true for "bisexual", "transgender", "intersex", "queer", and "LGBT". The Wikipedia page for "lesbian" shows up as the third result in a Google search, after two websites advertising lesbian videos. In the set of top ten Google search results for each LGBTIQ term, Wikipedia provides the only definition and etymology of each term, as well as links to visit their pages on related subjects and hyperlinked references.

Each LGBTIQ-related Wikipedia page has a sidebar on the right which states "Part of a series on Lesbian, gay, bisexual, and transgender (LGBT) people". Within that sidebar, the Wikipedian has provided related links to other LGBT Wikipedia pages organized by "Sexual Orientation", "History", "Culture", "Rights", "Social Attitudes", "Prejudice/Violence", "Academic fields and discourse", and the "LGBT Portal". Wikipedia defines "portals" as "...'Main Pages' for specific topics or areas…they are meant for both readers and editors of Wikipedia, and should promote content and encourage contribution" ("Wikipedia: Portal" 2012).

It is difficult to count the exact number of English-language Wikipedia pages that provide LGBTIQ information, let alone the number of non-English LGBTIQ Wikipedia pages. At last estimate, 15,000 LGBT Wikipedia entries exist (Rasberry 2012). People continuously add, edit, and delete articles as people come out, theories and laws change, and more LGBT cultural productions become public. For this reason, serious researchers and people interested in contributing to and editing LGBT content on Wikipedia should visit the LGBT Portal. It provides a list of categories and sub-categories of LGBTIQ content. As of December 2012, Wikipedia recognizes twenty-three main categories of LGBT content, including LGBT "stubs"—articles "deemed too short to provide encyclopedic coverage of a subject" ("Wikipedia: Stub" 2012). As of December 2012, there are nearly 800 English language LGBT "stubs" which need expanding and references.

STRATEGIES TO IMPROVE LGBTIQ INFORMATION ON WIKIPEDIA

With increasing frequency, Wikipedians are organizing Wikipedia parties to meet fellow contributors face to face, and to recruit new people. Traditionally, Wikipedia parties are held in libraries (Rasberry 2012)—particularly those on college and university campuses—which may discourage potential contributors from underrepresented groups. Some museums and archives also host Wikipedia parties. The reason for hosting these events at libraries, archives, and museums is not only to encourage contributors and editors to use quality resources for their research, but also to tap the academic subject specialists and the special collections of libraries, archives, and museums. Some institutions have even created the position of "Wikipedian in Residence" or have appointed a librarian, archivist, or digital humanist to serve as a liaison to their state Wikipedia group.

Outreach efforts to recruit new Wikipedians remains a challenge, simply because most people are passive visitors to Wikipedia. They do not know how to edit entries, even if they heard it can be done, and they do not always know how to get in touch with experienced Wikipedians. This is especially the case for people living in rural areas or those on the other side of the digital divide. Savvy Wikipedians meet each other online through the "Talk" and "Discussion" tabs on the page they work on together, through communication about article edits. In large urban areas where colleges, universities, and cultural heritage institutions are within close range of each other, Wiki MeetUp groups where new and experienced Wikipedians can meet face to face, often for casual social gatherings, have become very popular.

Some "best practices" to improve LGBTIQ information on Wikipedia:

1. If you would like to share your LGBTIQ expertise, develop your personal reputation as a Wikipedian. Create a Wikipedia account, search for your topic of interest, and edit or update the page. If the institution where you work has excellent LGBTIQ resources, link to them in the article.

2. If you would like to host a Wikipedia party but are unsure of your skills or expertise, invite knowledgeable colleagues to help facilitate.

3. When organizing a Wikipedia party, send personal invitations to the local LGBT Resource Center, the local LGBT cultural heritage institutions, all faculty on campus who teach LGBTIQ related courses, LGBT student and community organizations, community health and medical specialists, and all multicultural groups. Promote the event through all appropriate social media channels, and ask those invitees and organizations to spread the word.

4. Schedule the Wikipedia party during one of the "LGBT holidays" (LGBT History Month, National Coming Out Week, LGBT Pride Month, etc.) when community interest in LGBT topics are at a high.

5. Create an online topic guide for first-time Wikipedians. Rachel Wexelbaum of St. Cloud State University has created an example (Wexelbaum 2013). For first timers who might not have a topic in mind, show them the list of stubs on the LGBT Portal that need work.

6. To the best of your ability, make the party space a safe, inclusive space for all, in a wheelchair accessible building with gender-neutral bathrooms, free parking, public transportation access, and childcare. Whenever possible, find spaces outside the library that may prove more welcoming or more convenient for those individuals you may want to attract. Free food will also encourage people to participate!

Kate Wolf, Katie Herzog, Rich Yap, Adrianne Wadewitz

Adrianne Wadewitz, John Burtle, Sharp, Diane Kryszewski, Rich Yap, Kate Wolf, Adam Overton, Katie Herzog

Queers Online

Rich Yap, Kate Wolf, Adam Overton, Katie Herzog

Katie Herzog, Adrianne Wadewitz

Rich Yap, Kate Wolf, Adam Overton (on couch), Katie Herzog, Adrianne Wadewitz (standing)

Katie Herzog, ?, Adrianne Wadewitz, Allison Schulte, John Burtle

Queers Online

Adrianne Wadewitz

Adrienne Wadewitz working with Sharp on a Wikipedia entry

(Clockwise from left): Kate Wolf, Rich Yap, Katie Herzog, and anonymous participant collaborating

REFERENCES

Ashton, D. (2011). Awarding the self in *Wikipedia*: Identity work and the disclosure of knowledge. *First Monday, 16*(1-3). Retrieved from http://firstmonday.org/ojs/index.php/fm/article/viewArticle/3156

Baker, S. (2012). A place for Wikipedia or putting Wikipedia in its place. *New Horizons, 9*(1). Retrieved from http://jhepp.library.jhu.edu/ojs/index.php/newhorizons/article/view/23

Category:LGBT. (2013, January 9). Retrieved May 29, 2013 from Wikimedia Commons: http://commons.wikimedia.org/wiki/Category:LGBT

Cleanup listing for WikiProject LGBT Studies. (2014, Sept 2014). Retrieved from https://tools.wmflabs.org/bambots/cwb/alpha/LGBT_studies.html

Collier, B. & Bear, J. (2012). Conflict, criticism, or confidence: An empirical examination of the gender gap in Wikipedia contributions. *CSCW '12: Proceedings of the ACM 2012 Conference on Computer Supported Cooperative Work*, 383-392.

Community Engagement (Product)/Process Ideas. (2014, Sept 26). Retrieved from Wikimedia Meta Wiki: http://meta.wikimedia.org/wiki/Community_Engagement_%28Product%29/Process_ideas

Flock, F., Vrandecic, D. & Simperl, E. Toward a diversity-minded Wikipedia. Retrieved May 29, 2013 from Web of Science: http://www.websci11.org/fileadmin/websci/Papers/112_paper.pdf

Greenstein, S. & Zhu, F. (2012). Is Wikipedia biased? *American Economic Review: Papers & Proceedings, 102*(3), 343-348. Retrieved from http://www-bcf.usc.edu/~fzhu/wikipediabias.pdf

Hall, M.M., Clough, P.D., de Lacalle, O.L., Soroa, A. & Agirre, E. (2012). Enabling the discovery of digital cultural heritage objects through Wikipedia. *Proceedings of the 6th EACL Workshop on Language Technology for Cultural Heritage, Social Sciences, and Humanities*, 94-100. Retrieved from http://newdesign.aclweb.org/anthology-new/W/W12/W12-10.pdf#page=104

History of Wikipedia. (2013, May 29). Retrieved May 29, 2013 from Wikipedia: http://en.wikipedia.org/wiki/History_of_Wikipedia#2004

Lampe, C., Obar, J., Ozkaya, E., Zube, P. & Velasquez, A. (2012). Classroom Wikipedia participation effects on future intentions to contribute.

CSCW '12: Proceedings of the ACM 2012 Conference on Computer Supported Cooperative Work, 403-406.

Lim, S. & Kwon, N. (2010). Gender differences in information behavior concerning Wikipedia, an unorthodox information source? *Library & Information Science Research, 32*(3), 212-220.

Morgan, J.T., Mason, R.M. & Nahon, K. (2012). Negotiating cultural values in social media: A case study from Wikipedia. *HICSS '12: Proceedings of the 2012 45th Hawaii International Conference on System Sciences*, 3490-3499.

Nonbinary.org. (2013, May 24). Nonbinary.org. Retrieved from http://nonbinary.org/wiki/Main_Page

Okoli, C., Mehdi, M., Mesgari, M., Nielsen, F.A. & Lanamaki, A. (n.d.) *The people's encyclopedia under the gaze of the sages: A systematic review of scholarly research on Wikipedia*. Retrieved May 29, 2013 from the Social Science Research Network: http://papers.ssrn.com/sol3/papers.cfm?abstract_id=2021326

Portal:LGBT. (2013, March 16). Retrieved May 29, 2013 from Wikipedia: http://en.wikipedia.org/wiki/Portal:LGBT

Portal:LGBT/Categories. (2011, November 12). Retrieved May 29, 2013 from Wikipedia: http://en.wikipedia.org/wiki/Portal:LGBT/Categories

Portal:LGBT/WikiProjects and things you can do (2012, May 6). Retrieved May 29, 2013 from Wikipedia: http://en.wikipedia.org/wiki/Portal:LGBT/WikiProjects_and_things_you_can_do

SinhaRoy, S. (2011, Nov 1). Libraries tap into crowd power: Wikipedians "smartsource" at their libraries to improve online content. *American Libraries*. Retrieved from http://www.americanlibrariesmagazine.org/article/libraries-tap-crowd-power

Soules, A. (2012). Where's the bio? Databases, Wikipedia, and the web. *New Library World, 113*(1/2), 77-89.

Sundin, O. (2011). Janitors of knowledge: Constructing knowledge in the everyday life of Wikipedia editors. *Journal of Documentation, 67*(5), 840-862.

Tom of Finland Foundation. (2013). Tom of Finland Foundation: Promoting and Preserving Erotic Art. Retrieved May 29, 2013 from http://tomoffinlandfoundation.org/foundation/N_Home.html

Wikimedia Foundation. (2014, Aug 9). Frequently asked questions. Retrieved from Wikimedia Foundation: http://wikimediafoundation.org/wiki/FAQ/en

Wikimedia Foundation. (2012). Terms of use. Retrieved from Wikimedia Foundation: http://wikimediafoundation.org/index.php?title=Terms_of_Use&utm_source=TOU_top

Wikimedia Foundation. (2012). 2011-2012 Annual Report. Wikimedia Foundation. Retrieved from http://upload.wikimedia.org/wikipedia/commons/4/48/WMF-AR_2011%E2%80%9312_EN_SHIP2_17dec12_300dpi_hi-res.pdf

Wikimedia LGBT. (2013, May 17). Retrieved May 29, 2013 from Wikimedia Meta-Wiki: http://meta.wikimedia.org/wiki/Wikimedia_LGBT

Wikimedia LGBT Community. (2013, Aug 4). Facebook page. Retrieved Sept 25, 2014: https://www.facebook.com/WikimediaLGBT

Wikimedia LGBT/History. (2014, Jun 18). Retrieved Sept 25, 2014 from Wikimedia Meta-Wiki: http://meta.wikimedia.org/wiki/Wikimedia_LGBT/History

Wikimedia LGBT/Portal. (2014, Sept 14). Retrieved Sept 25, 2014 from Wikimedia Meta-Wiki: http://meta.wikimedia.org/wiki/Wikimedia_LGBT/Portal

Wikipedia:GLAM. (2014, Sept 27). Retrieved from Wikipedia: http://en.wikipedia.org/wiki/Wikipedia:GLAM

Wikipedia:Portal. (2013, March 13). Retrieved May 29, 2013 from Wikipedia: http://en.wikipedia.org/wiki/Wikipedia:Portal

Wikipedia:Stub. (2013, April 7). Retrieved May 29, 2013 from Wikipedia: http://en.wikipedia.org/wiki/Wikipedia:Stub

Wikipedia: Wikipedia Loves Libraries. (2013, Jan 10). Retrieved Sept 25, 2014 from Wikipedia: http://en.wikipedia.org/wiki/Wikipedia:Wikipedia_Loves_Libraries/2011

Wikipedia:Wikipedians. (2013, May 22). Retrieved May 29, 2013 from Wikipedia: http://en.wikipedia.org/wiki/Wikipedia:Wikipedians

Wikipedia:WikiProject LGBT studies. (2013, April 12). Retrieved May 29, 2013 from Wikipedia: http://en.wikipedia.org/wiki/Wikipedia:WikiProject_LGBT_studies

Wikipedia:WikiProject LGBT studies/Members. (2014, Sept 25). Retrieved Sept 25, 2014 from Wikipedia: http://en.wikipedia.org/wiki/Wikipedia:WikiProject_LGBT_studies/Members

WikiQueer. (n.d.) WikiQueer. http://www.wikiqueer.org/w/Main_Page

WikiQueer:FAQ (2013, February 25). Retrieved May 29, 2013 from WikiQueer: http://www.wikiqueer.org/w/WikiQueer:FAQ

"WikiQueer is Here." (2012, March 1). *The Outskirts* [web log]. Retrieved May 29, 2013 from https://thehostess.wordpress.com/2012/03/01/wikiqueer-is-here/

Wagley, C. (2014, Feb 6). Wikipedia becomes a battleground for art activism. *LA Weekly*. Retrieved from http://www.laweekly.com/2014-02-06/artbooks/wikipedia-becomes-a-battleground-for-art-activism/

Wexelbaum, R. (2013). Wikipedia: how to edit and create entries. [SubjectsPlus topic guide]. *Library: St. Cloud State University*. Retrieved from http://stcloud.lib.mnscu.edu/subjects/guide.php?subject=Wikipedia

Section Two

Transitioning from Print to Digital in LGBT Archives

Introduction to Section Two: Transitioning from Print to Digital in LGBT Archives

Some LGBT archives and special collections are small independent entities primarily run by volunteers without large budgets, while others may be considered national cultural heritage institutions. Their users, often members of the community that help build the archive as well as researchers, appreciate the content in these collections and sometimes are resistant to change. At the same time, physical formats do not last forever. Those unable to visit the archives in person want to view the materials from their phone, across the globe. They wonder why they can't just Google an archive and search their collections online. Younger generations, in general, are digital generations.

Some LGBT archivists feared that digitizing their collections would lead to shutting their doors forever, as they believed that visitors would no longer come to their physical locations. They also worried about the time, money, and expertise needed to digitize materials in different formats. Last but not least, the archivists would need to trace the origins and human subjects of millions of photos and other artifacts, as they would need permission to make these accessible online. Donors and community patrons often expected "their archive" to be a safe space where only LGBTIQ people would have permission to view materials considered crucial to teaching younger queer generations about "their" history.

The physical archives themselves each have a distinct history, worthy of recording for posterity. The history of the building and the people who worked in it runs parallel to the history of its digitization. In the first chapter of this section, Shawn(ta) Smith provides a history of the Lesbian Herstory Archives, the building of its online catalog, and a major oral history digitization project through personal interviews with the staff. Next, Rebecka Sheffield and Kate

Zieman of the Canadian Gay and Lesbian Archives describe their photo collections and the successes and challenges they have had thus far with digitization and access. Last but not least, Graham Willett and Steve Wright of the Australian Gay and Lesbian Archives discuss the legal and ethical questions surrounding digitization of people engaged in controversial social movements, and ownership of historical records and photos.

All libraries, archives, museums, and special collections grapple with these same issues when undertaking digitization projects. I believe that the writers in this section, by telling their stories, have shared recommended practices as well as cautionary tales.

Tape-by-Tape: Digital Practices and Cataloguing Rituals at the Lesbian Herstory Archives

Shawn(ta) D. Smith-Cruz

The Lesbian Herstory Archives (LHA) is a home for the many faces, lives, and experiences that encompass lesbian herstory. Physically, it is based in an historic limestone building in Brooklyn, New York and owned by the lesbian community. Contextually, LHA contains the images, writings, thoughts, wishes, and voices of lesbians from around the world. Women and men visit the Archives to see lesbian scrapbooks, magazines, photo albums, T-shirts, published articles, compiled biographies, community organizations, conference-worn buttons, favorite books, diaries, love letters, calendars, art and deeply loved ephemeral material. Students and researchers of varying disciplines utilize the Archives as a necessary source in their work. Tour-seeking out of towners, neighbors wanting a quiet place to read, interns developing projects, and newly realized lesbians also become dedicated users of the Archives. Users become volunteers. Through consistent volunteer participation from lesbian communities, and an uncompromising grassroots approach, the structure and heritage of the Lesbian Herstory Archives has developed a useable formula for archiving lesbian life.

This essay will outline the digital collections of the Lesbian Herstory Archives with an emphasis on process and workflow. The paragraphs below will describe the efforts put forth by the all-volunteer collective, and their dedication toward making materials accessible through the use of digital technology to preserve, catalog, and exhibit lesbian herstory. Interviews with Archive Coordinators, called "Archivettes," Saskia Scheffer on Photos, Rachel Corbman on the Online Public Access Catalog (OPAC), and Maxine Wolfe on Audio, will provide examples of LHA digital practices in the creation and maintenance of the Photo Collection, OPAC, and Audio Tape Digitization projects. Additional mention will include the Newsletter Digitization, Periodical Digitization, and the Subject File Digitization projects. Collaboration between LHA volunteers and outside institutions will prove successful for each of these projects. The complex relationship of money to digital initiatives will be examined. These overviews will provide insight as to how digital collections are created and considered at the Lesbian Herstory Archives.

ORIGIN

In the mid-1950s, the Daughters of Bilitis was the first lesbian organization of its kind to question how lesbians could exist within heteronormative society. They attempted to create spaces outside of bar culture. Although lesbian activists, lesbian playwrights, lesbian authors, and lesbian families always existed, the initiation of lesbian spaces forged community organizing that gave lesbians a new path for answering that ephemeral question, how do we exist? The Daughters of Bilitis constructed a tangible response to the criminalization of homosexuality. While formal organizing did not stop the bar raids, the imprisonment, or deaths of lesbians across the nation, twenty years after the founding of this organization and its many chapters around the country, lesbians gained increased visibility. During the 1970s, radical lesbian feminists, some separatist, created modern herstory by establishing small presses, music festivals, conferences, campus organizing, bookstores, barter exchanges, rallies and post free-love health consciousness-raising groups. Lesbians realized that this herstory had great cultural significance, and needed to be canonized, documented, and preserved.

In 1972 an alliance of activists, academics, and scholars affiliated with the City University of New York established the Gay Academic Union (GAU). GAU, had a mission to represent the concerns of gay and lesbian students, teachers, and workers. Following the trend in organizing during the 1970s, the women of GAU felt the need to create separate spaces to address the concerns of women. Their consciousness-raising groups were the breeding grounds for discussion points that have become the mission of the Lesbian Herstory Archives. One GAU subgroup, for example, included Joan Nestle and Julia Stanley who each believed that herstories were often documented through a patriarchal lens. This particular group felt strongly that lesbian culture ought to be gathered and preserved by lesbians themselves. Later that year, Deborah Edel, Sahli Cavallo, and Pamela Oline joined the group and together the women developed a new concept of beginning a grassroots lesbian archive.

In 1975, Joan Nestle's apartment in the Upper West Side of Manhattan served as the first home of the Lesbian Herstory Archives. In that same year,

LHA published its first free newsletter. For fifteen years, lesbians and some allies collected what was named lesbian herstory. Women from across the United States began donating the entirety of their lives, from their love letters to protest-worn sneakers. They began to archive —created accession forms, filed materials in acid-free boxes, and generated card catalogs. LHA eventually grew too large for the living room and bookcases of the Upper West Side apartment.

LHA moved to Brooklyn in June 1993. With money raised from house party fundraisers and small individual donations solicited by word of mouth, the lesbian community purchased an entire $300,000 four-story, turn-of -the –20th-century limestone townhouse in Park Slope, overlooking Prospect Park. On the day of the building's unveiling, a lesbian marching band paraded along 14th Street, women sang dyke songs, and long-time Archivette Paula Grant won the raffle to cut the ribbon. Both monetary and collection-based donations continued to pour in. Herstory quickly filled the walls.

The physical space of the building holds a strong place in lesbian herstory. While it houses the materials of the collection, the her and her sinks on the 2nd floor also exhibit lesbian memorabilia like denim jackets, buttons, dildos, and hand-crafted pillows, all which exemplify the dynamic artifacts that encompass what lesbians choose to donate. As not only an archive with a library and ephemeral exhibitions, but also as a community space, LHA continues to host various special events in order to encourage the use of materials. With the new building purchase, just as LHA was once inside the home of a lesbian, it is also home to a lesbian. A caretaker lives on the top floor of the archive, and forever walks around with a check-off list, carefully monitoring every transaction and delivery, on premises to oversee the collection.

LHA Principles

An introduction to the principles of LHA is necessary toward an understanding of LHA online. The founders alongside the lesbian community, made a life-long commitment to ensure the longevity of the materials specifically, and lesbian herstory and culture more generally. It was clear that LHA had to exist beyond a single generation. A statement of purpose and a set of principles to guide the development and preservation of the collection were created. These principles lead all existing and future projects, including the development and expansion of online access to LHA materials.

When created, the LHA statement of purpose was simple: To collect all and any materials relevant to the lives and experiences of lesbians. These materials included books, magazines, journals, news clippings (from establishment, feminist, or lesbian media), bibliographies, photos, historical information, tapes, films, diaries, oral histories, poetry and prose, biographies, autobiographies, notices of events, posters, graphics and other memorabilia.

The principles below are written verbatim, as derived from the many collectively run meetings since the initiation of LHA in 1974. Many of the principles are based less on standard archival practice and instead are focused on the LHA's commitment to living and nurturing lesbian herstory, to housing the past along with the present. The basic principles guiding LHA are:

- All Lesbian women must have access to the Archives; no academic, political, or sexual credentials will be required for use of the collection; race and class must be no barrier for use or inclusion.
- The Archives shall be housed within the community, not on an academic campus that is by definition closed to many women.
- The Archives shall be involved in the political struggles of all Lesbians.
- Archival skills shall be taught, one generation of Lesbians to another, breaking the elitism of traditional archives.
- The community should share in the work of the Archives.
- Funding shall be sought from within the communities the Archives serves, rather than from outside sources.
- The Archives will always have a caretaker living in it so that it will always be someone's home rather than an institution.
- The Archives will never be sold nor will its contents be divided.

("History" 2013)

All online access possibilities, as with additional LHA projects, consider the guiding principles first, before other modes of operation, including but not limited to archival principles or principles of queer theory. A collection housed onsite means that there is limited access for all lesbians to experience the materials. Addressing barriers of access to all lesbians make an online presence consistent with herstorical LHA practice. Ensuring that the LHA collection is sustained as a community-owned archive, while continuing to extend its access to additional communities is a new consideration for LHA online.

COMMUNITY-OWNED ARCHIVING

There are multiple ways that lesbians-as-community represent the process of archiving. In order to organize the constant flow of new material, LHA utilizes the guiding principle that the community should share in the work of the Archives. Materials that are donated then archived are representative of lesbian life. This means that a book in the LHA library may not be by a lesbian author, inasmuch as it means a lesbian donated it. The buttons are not made by lesbians, but worn by them. Although some formatted materials are lesbian-created, the majority of the collection is relational to the narratives that accompany the object.

Lesbians define themselves; this truism remains at the heart of the Archives. Therefore, who is constituted as a lesbian is fluid and changes over time. The multiple lesbian communities that are represented at LHA are inclusive of those who self-identify as lesbians, or have at one point in their lives chosen to donate as a lesbian. In addition, these same communities are sought to maintain the collection, supply labor and keep the collection growing and thriving. Lesbians are (primarily) the ones who donate the materials and the ones who archive the materials. An example of how this works is in our Subject Files, one of many collections. Subject files are classified as "Lesbians and ..." The ... in that equation may be Lesbians and Sports, Lesbians and Catholicism, Lesbians and Folklore, Lesbians and Bookstores, Lesbians and the 1950s, Lesbians and Fashion, the list goes on. With over fifteen hundred subjects, these files represent the diversity in the lesbian community, strategically catalogued by how the community views itself. Because lesbian communities are various, however, LHA acknowledges that donations and hard work may have been provided by those who do not (or no longer) identify as lesbians, but stand as committed allies, with a collective aim to maintain the LHA guiding principles.

Lesbians –As-Community and Access

The women who donate their lives to the Lesbian Herstory Archives are a part of an active, living culture. When considering that lesbian communities are relational to the entire world, access to the collection, then, must be accessible to all. Still, restrictions do exist. While some donors wish to be cited and wholly discoverable, others request anonymity; some may even choose to be closed to certain groups. Collections that are acquired and named for their donors, or "Special Collections," may have access clauses upon the request of the donor, such as "Do not open until I die or the year 2012, whichever comes later," or "To be viewed by lesbians only," as another example. LHA respects the wishes of donors by making an effort to consider their needs before adhering to any open access policy.

This question of access and permissions is one that affects all archival collections. Yet in the case where a collection of interest does not have noted restrictions, hands-on access is granted. Where most institutional archives have access policies that restrict users based on institutional affiliation, or accreditations, the Archives asks only that one displays interest in lesbian research. There is no way to predict anyone's personal identity at the door or via correspondence. Nor are people asked to "come out" before viewing materials. As long as one is a lesbian, is a part of the lesbian communities, or at best, expresses interest in lesbian research, he or she is welcome to access the LHA collection.

Gathering Materials

The first line of the statement of purpose is, "The Lesbian Herstory Archives exists to gather and preserve records of Lesbian lives and activities so that future generations will have ready access to materials relevant to their lives" ("History," 2013). To "gather" records of lesbian lives led to an open accession policy where the only criterion for receiving materials was that the donor ought to be lesbian, ought to have lesbian material to donate, or represent lesbianism in some form as it relates to evolving and herstoric definitions of lesbian communities. This collection of lesbian memorabilia from anyone who was a lesbian, including those who were not seen as famous, meant that any limitation of a concept of lesbian herstory was wholly subjective. Women sent emblems of their first kiss, documentations of their lives as partners with women, secrets that lived only in dark corners of their homes, testimonials of pride, and collective organizing tools like logos and catch-phrases that summoned lesbians across their town or the nation. This open gathering of materials was exciting, without boundaries, yet sealed with deep intention and consideration, as the call was to signify, a previously non-existent, definition of lesbian herstory.

Gathering of materials continues. Integral to the LHA mission, donations are still accepted. In multiple coordinator meetings, where Archivettes assemble quarterly to discuss LHA business, gathering materials has been placed on the agenda. The Archivettes currently question whether LHA should continue to accept materials. Should LHA announce itself as a collection of materials donated from 1974 to some chosen end date? Should a cap be placed on materials already owned by LHA? Although these conversations continue, LHA has not instituted an end to accepting donations. The only restriction on acquisitions has been for certain object types such as newsprint or large-scale visual art collections, whose format was difficult to preserve. Refusal of material is based on one of three factors: content, space limitations, and LHA capacity to preserve.

Gathering and preservation are key components to LHA's mission. This commitment to gathering and preservation is significant to the practice of housing digital collections. As time passes and the collection grows, more formats for archiving lesbian herstory appear. Now materials arrive as "born digital": photographs as jpegs on CDs, videos on DVD, or oral histories in MP3 and WAV files, to name a few common variations. In general, born digital materials are often grouped with materials digitally reformatted for preservation purposes. For example, films on DVD will be added to the VHS collection. As listed in the first line of the LHA statement of purpose, preservation is the focal point for digital practice: "…the Lesbian Herstory Archives exists to gather and preserve records of Lesbian lives and activities…" ("History" 2013). After gathering and preserving, the final step is providing access. Digitization and the use of online exhibition platforms, databases, content management systems, and social networking sites are explored at LHA for access to the physical building space, as well as materials in the collection.

LHA Today

Currently the Lesbian Herstory Archives contains over 420 Special Collections containing the papers of individuals and organizations. Researchers and visitors often come with knowledge of the Special Collections, but they also use over 11,000 books, 800 periodical titles (including journals and newspapers), 3000 oral history cassettes, 1,000 video tapes and DVDs, 12,000 photographs, 1,100 Tee Shirts, a large collection of graphics and music, as well as 1,500 organizational files, 2,000 unpublished papers (including creative writing, speeches, letters, short stories, and poetry), 1,500 subject files ("lesbians and…"), 500 geographic files ("lesbians in…"), plus a large collection of ephemera coined as "lesbiana" (buttons, board games, banners, datebooks, and other material types). As a result of the multitude of materials that exist at LHA, the dynamic position the collection holds in the oral tradition of lesbian herstory, each artifact representing an anecdotal lesbian experience, the creation of metadata and presence of digital collections aids in the real task of providing access to materials onsite and throughout the world.

The Photo Collection

On the 1st floor of LHA past the front parlor, is the main workroom. A rectangular, resizable, wooden table, flanked by six high-backed chairs, stands in the center of the workroom. On one side sits the main computer. To the right of the table stands a large filing cabinet that houses the photo collection, organized in acid free folders. In a walk-in closet beside the photo cabinet rests personal photo albums, large collections of photographers' original art, and film from past slide shows rest in their containers. Most researchers view the photos in this room, spreading them out on the large work table.

The Lesbian Herstory Archives is continuing to digitize its photo collection. It reflects the growth of the Archives since 1974. From the Photo section of the LHA website Digital collections page, "much of the materials came to [LHA] from women who simply wanted their images saved and their lives remembered" ("Digital Collections" 2013). This is true for much of the materials of the Archives' collection. Aside from the single purchased acquisition of the Red Dot Collection, acquired from the New York Chapter of the Daughters of Bilitis, all other LHA collections are donated, including the photographs. LHA holds snapshots, professional photography, photo albums, found images and everything in between. The Photo Collection sits separate as a formatted collection. Photos from Special Collections are added to the photo collection for ease of access and storage with a cross reference to the provenance.

Whether for the purpose of having a visual memento of their visit to LHA, or to provide herstorical proof of lesbian existence in an academic paper, users of the photo collection must gain permission to make a reproduction. Unlike newspaper clippings and writings, however, LHA staff cannot make immediate reproductions of photographs. In special circumstances, LHA Archivettes will allow the visitor to make a black and white photocopy, but not a professional reproduction usable for publication. Inquiries to publish images from LHA photo collections, or for quality reproductions, are forwarded to Saskia Scheffer, an Archivette who has taken personal responsibility for processing photos.

Saskia Scheffer also happens to be Head of Digital Conversion and Photographic Services Unit at The New York Public Library. She has been the designated Archivette or Coordinator for this collection for over eight years. Due to the increased interest in photos expressed by artists, genealogists, students, and anyone else interested in an image to reproduce and publish digitally, Saskia created a new email address specifically for photo inquiries. The email address imageslha@gmail.com is another example for how correspondence as well as material formats have turned to a digital realm (LHA has only had a public email address since April 2011; before then all inquiries were moderated by phone, snail mail, and fax). Saskia agreed to discuss the herstory of the Photo collection and the digitization of photographs for this essay.

SASKIA SCHEFFER WITH SHAWN(TA) SMITH-CRUZ ON THE PHOTO COLLECTION

Saskia, what made you decide to work with the photos at LHA?

I have been involved here for a long time. I am a photographer, and my job was in photography, so it happened almost automatically that I started to work with the photo collection. The plan to start digitizing a select part and offer access on-line came later, when another job gave me some insight on what would be possible. However, that other job, at NYPL, had the support of major resources and a custom built infrastructure, things that are not available at the Archives yet.

LHA has hundreds if not thousands of photographs, could you briefly describe the digital photo collection at LHA.

So far we have about 400 images available online [over 600 at the time of this publication]. They are in the form of JPGs. You get a thumbnail image which you can enlarge up to a certain size for better viewing. They have some metadata with them, bibliographic info, to indicate what they are and where they came from. The underlying software is CONTENTdm and the site is hosted by Metropolitan New York Library Council (METRO) [transferred to the New York Heritage Digital Collection]. We have a link to that collection via our homepage: http://lesbianherstoryarchives.org/digital.html

What was the process for choosing CONTENTdm?

Years ago, a grant was provided by the Spark Plug foundation, and at first, we didn't know what to do with the funds. The collective agreed on applying it to online access of our photos. We picked CONTENTdm because it was recommended by people we trust, and it was offered through OCLC, an organization that is respected in the field. The interface has the combination of viewer ease and access to metadata. Generally, coordinators wanted to work with a company that could help troubleshoot issues when they came up. There was a bit of a learning curve, and financially it is best to be associated with an organization that can do the hosting, since that part of it is very expensive to do independently.

It took a long time to put the images up. I'd average that it takes about 1/2 hour per image to do. This includes the time to collect the background information on the image including donor information, collection it belongs to, what it is, what the rights are, the tags or keywords, the actual scanning and then to upload them onto the server.

I know we had a recent intern, Corinne Klee, but what was the workflow like for the beginning of this project?

I learned a lot since taking on this project. The first two volunteers to help, Ellen Eisenman and Cecelia Martin, started the scanning and did quite a few images. I started a metadata system and if I were to do it over, I would do the metadata first and then scan. That way you can keep much better track of what you have, and the use of tags and keywords will let you associate images with other images. Our photo collection had no real finding aid, which soon became a problem. Some of that first scanning work is online, some of it is still waiting for inclusion. Issues such as copyright were not resolved, information was lacking. We were not aware of this when we started. And the collection needed physical care as well. The next intern, Jabu Pereira, started that work, meticulously going through the folders, putting the photos in sleeves, creating a level of protective organization. And most recently Corinne Klee, another intern completed the photo sleeve process after which she worked on the actual finding aid, describing images and bringing all available information into a spreadsheet.

Many images have very limited information. In the early years of the archives we collected, put photos in folders, and had no system to include the 'who' and 'what' of every picture. Gathering what is there takes enormous focus and a concentrated amount of time. But by doing so the collection will be protected and accessible in a different way for browsing, with less risk for damage. This entire process of digitization is about preservation as well. If everything is online, you can bypass the browsing of the many original photos. We can also send people images without them having to come into the Archives. Viewing images can be made much easier this way.

What is the process for choosing which photos are digitized, once the collection is organized and tagged?

The 400 already digitized [in 2012] were based on a couple of things such as requests for certain images. Fulfilling such requests gave us an idea of what was interesting to the community. And we try to select informative images, or material that is not readily available elsewhere. Also photos that gave us sufficient information, enough that we could give it keywords or tags and make them discoverable were prioritized. Our photos come from all kinds of sources. From Polaroids to the 4 x 5 Brownie snapshots to the 8 x 10 professional prints, and everything in between.

Tell me how you prepare the images.

Some of the older material faded a bit and required some work to make the images easier to read. Once a photo is chosen for scanning, we produce a .TIFF file as the archival file. Then it gets linked to the metadata. We do this by providing unique image IDs for the images, and making that image ID part of the metadata. We may do a little photo editing, you know, make it a little lighter, add a little contrast, things like that, to recognize features in people's faces. This we save as a copy of the original file, and use it as a .JPG for web delivery. That happens in the ContentDM process.

I'm aware that we have in the past collected money for photo reproductions. Tell me about how the photo collection has acted as a source of small-scale fundraising.

We can make images available for publication and charge a permission or publication fee. This provides us with a little fundraising possibility. But if you realize what it all costs to do this, I would say that we are not even at the point of the effort paying for itself. Maybe that will come in the near future, as we keep adding images to the on-line collection. The fee is an interesting aspect of the work. In the community, people are often expecting that things are done for free. Researchers will pay the regular fee to large institutions but frown at LHA for charging. There is a big concept that this is a free service. The demand for images is high. The possibility of generating some money is important as it might actually pay for itself, and enable us to keep offering this service.

(S Scheffer, personal communication, August 21, 2012)

The Online Public Access Catalog (OPAC)

LHA strives to provide as much information about the processing rituals as possible or necessary. Each collection has its own cataloguing system, is housed in its own database, and is described by multiple people over time, but generally overseen by a single Archivette. A unique cataloguing system is used, answering the questions necessary for each material type.

The first cataloguing software used by LHA was Q&A, a software that was commonly used in the mid-nineties. All of the cataloguing was done in-house by Archivettes. The goal for cataloguing was to process the collections by donor name, allowing the discoverability of item-level searches to be based on the donor, not the object itself. After Q&A, InMagic, was chosen as the internally used computer database and is still the current database used on onsite computers. Catalog entries come out of the in-house InMagic database, which stores all material records.

LHA is in the process of moving its in-house database, InMagic/DBTextWorks, to an online web-platform, WebPubisherPro, software that is distributed by DBTextWorks, the same company that creates InMagic. LHA chose WebPublisherPro software, the online version of DBTextWorks, to create an Online Public Access Catalog similar to the reasons for choosing CONTENTdm for photos. The choice to use this proprietary software came from the need to maintain consistent technical support for a fluctuating user-base.

Open source software, cost efficient in some ways, was a risky option when primary concerns were troubleshooting potential database issues. As a volunteer collective, with a workgroup of community members with no assumed expertise, the ability to work with a company who could troubleshoot issues was a major factor in software selection. This critical need made available open source software unlikely candidates. WebPublisherPro was chosen, and in the end, provided a controlled environment, for the transfer of metadata from our multiple collections.

A comparative example is the entry for Books, already migrated and formatted for the general OPAC compared to that of T-Shirts in the standalone database. Noticeably, the structure of the information, if merged, would require a renaming of field, a reformatting of standard entries such as title case and date. All 11,000+ books are catalogued with the same structure, just as all 1000 t-shirts have similar cataloguing structure. Issues of migrating data, however, are at the center of the OPAC development process.

Books Collection item entry chosen at random:

Collection Name	**Books**
Title:	No Turning Back: Lesbian and Gay Liberation For The '80s
Author:	Goodman, Gerre, et al.
Place:	Philadelphia
Publisher:	New Society Publishers
Pubdate:	1983
Format:	Book
Holdings:	HER

Other field names could include, Subtitle, ISBN #, Storage Identifying #, Box Number, and if there is a special note in the field "summary" which will denote any type of inscriptions or any other relevant portion of the book's format.

Compare the Books item entry with T-Shirt item entry chosen at random:

Box No	4
Date Entered	9/1/1998
Overall Design	TG
Location of Text	FB
Location of Design	FB
Type	SS
Color	GRAY SHIRT; BLACK PRINT
Text	**OUTLAW OUTRAGE OUTRIGHT OUTSPOKEN OUTRAGEOUS OUTSTANDING, THE RALLY ; (ON BACK):HOT 97 FM JAMS!**
Graphic	INVERTED TRIANGLE, 1/2 GREY; 1/2 BLACK WITH WORDS OVER IT/HOT 97 LOGO
Event	**LESBIAN AND GAY PRIDE RALLY**
Organization	HERITAGE OF PRIDE
City	NEW YORK
State	NY
Major Category	LG
Primary Subject	PRD EVTS
Secondary Subject	BUS/ADV
Also See	SUBJECT FILES FOR PRIDE EVENTS; ORG. FILES FOR HERITAGE OF PRIDE
Date Modified	2/25/2012
ID	28

The development of the OPAC is still in process as the collective devises ways to merge fields of varying collections from each individual InMagic database to the single OPAC database. Since 2011, Archivettes, and interns, have successfully migrated fields of the following collections: Books, T-Shirts,

Graphics, and Film/Video. The Periodicals collection was scheduled for July 2013, and so forth. A beta version exists online, but these collections are not yet open to the public for searching. Even post-migration, the data is inconsistent and must be cleaned prior to public use. Archivettes and interns have been working on cleaning up the data before the database is opened to the public. In addition to cleaning up the databases, many catalog entries will have accompanying .JPEG files to view, namely over 1,000 t-shirts which amount to 6 gigabites of t-shirt images, all of which must be reformatted in order to be viewable on the web.

Since the T-Shirt collection will have accompanying images, each with unique identifiers and field names, there is discussion about possibly providing this to users as a stand-alone collection with its own searchable database. This will be decided once the image conversion is complete and links to the images have been uploaded to the T-Shirt database. If it is agreed upon, the T-Shirts OPAC will be ready for the public sooner than the all-in-one OPAC of additional collections.

Rachel Corbman, a Coordinator overseeing LHA Special Collections, offers a further contextualization of LHA collection development and cataloguing practices. Through WordPress, Rachel created a list of processed Special Collections, organized by accession number, or chronological order, and again by collection name for public access, separate from the OPAC's reveal. The following interview is a glimpse of Rachel's understanding of the coordination of LHA collection development policies, as well as an attempt to answer the questions that put LHA to task among the larger archival community. Rachel is a doctoral student in Women's and Gender Studies at SUNY Stony Brook. She also holds a MA in the Women's, Gender, & Sexuality track of the Graduate Center of the City of New York Masters and Liberal Studies MALS Program.

Rachel Corbman with Shawn(ta) Smith-Cruz on Cataloguing Rituals

Rachel, firstly, how did you get involved with LHA?

I had heard about LHA by virtue of the fact that my research is centered on the history of American feminism. Because the archive was so connected in my head with a particular brand of 1970s feminism, I am not entirely sure that I even knew if the archive was still around. I was asked to stay on as an Archivette after completing my internship. And a few months after that, my former supervisor Maxine Wolfe asked me to take responsibility for the archive's special collections so that she could concentrate on the spoken word audio collection.

Can you describe what Special Collections are, and some strengths and weaknesses that you've found as you've been going through them?

Special Collections are the personal papers that are donated by people and organizations or groups. If someone wants to donate their lives to the Archives, we call this a Special Collection, for example. We have more than 400 Special Collections, in all about half of which have been completely processed. Donors range from well-known lesbians – such as Adrienne Rich and Audre Lorde—to Vanessa the anonymous lesbian prostitute. The sizes of the collections also vary widely, ranging from collections that fit into one small archival box to collections that are comprised of more than 50 large archival boxes. For better or for worse, there is a geographic bias towards New York and a temporal bias towards post-1970s. This isn't really by design so much as it reflects the fact that LHA does not appraise or actively solicit collections. Particular strengths include 1970s feminist activism, AIDS activism, the history of Women's Studies, women's music, activism for lesbian custody of children, and Daughters of Bilitis, the first lesbian organization in the United States founded in San Francisco in 1955. Let's talk weaknesses now. We don't have much material in the Special Collections that predates the 1950s. An exception to this rule is the Katherine Susan Anthony collection, which consists of the research that the donor did on Anthony. Anthony was a writer who was born in 1877 who openly lived with her partner in the Village for more than 30 years. For obvious reasons, we also don't tend to have the papers of famous closeted or semi-closeted lesbians such as Patricia Highsmith, Lorraine Hansberry, or Susan Sontag.

Wait! Lorraine Hansberry was a lesbian?!

Well, we can't "prove" that she identified as such, because she wasn't around to donate herself to the collection. But we do have the May 1957 issue of *The Ladder*, the first nationally distributed lesbian magazine where an editorial signed L.H.N., is available for viewing.

Can you discuss how the collections are organized? I'd like you to unveil, rather carefully, the ways in which LHA applies archival standards to its collections, namely, the Special Collections.

One of the things that intrigue me about Lesbian Herstory Archive's Special Collections is its gradual movement towards archival conventions. Special

Collections date back to 1979 with the Adrienne Rich collection having the distinction of being the first collection accessioned, albeit much of the material was collected earlier. Judging by the records included with older collections, we always organized material into folders that were housed in archival boxes. However, the early collections do not have traditional looking finding aids. They either have nothing or they have inventories that list everything in each box on an item level. It looks as though Joan Nestle was the one to create these inventories. The first example of a finding aid that I am aware of was created in 1984, probably by Polly Thistlewaite, who is currently the Chief Librarian at the Graduate Center of the City University of New York. In Ann Cvetkovich's *An Archive of Feeling*, the writer makes what I think is a very apt point that we can spot the involvement of librarians such as Polly, Lucinda Zoe, Amy Beth, and Desiree Vester in the ways in which LHA catalogues its collections. Needless to say, you, I, and others can be added to this list.

Yes, LHA does have lots of librarians who work there now, but librarians did not necessarily create the standards that we use?

The archive's current approach to organizing its Special Collections was engineered by Maxine Wolfe –who I believe you are interviewing next about audio?

Yes, that is correct.

Maxine designed a finding aid that both closely resembles standards, but also diverges from them in a number of ways. Standards were first set in place in 1977. Prior to this, there were two generally agreed upon philosophies for how one organizes archival collections. First, provenance, which stipulates that papers produced by a particular entity should be kept together in one collection. Second, respect des fonds, which means that the papers should be organized in a way that corresponds to the original order that they were kept. According to Francis X. Blouin Jr. and William Rosenberg, other than these two principles, "most archival institutions had their own idiosyncratic methods for description and access, based on the uniqueness of the collections, their history, and their resources." It is interesting to consider LHA's evolving approach to its Special Collections in light of this since, first of all, the Special Collections only came into being in 1979, two short years after the advent of universal standards. At present, the finding aids that LHA produces are a less labor-intensive version of traditional finding aids. The majority of the fields in our finding aids are the same or a slight variation on the ones found on finding aids produced in compliance with archival standards. Perhaps the biggest difference is that, though we have an infrequently used subject field, the subjects of our special collections do not need to be found in the Library of Congress' official list of appropriate subject headings, which are in a specific order that we don't necessarily comply with at LHA. The second major similarity is that we do folder rather than box or item level description of the collection, though we don't break the folders into series as is standard for more traditionally processed collections.

Thank you for that detailed description of how our archiving is similar and different than the larger field. Is there anything else you'd like to add, specifically on how we are both a community-based archive, and accessible to the archival community?

Well, if we consider the ever-increasing academic legitimacy of Lesbian and Gay Studies and Feminist and Queer Theory, the Lesbian Herstory Archives is constantly inundated with offers to collaborate with larger and well funded institutions. A few recent examples include: our work with Thomson/Gale to microfilm our newsletters, newsprint, subject files, and organizational files; as well as Lesbian Herstory Archives' contributions to EBSCO's LGBTLife database; and, finally, the relationships that LHA has developed with library or archival programs in local universities, including Pratt and NYU's MIAP program, which are working to digitize our spoken word and video collections, respectively. With this in mind, it should come as no surprise that LHA has opted to closely align itself with archival standards, perhaps especially in the case of the special collections. Divergences, when they emerge are likely either the result of LHA being woefully underfunded or, on the contrary, a willful and conscious decision to break with tradition.

Thank you Rachel, I'm going to include an overview about the things you've just mentioned, specifically in relation to the Online Public Access Catalog.

You're welcome. Don't forget to mention that, although, not complete with finding aids, descriptions of the Special Collections are now browsable online: http://herstoryspecialcollections.wordpress.com/.

Thanks Rachel, I will!

(R. Corbman, personal communication, March 11, 2013)

Discoverability is the goal for the OPAC and will come in many forms. Just as the T-Shirts catalog may be separate, the WordPress edition of the Special Collections, created and unveiled during the writing of this article, will have duplication with the eventual OPAC. The goal behind creating an Online Public Access Catalog was to provide online access to materials thereby revolutionizing the way the public utilizes and discovers LHA collections. The pilot year of this multi-year project was initiated by the $15,000 awarded from the Rockefeller Brother's Fund which allowed for the development of an internship training program for additional year replication, data clean-up for the three largest collections, purchase of Online Public Access Catalog software and design, and implementation of an OPAC.

Below is an edited excerpt of the annual report sent to the foundation, compiled by the OPAC committee after a year of planning, then implementation. The committee was led by Archivette and Caretaker, Desiree Yael Vester. Committee interns were: Barbara Bieck, Bit Blair, Amalia E. Bultler, Jackie Coffey, and Marianne Williams. The paragraphs below describe how grant funds were used and the results of the project.

January – May 2011 – *Strategic Cataloguing Plan, OPAC Software, and Interns*

During the first months of the grant year, the work of the volunteer collective was focused on developing a plan to ensure adequate transfer of the catalog into an online format. This process included an assessment of current holdings particular catalog records, a decision to purchase OPAC software that could represent this multi-formatted collection, and a plan for the distribution of labor to implement these next steps. A decision was made to employ interns for the summer and fall, who although were unpaid, could for course credit format and upload the collection onto an online forum.

Strategic Cataloguing Plan –Creating an OPAC meant cataloguing format by format, so as to ensure a catalog that was inclusive of the entire collection. In addition, adjustments to the current catalog meant the creation of an OPAC Working Group whose mission it was to assist with database cleanup, OPAC design (creation, implementation, testing), indexing, cataloging, website maintenance, roll out promotion, and catalog demonstration.

Decision to Choose OPAC Software –The Strategic Cataloguing Plan required the creation of a catalog that was compatible with an integrated library system software that fit into three criteria: an advanced search capability, ability to merge the pre-existing intranet Inmagic software, and technical support service once the transfer was complete. A formal call was not created; instead, research was implemented to consider which companies fit into this rubric. Two presentations were provided to the collective. In the end, DBTextWorks was chosen as the integrated library system with the most compatibility.

Employment of Interns and Internship Training Program —As an all volunteer collective, the implementation of an internship program where archivists-in-training could work with professional lesbian activists, archivists, and librarians was in direct allegiance with the mission of LHA, and acted as the basis for the OPAC project. A call was set out to employ unpaid interns for two semesters. An internship requirement was completion of at least one introductory cataloguing course.

Membership in associations such as Metropolitan Library Council as well as the Society of American Archivists, made it possible to place a call for interns with library science programs. Interns experienced collections processing, cataloging, indexing, participation in the OPAC Working Group, and the preparation of printed and online collection guides.

June–November 2011 —*Collection Areas, Catalog Implementation and Testing*

Library Science interns were employed to survey, process, and catalogue collections. Examples of procedures for formatting these collections are: organizing hard-copy materials, scanning and digitization, indexing, data transfer and database cleanup in LHA catalog, and preparing materials for shipment to off-site storage as needed. Collections that received the most in-depth processing are the video collection, periodicals collection, books and the Red Dot collection, Gale group subject files, and the T-Shirt collection, listed in detail below.

The Video Collection: Due to the support of the RBF funds each video received notation for its title, director, producer, writer, cast, copyright year, and length. By the end of the grant year, the video collection in its entirety is successfully cataloged. The collection now includes the donation of some L Word promotional material, the Lesbian Herstory Archives/Daughters Of Bilitis Project tapes, Irish Lesbian and Gay Organization videos, and the *In The Life* tapes. There are 13 boxes of videos and 1000 entries in the spreadsheet, which originally had approximately 120 videos listed. Duplicates were stored off site at Iron Mountain, the LHA archival repository. Audiotapes, betas, CDs, and other material were included with the processing of videos.

The Periodicals Collection: Newsletters were originally indexed in a cardex, a hand-written card catalog. Using the Cardex as a guide, each record was transferred to the DBTextWorks intranet software for an eventual upload into the OPAC by intern Amailia E. Butler. Pre-existing records were edited for uniformity and where additional information was added. Incorporated was volume and/or issue numbers, regions (self-defined with map for reference), subjects (primary from WorldCat/OCLC/Library of Congress), address, publisher, and comments.

Books and the Red Dot Collection: The Lesbian Herstory Archives maintains two catalogs for books: General Books and the Red Dot Collection equaling 9,191 records. The Red Dot Collection is the collection of books secured from the New York chapter of the first lesbian organization in the country –the Daughters of Bilitis. 798 records have been surveyed and updated, covering the entirety of the Red Dot Collection, among others. Books include self-published poetry, novels, course readers, unpublished screenplays, and other resources unique to the collection. Many of these single-issue items are only available at the LHA. As a result, original cataloguing was also a part of this processing.

Gale Group Subject Files: In 2004, Gale®, part of Cengage Learning, a world leader in e-research and educational publishing for libraries, digitized the subject files and newsletters of LHA as part of their Gay Rights Movement Series. Subject files are the first stop for most researchers, some of which date back to 1970s and are primary source documents or include correspondence and publicity materials from other gay and lesbian archives from several countries. There are 17 CDs of scans from the Archives' files, with approximately 190,000 digitized files in total. Although Gale digitized these files, they were never before searchable in an online catalog. Due to the RBF grant, entries were created into the database for online searching.

T-Shirt collection: The Lesbian Herstory Archives has a collection of over 900 t-shirts, sent by friends and donors who acquired them at protests, college student groups, music festivals, concerts, bookstores, and coffee shops; a few of them are handmade. Xerox copies of all T-Shirt designs have been scanned to a hard drive in two formats -.tiff (for preservation) and .jpg (for easier manipulation).

Administrative Access to the Catalog: Crew Noble was chosen as the web designer and host for the OPAC. The One Archives (OPAC) and June Mazer (OPAC), two very influential LGBT archives also use Crew Noble. To eliminate the need to update between the LHA hard-drive and Crew Noble, there is an edit function, which will ultimately switch the primary editing location.

This will allow the ability to edit the DBTextworks online databases via a web browser. The goal is to eventually shift the collections completely to Crew Noble servers and have all editing occur online. Scans have been added of t-shirts with links to those t-shirts in the Image URL field. Users can click the link to get a larger version of the scanned image.

Audio Digitization and Online Exhibitions

On November 17, 2012, for twelve hours from noon to midnight, LHA hosted a Marathon reading of the works of Audre Lorde and Adrienne Rich. The event marked the year of Adrienne Rich's passing and the 20th anniversary of Audre Lorde's passing, two transitions that led these two iconic women to becoming community ancestors. One pivotal resource that helped to steer the reading was the use of audio. Event co-coordinators Archivette, Flavia Rando, community member Alexis Clements and I, Shawn(ta) Smith, along with a committee of community members chose to digitally record the readings amplified inside of the Archives' limestone. These recordings are currently audible on the LHA website as an archive of the event. In addition, a listening station of previously digitized audio was accessible on a touch screen tablet with clips of Lorde and Rich in conversation, as well as individual clips of each poet reading and speaking to large audiences. Elizabeth Lorde Rollins, Audre Lorde's daughter, called the Archives, and then sent a letter, both thanking us for the receipt of her mother's voice in digital form. This audio access was possible because weeks before the event, Lorde's collection of audio was completely digitized. This digitization effort was a collaborative effort between LHA Coordinator Maxine Wolfe, Pratt School of Information and Library Sciences (Pratt SILS) Professor Anthony Cocciolo, and students from his digitization course. Since 2008, this partnership has led to the online exhibition Herstories: A Digital Collection, hosted at the Pratt Institute on Omeka software. It contains some digitizations from the 3,000 oral history cassettes in the Archives' collection.

During her twenty eight years as an Archivette, Maxine Wolfe has maintained multiple collections, organized the digitization of the periodical and subject files, and organized and facilitated monthly Special Collection workdays to process collections of personal and organizational papers and create finding aids. Maxine orchestrated and supervised the digitization of Spoken Word cassettes. She also staffs on a regular basis. In the following interview, Maxine describes the LHA audio collection, as well as the audio digitization project that has made the voices of Lorde, Rich, and many other lesbians from our audio collection accessible.

Maxine Wolfe with Shawn(ta) Smith on Audio

Maxine, can you give us an overview of the audio as it exists at LHA?

The Lesbian Herstory Archives already holds about 3000 cassette tapes that range from oral histories, to panels at conferences, to conversations between two women, correspondence between women, readings by poets and writers, and poets performances. There are also excerpts of radio shows including the entire WBAI Womens and Lesbian programs between the 70s and 80s. However, all are on cassette, which have a short life, although very few have expired. This is a monumental job for cataloguing. Over 1300 are currently catalogued.

What was the process for putting them into a digital format?

Firstly, I must say that digital reformatting is not the beginning and end of how these materials should be preserved. We still don't know the life of digital materials. Before, everyone was in a rush to transfer information to discs, now from discs to flash drives. Eventually, flash drives will be an unusable format, so these are things to keep in mind when digitization is for the purposes of preservation.

And online access, what was the impetus for not only digitizing the audio, but also making them accessible online?

It is important for people to get the information and to hear it, that's why putting the materials online is so important. It's not just digitizing the tapes, but putting them into context with metadata. Just hearing what people say, but not having access to any information about them is limiting.

With over 3000 audiotapes, this is a daunting project. What was the process like to work with Anthony and Pratt, specifically, or for getting others involved in the project generally?

Anthony Cocciolo, a professor at Pratt Institute in library science, put out a notice requesting oral histories for a project for his new digitization courses. Amy Wolfe, my daughter, happened to be a librarian at Pratt at the time, and so, was still on the Pratt listserv. Naturally, she told her mother that this opportunity existed, and I knew it was not one to pass up. I called Anthony without much hesitation and said that LHA had 3000 oral histories, all of which needed digital preservation.

Were there any initial concerns when creating the partnership?

During our conversation, Anthony revealed that the digitization was a part of a class project. My concern wasn't for class participation in general. However, as a lesbian archive, we have very sensitive stories. I made it very clear that we are a lesbian archive and do not want to deal with homophobic people. He assured me that his students would be sensitive to the collection. Usually, I would have been more skeptical, I mean, how could he know the responses of his students. He replied: Don't worry, I am a gay man, and will take responsibility for this.

What luck! So, on some level, it remains inside of the community.

To work with an outside organization, these are the questions that we need to have. We as an organization, and lesbians herstorically, have dealt with abuse our whole lives, and won't put up with it just to digitize a tape. We won't compromise. And we didn't have to. The entire collection has been catalogued by lesbians, and in some instances like this one, allies have been huge supporters.

And it proved to be a fruitful venture. Tell me about the process for digitization.

Each semester began with the students coming to the Archives to receive a tour, so that they could get a sense of where these interviews came from. After that, the students did all of the work. 2010 was the first year that it was completed, and the collection used was all of the Mabel Hampton interviews. They digitized all of the tapes, scanned the photographs, gave a small synopsis, an introduction about who Mabel was and did the research, all using the materials of the collection. 37 interviews were done in the first semester, then a website was created.

What made you choose the Mabel Hampton collection as the first?

When creating an online exhibition, we have to consider the rights of the materials. We have the rights to all of the Mabel Hampton interviews since they were conducted with Joan Nestle and Mabel was a part of the Coordinating committee. This collection made sense to begin the first round. Second, we wanted to consider demand. In 2011 most of what we had on Audre Lorde most were tapes of readings at benefits, a conversation between her and Adrienne Rich and recordings of her speeches. We have close contact with her family and her estate is readily accessible, so we decided this complete collection would be useful for the course. With the Boots of Leather, Slippers of Gold collection, we asked Madeline Davis if she would be interested in us working on her materials and she said yes! 137 Boots of Leather tapes will be completed this year. Next summer, Anthony and his class will do the Daughters of Bilitis interviews.

What are the next steps?

Once this project began, we decided to digitize ourselves on site at the Archives. We used Audacity audio editing software, which is the same that Anthony used with his students, which is great because it is free and user-friendly. I worked with Colette Montoya-Humphrey to create a SPW [spoken word] project and audacity protocol manual. Anthony does not use any noise reduction but we discovered that in archivist circles, the discussion is to whether you should use noise reduction or not, to alter the audio, or keep the original sound. We decided on site that we would preserve the voices by reducing the noise when necessary. Still, with the large, archival .wav files, we chose not to reduce noise. Noise reduction is useful to ensure that we can hear what people are saying. When we make .mp3s for people to use at the archives, then we apply some editing. The materials currently live on a hard drive at the Archives. Once digitized, on the hard drive, CDs are created from the wav into mp3s. The metadata is being compiled simultaneously.

Of the 3000 interviews, it's difficult to mention them all. We are going tape by tape, and specifically those with releases and permissions. For example, other interviews we have are lesbians and fashion, the Radical Rose recordings which recorded everything that happened in Minneapolis which all have releases. So while the class is busy digitizing and putting things online, we are continuing to catalog all of our tapes, and digitize the regular collection.

Can you tell me about the other collections at LHA, and how digitization is taking form?

Generally we've catalogued our 10000 books. Our Periodicals have been digitized and are available with EBSCO's LGBT Life full text database, which people can view onsite, or at local libraries. The New York Public Library and some CUNY campuses have access, for example. We've learned from the process of working with a company that negotiating a contract where you get a copy and they don't own it is the most important part of the process. Our Newsletters (2006) & Subject Files (2004) are processed by Thompson Gale as the 2004 Gay Rights Movement Series.

They scanned them and then transferred them onto microfilm. As a result of our contract with them, we receive royalties of about $6k per year.

One more thing, if you look to the EBSCO database, all of the articles are not full-text because of the ability to get copyright, so they've abstracted an index of the database. We do have, however the digital copies of each periodical, full-text, onsite. Unfortunately, we don't have the server to place them online. In January 2013, Thompson Gale begins a similar process with the Newsprint newspapers with a similar type of contract, specifically for titles that were not already being archived elsewhere, like *The Advocate* for example. We do still need a server or some way to host all of our digital holdings. And then, someone has to index the periodicals. I believe EBSCO can do it.

(M. Wolfe, personal communication, December 16, 2012)

Tape-by-Tape – Online at LHA

As Maxine hinted, the multi-step process for digitizing and placing items online occurs item-by-item, or tape-by-tape. The process for preserving these rich materials hasn't changed very much in almost 40 years of lesbian archiving. The women volunteer time and utilize community resources to allow for continued preservation and access.

Online presence is a conversation that must include both preservation and access due to the influx of newly acquired materials, and expanded programming. In addition, there is interest in 484 14th Street as a community space beyond the Archive, where readings, book launches, courses like the Lesbian Studies Institute, or art gallery exhibitions, to name a few become integral to LHA programming. The collection still persists, and the group of Archivettes—while small—remain consistent. Online communication as a form of access also achieves the goal of increasing the number of women who can work on these projects. They will be the future Archivettes –Coordinators, staffers, interns, and volunteers — who will all play a role in the many facets of LHA –our archiving and our programming.

With the newly created email address lesbianherstoryarchives@gmail.com, and the ongoing efforts of the LHA's very part-time webmistress Heather Stewart, the online presence of the Lesbian Herstory Archives is thriving. As new demands for social networking opportunities increase, LHA has published a Facebook page, launched digital exhibitions, used Crowdrise for fundraising campaigns, and sent out periodic e-newsletters. Requests for access to these rich materials from anywhere in the world is in great demand. At LHA, and likely in the world of community LGBT archiving, we will meet the online demands one step at a time, tape-by-tape.

REFERENCES

Carlomusto, J., Pérez, D., Saalfield, C., Thistlethwaite, P., Not Just Passing Through Productions., & Women Make Movies (Firm). (1994). *Not just passing through*. New York, N.Y: Not Just Passing Through Productions.

Edel, D. (1990, Spring). The Lesbian Herstory Archives. *Women of Power* 16, 22-23.

Lesbian Herstory Educational Foundation. (2013). Digital Collections. Retrieved from http://lesbianherstoryarchives.org/digital.html

Lesbian Herstory Educational Foundation. (2013). History. Retrieved from http://lesbianherstoryarchives.org/history.html

Nestle, J. (1998). The Will to remember: The Lesbian Herstory Archives of New York. *Journal of Homosexuality*, 34 (¾), 225–235.

Smith, S. (2011). The Lesbian Herstory Archives. In *Qualia folk: ... dedicated to LGBT scholarship*. Retrieved from http://www.qualiafolk.com/2011/12/08/lesbian-herstory-archives/

Privacy, Context & Pride: The Management of Digital Photographs in a Queer Archives

Rebecka Sheffield & Kate Zieman

Introduction

The Canadian Lesbian and Gay Archives (CLGA), founded in Toronto as the Canadian Gay Liberation Archives in 1973, is the largest queer[1] archives in Canada and the second largest in the world. The CLGA grew out of the working files of *The Body Politic*, Canada's gay liberation newspaper of record from 1971 to 1987. For many years Pink Triangle Press (the collective that published *The Body Politic*) and the archives were physically and operationally intertwined. After gaining physical independence from Pink Triangle Press in 1992, the CLGA went on to occupy a number of cramped offices before acquiring, renovating and moving to a heritage home in 2009. This shift to a larger and more accessible space has occasioned a renewed emphasis on public engagement. The CLGA's profile in all communities steadily increases through tours, open houses, lectures and a robust exhibition program. The Archives has also forged stronger links with community organizations like Pride Toronto and the Inside Out LGBT Film Festival, and its online presence has grown through its website and use of Facebook, Twitter, and other social media applications.

---

1   Like Barriault and Sheffield (2009), we deploy 'queer' in this project in its most inclusive meaning as a way to discuss all people whose gender and sexuality has been historically understood as non-heteronormative. This includes, but is certainly not limited to those people who identify as lesbian, gay, bisexual, trans, and two-spirited. We have used the terms 'gay' and 'lesbian' where we wish to convey more specificity about the people and events that we are describing. We recognize, however, that each of these terms is contestable.

As the CLGA has raised its public profile, volunteers have observed an increased demand for archival and contemporary digital images. Some requests have come from academic researchers, but most are from media and community organizations hoping to include images in their publications and promotional material. Currently, the CLGA's photograph collection includes thousands of items including prints, negatives, postcards, and halftone reproductions. Photographic material from *The Body Politic* forms the core of the collection, and as one longtime volunteer has noted, these records constitute one of the "gems" of the Archives (Miller 2012). Pink Triangle Press was one of the only queer media producers operating during the 1970s and 1980s; it documented much of the Canadian gay liberation movement's activity including demonstrations, conferences, and social events. Photographs that appeared in *The Body Politic* made their way into the archives, along with negatives and contact sheets featuring many images never seen in print. Over the years, acquisitions from individuals and organizations have broadened the scope of the photograph collection; of particular note is a donation from Lynnie Johnston, which includes several photographs documenting both the 1981 raids on Toronto's gay bathhouses and the massive demonstrations that followed (the Bathhouse Raids, as they have come to be known, are often referred to as 'Canada's Stonewall' [CBC 2013]). The CLGA's photograph collection now features thousands of images of demonstrations, conferences, performances and social events in cities across Canada, and it has become an invaluable visual record of 20th century Canadian queer history. Considering the revitalized commitment to public engagement and the increasing demand for photographic material, it should come as no surprise that the CLGA wishes to further leverage this valuable collection.

Of roughly 10,000 items, only a handful have been digitized and made available to researchers, often without clear instructions for crediting the Archives for its services. In several cases, these same few images have been digitized on multiple occasions for different projects, betraying a lack of efficient management of the digitized files. Such poor practices have led to unnecessary handling of the photographs and raised concerns over their conservation. At the same time, some volunteers have also expressed worry over the privacy of third parties depicted in some images, particularly those documenting early activism. Disclosure of sexual orientation can still put people at risk for harm. Questions about intellectual property plague researchers, and the CLGA is not always able to provide enough contextual information to identify the rights holder of each photograph. Resource constraints are also a challenge; volunteers have always run the Archives, though in recent years the CLGA has hired a general manager to oversee daily operations. Some scanning technology is available, but the staff often lacks the specialized knowledge required to properly manage a digitization project. It is within these political and socio-technical contexts that we begin our discussion of some recent challenges that the CLGA has encountered with regard to its photograph collection and a mounting desire to make these images available online.

The Persistence of Analog Realities

As de Rond and Miller (2005, 321) have suggested, "there are few more familiar aphorisms in the academic community than 'publish or perish'". Scholars either venerate or dread the 'publish or perish' principle, which has become a way of life for many researchers. Archivists are similarly haunted by a 'digitize or disappear' principle, the bane or boon of the archival community, which suggests that the importance of an archives is primarily a function of how much of its holdings are accessible online through digital media. Archivists are often confronted with the unenlightened question, 'Why don't you just put it all online?' If only it were that easy! Although we would welcome the benefits of large-scale digitization such as improved accessibility and preservation of originals, we would be remiss not to examine some of the obstacles inherent in such a project.

For more than three decades, the CLGA primarily served scholarly researchers, journalists, and other media professionals. Few people outside of these professions accessed the holdings, although many profited from the journalistic and scholarly research that took place. Recent cultural and political advances have sparked much broader interest in queer histories, both within and outside of the academy. At the same time, the proliferation of digital technologies has pressured queer archivists to respond to an ever-increasing demand for digitally-mediated access to the material records in their custody. Although reference services take place in person, the CLGA has established a strong web presence and made some of its finding aids available online. The organization does not, however, provide online access to its central database, nor does it currently make partial or entire collections available on its website. The few digitized records that are posted on the website (mostly photographs and periodical covers) are there either for aesthetic reasons or as examples of the type of records held by the CLGA.

The Society of American Archivists defines digitization as the process by which analog information is transformed into binary electronic form, or made digital through conversion technology, such as scanning and optical character recognition (OCR) (Pearse-Moses 2013). The term 'digitized' also distinguishes materials that have been converted from analog to digital from materials that were originally created in a digital media. This is a noteworthy distinction because the overwhelming majority of records collected by the CLGA are analog in nature; few, if any of its photographic records are 'born digital'. Thus, the first step in making more of its holdings accessible online is to digitize analog records, a daunting task that would consume a significant portion of the already-limited human resources and technical capacity of the CLGA. As of this writing, the Archives is not in the habit of actively acquiring born-digital records, as there is no capacity within the current structure to preserve or make accessible digital information. One might assume that the will to engage with digital technologies is weak, but, this is not the case. The number of difficulties facing archivists who desire to digitize and make accessible records online is daunting enough to dampen much of our enthusiasm.

Although this is not the appropriate forum to adequately describe the full range of challenges that digitization presents, we do want to dispel some lasting myths. First, we stress that digitization is always a fraught activity. Archivists must consider resource allocation, facilities, and infrastructure, as well as the impact of changing technologies over time. They must also prepare disaster and recovery plans in the event that the data is lost through disk failure or accidental erasure. In addition to these pragmatic concerns, archivists must also consider how to capture the significant properties of a tangible object in a digital format. As Wendy Duff (2010) argues, the amount and type of metadata that is captured about a record affects its authenticity, legal admissibility, artifactual value, ease and convenience of use, and aesthetic qualities. Archivists must decide which preservation strategies will best preserve these significant properties over time and which will be lost or altered over time through normalization or format conversion. Considering the burden digitization places on human resources, archives must also prioritize which collections will be done first, a process with political implications. For example, does one digitize the records that are most commonly accessed, or give priority to an important collection that is rarely used because it is either difficult to access or it is relatively unknown to researchers?

An additional myth is that all records can be digitized and that the digital copy can stand in for the original. As a corollary, digitization does not open up space for new acquisitions, as the original record should be kept. While it may be easy to digitize some paper records, important metadata can still be lost or obscured throughout the digitization process. Although scanning technologies have improved significantly over time, three-dimensional objects such as matchbooks and t-shirts are not easy to digitize. A pin button from the CLGA, for example, cannot be run through a scanner as a whole object. Rather, as the CLGA volunteer curator Wil Craddock has done for The Pin Button

Project[2], we can take a photograph of the button's front face and describe this image using metadata such as the pin's dimensions, the year it was created, or the organization that created it. Other data about the type of metal used in the pin back, or the quality of the paper used to make the pin face, might not be captured because the archivist deems it to be superfluous even with the understanding that the needs of the future researcher are impossible to predict. Thoughtful, but ultimately arbitrary, limits have to be set in an effort to ease the burden on the human resources that carry digitization projects forward.

Some of our anxiety about digitization has been quelled by a constellation of available technologies, policies, allocation mechanisms, coordination, and skilled people that makes digital preservation possible (or makes it much less expensive and reliable). The decreasing costs associated with digitization technologies are also complemented by the development of standards to help guide decision-making about the adoption of technological infrastructure and metadata capturing processes. Digitization, as Conway (2008) points out, usually requires a guideline that sets out the agreed-upon technical specifications that determine how the new 'digital original' or preservation master will be preserved, which metadata are essential to capture for future information retrieval, and the extent to which the archivist can intervene in the creation of the new 'digital original' by adding new or complementary descriptive data. Such consensus-making also requires resources and can involve any number of stakeholders, from members of the Board of Directors to long-term volunteers. Best practices, for example, have now been enshrined in ISO 13028:2010, an internationally recognized standard that establishes guidelines for creating and maintaining records in digital formats. Many archives, including the National Archives and Records Administration (NARA) of the United States, and Library and Archives Canada (LAC), have their own technical standards for digitization (see Puglia, Reed and Rhodes 2004; LAC 2008). The CLGA, therefore, has plenty of resources to reference in the event that it develops its own policy and procedures for future digitization projects.

What continues to prohibit the wholesale adoption of digitization is not archivists' reluctance, technology costs, or concern over standards, but rather

---

2   The Pin Button Project is an online interactive exhibition and oral history project featuring pin buttons from the collection at the Canadian Lesbian and Gay Archives. The pins were selected, photographed and presented online by a team of volunteers led by curator Wil Craddock. The exhibition is accessible online at www.clga.ca/thepinbuttonproject, and visitors read the histories of each button, leave comments, and 'adopt a button' with a charitable donation to the project. The Pin Button Project is co-sponsored by the Community One Foundation, Xtra!, and the Mark S. Bonham Centre for Sexual Diversity Studies through the Michael Lynch History Grant.

the ambiguities around the management of rights and responsibilities. The following sections will discuss two of the most pressing concerns related to our rights and responsibilities: the intellectual property rights endowed in the photographs, and the privacy rights of those depicted therein.

Intellectual Property and Digitization

With few exceptions, the CLGA does not own the copyright to the records in its possession. This is true for most community archives, whereby records are collected from multiple provenance and collections include ephemera and other records where the rights are ambiguous. Researchers are made aware of this fact when they sign a research agreement, whereupon they agree to the terms of the CLGA's research policies and acknowledge that the Archives is neither responsible nor capable of granting permission to copy under the provisions of the *Canadian Copyright Act*. Researchers must therefore seek permission directly from the rightsholder should they wish to use the material in any way protected by the *Act*. While volunteers may assist researchers with obtaining information about rightsholders, the onus for clearing any permissions for the use of intellectual property rests squarely with the researcher.

As one might imagine, researchers often find it frustrating to learn that the CLGA cannot easily grant permission to republish or make copies of records in its possession. Worse still, the Archives does not always have accurate or complete information about the copyright of its records. In the case of the photograph collection, few records have been described at the item level. This is actually standard practice in archives, where records are less managed and less manageable than library materials or museum objects due to their intellectual scope and the volume of individual records that comprise a single fonds.[3] At the CLGA, most photographs are part of a larger series of fonds of personal or organizational records. As a result, they are usually described at the series level, which gives researchers contextual information about an entire aggregate group, but does not call attention to any single photograph in this series. Information about the particular people and events depicted in each image is not always forthcoming. Unless the donor has specifically indicated the name of the rightsholder (e.g. the photographer or the organization commissioning the photograph[s]), then the description will also lack vital information about

---

3 The term 'fonds' refers to an entire body of records created or accumulated by an organization, family, or individual. This differs from 'collection', which refers to a body of records collected from more than one provenance.

the copyright holder. It cannot be assumed that the donor owns the copyright to any of the photographs that reside in the collection, nor should it be assumed that the CLGA retains these rights.

To further complicate matters, the assignment of copyright is not always clear, even if the Archives has identified the person who took the photograph. While a thorough review of intellectual property legislation is worthy of a much longer discussion, it is worth noting that laws remain relatively confounding for both the professional archivist and the archival researcher.

Copyright Law in Canada

In Canada, the *Copyright Act* covers all matters related to the development, use, reproduction, and translation of materials. Section 3 (1) of the *Act* defines copyright as "the sole right to produce or reproduce the work or any substantial part thereof in any material form whatever, to perform the work or any substantial part thereof in public or, if the work is unpublished, to publish the work or any substantial part thereof [...]"(*R.S., 1985, c. C-42*). As Murray and Truscow (2007, 163) explain, photography is included under Section 2, which defines the type of "artistic works" that are protected. In this sense, the Act recognizes that photography is a range of practices that, like writing or filmmaking, results in a creative work worthy of protection.

The assignment of intellectual property rights to photographers, however, is less straightforward than those assigned to writers or other visual artists. As Murray and Truscow point out, photography emerged in the late 1800s as a technical practice and thus, early legislation treated photographs much as it would the product of a mechanical or technical routine. As such, photographers have not always owned the intellectual property rights to their work by default. If a photographer were commissioned to take a photograph and did not explicitly assert copyright in a contract, then rights were automatically waived. At one point, intellectual property rights were first assigned to the owner of the camera—a perfectly reasonable assignment of rights for a period when such equipment was usually owned by a professional and used by several employees (Murray and Truscow 2007). This also worked in the case of the amateur photographer who lends out a camera to a stranger to take a family picture; however, it also meant that anyone who borrowed or rented equipment were not guaranteed rights to any photographs taken using this equipment.

In 1999, the *Act* was amended to provide more clarity for the intellectual property of photographs. A revised Section 10(2) granted authorship of the work to the first owner of the plates or negative, whether or not that person took the photograph. The term of copyright was expanded from 50 years after the end of the year in which the image was made to the end of the year in which the author died plus 50 years, if the author was a natural person. Section 10(13) also clarified that if the photograph was commissioned, authorship was automatically assigned to the person by whom the plate or other original was ordered. This treatment of photographers differs slightly from other creators because it assumes that the author and the creator of the photograph are two distinct legal entities, whereas the creator of a manuscript, for example, is by default the author of said manuscript. At the time of this writing, revisions to *The Copyright Act* introduced to Parliament in Bill C-11, bring photographs in line with other artistic work, such as poetry or prose: photographers are now considered the first owner of any works they produce and these rights may be assigned to another person or organization (Bill C-11, 2012). The harmonization of authorship rights will no doubt benefit professional photographers (and more likely their heirs) as this will clarify their rights to the photographs they take.

Nevertheless, the amendments to the *Copyright Act* are not necessarily as favorable for archivists and historical researchers as they are for photographers. As Murray and Truscow (2007) suggest, the confusion around authorship and creatorship have had dire implications for archives and their users. They write, "when we are dealing with historical photographs, photographers are particularly difficult to identify—-compared, say, to the authors of letters or books: the date, venue, and subjects of old photographs are hard enough to determine, and the finger on the shutter even more elusive" (163). As a result, it was much easier to make use of historical photographs before the 1999 amendments because the term of copyright was simply 50 years from the taking of the photograph.

Legal Implications for the CLGA

Even copying a photograph for research use carries with it a responsibility that most volunteers at the CLGA are uncomfortable taking on. As Dorey (2009) notes, the federal government has made some specific exceptions to allow educational institutions, libraries, archives, and museums to make reference copies of material subject to copyright. In accordance with Exception for Educational Institutions, Libraries, Archives and Museums Regulations (*SOR/99-325*), archivists can make copies for consultation, reference, and research use. They must document which works were copied and make this information available for 28 days for public consultation. In addition, they must keep this information for three years and inform any copyright holder of use on an annual basis. This assumes, however, that the copyright owner is known and can be contacted. In many situations, the CLGA struggles to identify the copyright owners of photographs in its collection. If the copyright holder cannot be located, then the Archives would have to contact the Canadian Copyright Board (CCB), an economic regulatory body, and seek a licence to copy a work for which the rightsholder cannot be traced. According to the CCB (2001), it will issue a license after all steps to locate the rightsholder have been exhausted. For archives, however, this procedure is not always helpful because, as Dorey (2009) so trenchantly notes, the CCB cannot grant permission to copy unpublished works that do not fall under its purview. Although some of the CLGA's photographs have been previously published, namely those that are collected from the organizational files of the Pink Triangle Press, most have never been published.

Moral Rights

The prickly problem of moral rights also poses challenges for archives and their users. Unlike the United States, Canada has established moral rights as part of its intellectual property rights. Moral rights allow a creator to control how their artistic work is used even if copyright has been assigned to another owner. In doing so, the creator can benefit economically from the assignment of rights and still dictate how their work will be represented. Perhaps the most famous example of a creator exerting moral rights is the case of *Snow v. The Eaton Centre Ltd.*, in which the Ontario High Court of Justice affirmed the rights of artist Michael Snow by finding that a downtown Toronto mall had violated his moral rights when they put Christmas bows around the necks of geese in a sculpture that he had created. Although the sculpture, entitled *Flightstop*, was a commissioned work for which Snow was assigned copyright, he objected to the alterations because it devalued the artistic integrity of the work. As Harris explains, the assertion of moral rights is also what allows Canadians to insist that they be accurately credited for contributions to creative work and prevent anyone from using their works "in association with a product, service, cause, or institution" that could damage the creator's reputation (Harris 2010). In the case of archival photographs, the researcher must tread through muddy waters to obtain permission to use photographs and ensure that moral rights are upheld.

Considering the noted obstacles, queer archivists at the CLGA would still like to share the rich content of the photographic collection with a broader audience via digital technologies, but the lack of contextual data is testing the limits of volunteers' expertise and patience. Much of their time is spent attempting to search for photographs that document particular events, people, and places of historical interest to the community. In addition, digitization projects have also exposed the vulnerabilities of the CLGA as a volunteer-run organization that has not always operated with professional oversight.

Case Study 1: Delivering Context From Chaos

In one recent case, the Chair of the Community Engagement Committee met with the creator of a new free mobile phone app that had received attention in the local press. The app, called 'Zeitag TO', integrates archival photographs into an interactive map. Seeing an opportunity to educate the public about Toronto's queer past, the volunteer made arrangements to supply the app's creator with photos of 20 locations that had significance to the city's LGBTQ community. This proved to be more complicated than anticipated. Initially, the chief obstacle was the chaotic state of the photograph collection, which made it nearly impossible to find anything through the database. Over several evenings, a team of three volunteers made unsuccessful attempts to match catalogue records with physical photographs. Eventually they abandoned the database entirely and sifted through hundreds of photographs by hand. One volunteer also reviewed dozens of digital scans that had been saved on a hard drive. These scans made over several years for a number of purposes (e.g., user requests, exhibitions, etc.), had not been named according to any established conventions, and were impossible to identify without recourse to the physical holdings and a largely-obsolete finding aid from 1992.

After several candidate photos had been chosen and (if necessary) digitized, the project leader began the thorny task of determining copyright. Many of the images were pulled from the records of Pink Triangle Press. Due to the close association between the archives and Pink Triangle Press, the clearing of copyright for this material has traditionally been casual. In most cases, the CLGA is free to use material for any purpose that promotes the work of the archives. Only one photographer who published in the *Body Politic* has ever refuted this agreement and asked that his images not be used, though it is often impossible to distinguish which photographs were actually taken by him.

Unfortunately, neither this loose copyright agreement with Pink Triangle Press nor the restrictions on the lone photographer's work have ever been documented in an official capacity, but long-time volunteers and the President of the Board are generally available for consultation. When contacted about the Zeitag TO project, the President stated that he was fairly certain that the CLGA held the rights to a number of the photographs, but the lack of clarity caused the project leader to also contact Alan Miller (a trained librarian, one of the Archives' longest-serving volunteers) as well as Paul Leatherdale, the archivist who maintains some jurisdictional responsibility for the photograph collection. Based on their knowledge of the community and the collection, Miller and Leatherdale recommended which photos would be acceptable to use and which were best avoided. Miller also provided contact information for the photographers that he knew personally, so the project leader was able to write to them for explicit permission. In one case, a rightsholder complained that she had been contacted many times over the years and always gave permission, but this was not recorded in the relevant finding aids. Ultimately, the team was only able to find and clear 12 photos, rather than the original 20 that had been promised.

Recommendations

While exasperating, the Zeitag TO experience was instructive in that it highlighted a number of key areas for improvement. First and foremost, the collections need to be properly arranged and described because it is nearly impossible to locate any particular image using the existing finding aids or database. As noted above, the work required to bring these photographs under intellectual control is daunting. Nevertheless, queer archivists at the CLGA know that there is incredible value in these photographs and making them available online would spark a surge of new support for the organization. Sharing these images widely through digital technologies also helps meet the mandate of the Archives as an agent of social change, and emphasizing this to the Board of Directors (none of whom are information professionals) might help move things along. Second, it is imperative that volunteers work toward acquiring the crucial metadata that can illuminate the status of these records with regard to rights, restrictions on use, and contextual meaning. Relying on the recollections of volunteers and other community members is not a practical strategy, particularly for an organization striving to situate itself as the principal source of information about queer Canadian history. The CLGA would be wise to gather this kind of information while the now-elderly donors are still alive, and to make it an integral component of donor agreements for any forthcoming accessions. Third, the CLGA needs to leverage its existing digital scans so that future volunteers do not repeat digitization work already completed. Creating a standardized database to house these digital surrogates and developing a tool to ensure long-term compatibility and preservation would be ideal. Finally, the Archives needs to develop a protocol for engaging with researchers on digital projects that use archival photographs. Who owns the rights to the photographs once digitized? How is the CLGA credited in the project? How is the Archives compensated for costs associated with digitization (e.g., new scanners, data storage)? Who is responsible for ensuring that the privacy of any third parties depicted in the photographs is protected or respected? What kinds of projects are beyond the scope of the Archives and which would be most beneficial? How does the project contribute to the advancement of queer scholarship and celebrate the lives of queer people in Canada and abroad? Once these changes are in place, the process of digitizing and sharing the photograph collection will proceed much smoother.

PRIVACY & THE (AB)USE OF ARCHIVAL PHOTOGRAPHS IN A DIGITALLY MEDIATED ENVIRONMENT

Another pressing concern for queer archivists engaged in digitization work is that they will inadvertently harm an individual by placing their photograph online for a mass audience to see. In fact, the fear of 'outing' any person is often enough to prevent queer archivists from using the image unless all persons depicted are well known to the LGBT community. Such conservative inclinations seem to run counter to the activist mandates of queer archives as agents of social change; however, as one long-time volunteer reminded us, this hesitancy is a reflection of the collective experiences of queer archivists, many of whom came of age during the pre-Stonewall era when the disclosure of one's sexual orientation put one at great risk. Outing remains a contemporary concern as well. Despite legal and social advances over the past four decades, many queer people remain private about their sexual orientation because disclosure can impact their ability to retain housing, employment, and access to children, as well as their capacity to participate fully in their own communities. Thus, the right to live a closeted life is philosophically and pragmatically defensible.

Warren and Brandeis (2005 [1890]) first articulated the concept of privacy in the notable paper, "The Right to Privacy". Published in 1890, the much-touted article responded to Michigan Supreme Court Justice Thomas M. Cooley's statement that people have the right to "be let alone" (210). The authors, both Harvard Law School graduates, stressed that common laws have evolved to safeguard the individual on many different levels, from physical injury to a loss of reputation, as in the case of libel and slander, and they suggest that the invasion of privacy is akin to a violation of individual rights because such acts can result in harm due to "mental pain and distress" (211). The authors also urged citizens to be wary of new technologies, such as inexpensive cameras and 'gossip' newspapers that expose private details that those involved may not wish to be revealed. Privacy, therefore, is conceived as both a right to seek solitude (e.g. physical isolation from others) and to control when, how, and where intimate details are disclosed.

As the Harvard graduates predicted, the right of privacy has become increasingly important over the last century, as technological advancements have made it even easier to collect, store, and disseminate private information. Privacy has also migrated from the ethical sphere to the legal sphere, although the two are not mutually exclusive. Until recently, Canada addressed invasion of privacy complaints through the laws of tort; however, the courts have not always recognized the capacity for plaintiffs to sue based on these laws. Nevertheless, the adoption of the federal *Privacy Act* in 1980 has achieved more clarity with regard to the government's position on privacy. The law, which has been amended several times since its enactment, provides additional protection for Canadians with respect to their personal information held by government institutions. Additional federal and provincial legislation also extends privacy protection to individuals whose personal information is held by private agencies and health institutions. Together with legislation enacted by municipal governments, the privacy of Canadians is well protected and provincial and federal oversight offices ensure that those who collect personal information hold up these rights.

Queer archives, particularly those that emerge and persist outside of Canada's established archival system, do not easily comply with any of the jurisdictional limitations set out in privacy law. They are neither government nor public institutions, and while they may house records containing personal health information (e.g., in the personal records of community members who died with AIDS or private accounts of those subjected to psychological treatments for homosexuality), they do not act as custodians of these types of data in the same manner as a hospital or a healthcare professional. In the case of photography, the legislation is even less relevant, as most of the images deposited in the Archives are those taken at Pride celebrations, political demonstrations, and other events that take place in public. There is little privacy protection for people who happen to appear in the background of a photograph of a Pride parade, for instance, or sitting in the bleachers at a gay baseball game.[4] Protecting the privacy of all individuals in an image of a crowded street corner would be logistically impossible and preclude any journalistic or documentary record-making. Consequently, any protection of privacy measures enacted by the CLGA, such as redacting photographs to blur out faces or removing

---

4   In 1998, the Supreme Court of Canada in the case of Aubry v. Éditions Vice-Versa, [1998] 1 S.C.R. 591, confirmed the right to privacy of individuals in limiting publication of photographs without their consent, unless there is a valid reason to publish the photograph to protect the public's right to information. That is, if a photographer is documenting an event or a public place and the photograph captures individuals as passers-by, then the privacy of these individuals is subordinate to the informational value of the photograph. If an individual subject is the primary focus of the photograph, then the artistic expression of the photographer is subordinate to the privacy of the individual and, thus, the photographer must seek consent to use the image. The images in the CLGAs collection that are most requested were taken prior to the 1998 ruling that consent was required and, in most cases, were meant to document an event or place and thus, convey information of value.

identifying information from descriptive metadata, are done for ethical reasons and not because the organization is obliged to do so under the law.

In an offline environment, the protection of privacy was fairly easy to balance against the Archives' mandate to promote queer visibility and scholarship. Before the introduction of digital technologies, a researcher would have to make an appointment to visit the Archives and meet with a reference archivist. This meeting would help the archivist understand the nature of the research, determine which collections might be of use to the researcher, and provide an opportunity to introduce the researcher to the mandate and policies of the Archives. The reference archivist physically controlled access to the collections and could personally inform the researcher if certain records should not be republished. If the researcher did wish to use a photograph in a publication, the risk of exposing someone was more easily weighed against the potential benefit of having this image used because its use was limited in scope and scale. The proliferation of digital technologies, however, has greatly enhanced the impact of photographic images. Those published online can be seen by an inestimable number of viewers from around the world and their subsequent re-use is difficult to manage. Once a photograph is online, its future use is out of the archivist's control. As we have seen over the past few years, digitized photographs are easily copied from the CLGA's blog and re-posted elsewhere. Our photos have turned up in other organizations' blogs, and in video clips without our explicit knowledge or permission.

Concerns around privacy are not only restricted to the re-use of archival photographs; in fact, many of the same issues impinge on the Archives' capacity to promote its contemporary activities online. Some of our supporters wish to remain offline because the reach of the Internet is considered unsafe. In other cases, even if individuals are comfortable coming to the Archives in person, they do not wish to have their personal information become part of its online environment.

Case Study 2: Visibility v. Privacy

The CLGA hosts a number of events throughout the year, and there is always a volunteer photographer present. Photographs taken here may end up on the blog, in the newsletter, or on the Flickr site. The photographer usually asks people who are posing if they are comfortable with the images being made public, and those who are not can decline. Photos of crowds are also occasionally taken, and in these cases the photographer has not been able to inform everyone in the room that their image may end up online. After one recent exhibition opening, a board member who had been helping to identify people informed the photographer that she suspected one person depicted in a crowd shot was not out. She asked that the image be deleted, and the photographer complied though the request made her uncomfortable. This situation raises several questions: Should an organization whose mandate hinges on queer pride and visibility be expected to help a visitor conceal their sexual identity? Is it a volunteer's responsibility to inform each and every person at a public event that their picture may end up online? Would somebody really still be considered queer merely by virtue of their presence at a queer archives? Without any policies in place to facilitate these situations, the tendency at the CLGA has been to err the side of cautious conservatism. While this is anathema to most volunteers, particularly those who have spent the better part of their lives struggling for visibility, there seems to be a lingering fear of social and legal repercussions.

Recommendations

Although the responsibility to protect privacy at the CLGA is more ethical than legal, the establishment of a clear organizational-level policy is essential. The situation described above could be easily avoided by posting signs informing visitors that they may be photographed in several places around the building; this would effectively place the burden on the visitor to make it clear that they did not want their picture taken, rather than expecting volunteers to make decisions based on speculation. As for material in the collection, a research agreement that transfers the burden of permission and clearances from the Archives to the researcher does well to indemnify the Archives in cases where intellectual property rights have been violated by the researcher, but it does not necessarily resolve issues of privacy. An organizational policy, on the other hand, could provide guidance about which photographs or collections of photographs can be published and in which circumstances this publication may be allowed. For example, the Archives may choose to distinguish between photographs that are part of personal records collections (*i.e.,* those that are included in donations from private individuals) and those taken by organizations to document their work (i.e., photographs of rallies that are donated along with a political group's organizational records). The Archives might also choose to make available for publication photographs that belong to a collection for which the donor has explicitly provided permission to republish the images online or in print. This does not protect third parties who may appear in the images, but it would ease some of the fear that publishing would harm those depicted, as presumably the donor would have removed any photographs not appropriate for publication. Alternatively, the Archives might also decide that all photographs in the repository should be available for digitization because the proliferation of material culture that references queer lives is central to the mandate of the organization.

Conclusions—Creating Clear & Effective Policy

It is imperative that the Archives gain intellectual control over the photograph collection, as accurate metadata will make it much easier to determine and clear copyright. Fortunately, a team of volunteers who will focus exclusively on this task is currently being assembled, and a two-step process has been designed. First, volunteers will develop brief skeleton records for everything in the collection (title, date, box number, names, and locations) so that material can at least be located. Once this has been completed, the volunteers will go back and write complete RAD-based descriptions. It is unlikely that the second step will be completed by 2014, but at least the first step will be well underway. Ideally, the team working on the photo collection will take the time to identify and research the 'greatest hits' (namely the photos that are asked for every year), and to have those scanned, catalogued, cleared and ready to go.

More generally, the CLGA must enforce the existing policy governing research agreements, and they should encourage donors to discuss any restrictions or privacy sensitivities at the time of donation. Finally, it would be advisable for the Archives to develop a clear policy around event photography, and to act quickly to post any relevant warnings in the physical space and on the website.

Works Cited

Aubry v. Éditions Vice-Versa. (1998). 1 S.C.R. 591. Retrieved 17 November 2012, from: http:// scc.lexum.umontreal.ca/en/1998/1998rcs1-591/1998rcs1-591.html.

Barriault, M., and R. Sheffield. (2009). "Note from the guest editors." *Queer Archives.* Spec. issue of *Archivaria* 68: 119–121.

Bill C-11: *An Act to Amend the Copyright Act.* (2012). Received Royal Assent, June 18, 2012, 41st Parliament, 1st Session. Ottawa: Public Works and Government Services Canada. Retrieved 12 January 2013, from http://www.parl.gc.ca/LegisInfo/BillDetails.aspx?Mode=1&billId=5134851&Language=E

California Digital Library [CDL]. (2005). *CDL guidelines for digital images.* Retrieved 17 January 2013, from: http://www.cdlib.org/inside/diglib/guidelines/bpgimages/cdl_gdi_v2

Canadian Broadcasting Corporation. (n.d.). "Same-sex rights: A timeline". Retrieved 12 January 2013, from: http://www.cbc.ca/news/background/samesexrights/timeline_canada.html

Copyright Act, Revised Statutes of Canada, 1985, c. C-42. Retrieved 17 January 2013, from http://laws.justice.gc.ca/en/C-42/index.html

Canadian Copyright Board. (2001). *Unlocatable copyright owners.* Retrieved 17 January, 2013, from: http://www.cb-cda.gc.ca/unlocatable-introuvables/brochure2-e.html

Conway, P. (2008). "Best practices for digitizing photographs: A network analysis of influences," *Proceedings of archiving 2008*, Bern, Switzerland. Washington: IS&T: 94-102.

De Rond, M., and A.N. Miller. (2005). "Publish or perish bane or boon of academic life?" *Journal of Management Inquiry*, 14(4): 321-329.

Dorey, J. (2009). Is this the future of archived photographs? An analysis of the impact of *Aubry v. Éditions Vice-Versa*, [1998] 1 S.C.R. 591 on copyrighted photographs in Québec-based archives. Presentation. May 27, 2009. Montreal: Annual McGill ACA Colloquium.

Harris, L.E. (2010). "Moral rights in Canadian copyright law," *LawNow* (May/June). Accessed 17 January 2013, from: http://www.copyrightlaws.com/us/the-lesser-known-subject-of-moral-rights-in-copyright-law/

Leatherdale, P. (2013). Personal Communication. January 12, 2013. Toronto, Ontario.

Miller, A. (2012). Personal Communication. July 19, 2012. Toronto, Ontario.

Murray, L., and S. Truscow (2007) *Copyright in Canada: A citizen's guide.* Toronto: Between the Lines.

National Archives and Records Administration, S. Puglia, J. Reed, and E. Rhodes. (2004). *Technical guidelines for digitizing archival materials for electronic access: Creation of production master files – raster images.* Washington, DC: National Archives and Records Administration. Accessed 17 January 2013, from: http://www.archives.gov/research/arc/digitizing-archival- materials.html

Pearse-Moses, R. (2013). "Digitization." *A glossary of archival and records terminology.* Chicago: SAA. Accessed 14 January 2013, from: http://www2.archivists.org/glossary/terms/d/digitization.

Pride Toronto. (n.d.). "About us". Accessed 17 January 2013, from: http://www.pridetoronto.com/about/

Society of American Archivists. (n.d.). "Fonds". Accessed 12 January 2013, from: http://www2.archivists.org/glossary/terms/f/fonds

Warren, S.D., and L.D. Brandeis. (2005 [1890]). "The right to privacy". In A.D. Moore (Ed.), *Information ethics: Privacy, property, and power* (pp. 209-225). Seattle, Washington: University of Washington Press.

Copyright, Copywrong, and Ethics: Digitising Records of the Australian Gay and Lesbian Movements from 1973

Graham Willett and Steve Wright

Introduction

1973 was an important year for gay and lesbian politics in Australia, marked by a series of significant events that culminated in the celebration of Gay Pride Week in major cities across the country. Gay and lesbian activism began in Australia later than in other similar societies. It was only in 1969 with the formation of the Daughters of Bilitis in Melbourne and the Homosexual Law Reform Society in Canberra, and then in 1970 with the formation of the Campaign Against Moral Persecution (CAMP) in Sydney and its spread as a national organisation thereafter, that gay people began to speak for themselves in any very public way. Those inspired by the success of CAMP, and frustrated by what they saw as its limitations, established Gay Liberation, Radicalesbians, and a plethora of other groups. 1973 was in many ways the highpoint of this opening stage of the struggle (Willett 2000).

To commemorate that time from forty years ago, we have begun assembling suitable materials for an online archive. One of us (Willett) researches lesbian and gay history, and has been a committee member of the Australian Lesbian and Gay Archives for nearly twenty years. The other (Wright) researches the creation and use of documents in social movements. The purpose of the archive is twofold: to provide wider access to significant primary sources from that year, and to provide space for participants and others to reflect upon its legacy and significance. At this stage we are working on a pilot project, details of which are discussed below. In our efforts to gather suitable materials for this archive, we have had to consider a number of questions that lie at the intersection of legal rights and ethical obligations. In this chapter we will begin to explore these questions, bearing in mind that answering some of them may only raise further questions in turn.

WHY AN ONLINE ARCHIVE?

The past fifty years have seen the emergence or re-emergence of social movements across the globe. They have shared a common mission to challenge the assumptions and practices that underpin prevailing social norms. In their efforts to analyse existing social structures and mobilise popular forces against them, participants in such movements have generated their own rich outpouring of documents. People employed these materials – newspapers and journals, more ephemeral items such as leaflets and pamphlets, as well as posters, lapel badges, bumper stickers, and ever more diverse forms of communication – for broad public engagement. For much of those fifty years, such documents were produced primarily in printed formats; over the past generation, they have increasingly become of a digital nature.

Whether for making history or writing it, documents remain indispensable. Documents specify the rights and obligations of citizens and residents. They regulate the terms through which the everyday business of the market and state is conducted, and they provide much of the information needed for daily survival. In this respect Hartland, McKemmish, and Upward (2005, p. 75) are correct to insist that 'We live in a web of documents and have done so ever since civil societies first began to emerge'. Little wonder that historians have been so keen to collect, collate, preserve, and analyse them, regardless of whether they study nations or other large-scale communities, historical events, individuals, or social and political movements.

Traditionally, these documents were published in what we would now call "hard copy". But in our present online age, it becomes increasingly feasible for social movement archives to digitize and preserve some of their holdings of primary sources for public access. The advantages of this form of collection are obvious. In the past, archives could only exhibit a limited part of their collections at any given time, mainly to those individuals able to visit them in person. Through digitisation and display online, archivists can bring materials languishing in filing cabinets to the attention of a variety of audiences. These primary sources will help those actively or passively involved with social movements to better understand the evolution of processes through which the movements' main goals were formulated, as well as to identify possible alternative pathways that were ultimately abandoned or left undeveloped. For those students, researchers, or activists first learning about a social movement, access to these primary sources offers another layer of meaning, beyond the narratives provided by secondary accounts. The provision of a significantly wider range of archival documents to all interested parties has considerable benefits. Texts commonly held in social movement archives yet less widely discussed in retrospect – leaflets, newssheets, and other kinds of materials typically produced and circulated in the routine of political activism – can provide key insights into how broad layers of the movements grappled day to day with the task of making their shared hopes a reality.

The challenges are not merely technical

The task of presenting social movement primary sources online raises its own unique challenges. The website must be designed in such a way that it is accessible to the range of audiences that may choose to utilise it. While the intelligent use of metadata can greatly aid both the organization and retrieval of the online archive, the generation of such metadata is a labour-intensive exercise, and may demand resources beyond the means of the largely volunteer-based organizations that typically make social movement archives possible in the first place. On the other hand, the increasingly interactive nature of web technology can, if used with thought and care, make it possible for online projects to draw upon the knowledge and expertise of a site's 'users' as a fundamental means of providing much of the contextual information needed to support the effective presentation of primary sources.

No less important, however, are the legal and ethical questions bound up with a project of this kind, especially given that archives are 'always political sites of contested memory and knowledge' (McKemmish, Gilliland-Swetland, and Ketelaar 2005, 147). These questions include:

- To whom do the documents produced by the individuals and groups that constitute social movements 'belong'?

- In what ways (if any) do claims of ownership and control of the digitised forms of these documents need to be managed by those committed to their preservation and public reproduction?

- How can historians, creators, cultural heritage professionals and the like navigate the legal issues of copyright ownership as against the claims of a community to its own past?

- What rights exist to the information contained in the various kinds of materials we have identified as holding that past? What rights *should* exist? (And here we are talking not simply about legal rights, but also about ethical claims.)

- What happens when rights conflict? What opportunities exist for developing alternative regimes of rights that might address these and associated problems?

LEARNING FROM OTHER EXPERIENCES

Access to past cultural artifacts is commonly taken to be a right as well as a necessity in social movements and beyond, though not all those producing historically-significant materials would agree, as the following case illustrates. In June 2009, the Organization for Transformative Works, a 'nonprofit organization run by and for fans to provide access to and preserve the history of fanworks and fan cultures', announced that it was working with the University of Iowa on a project that would digitise works from the University's extensive collection of zines and make them available online 'in order to preserve them and make them accessible to wider popular and research audiences' (Organization for Transformative Works 2009). To recognize copyright the project would only upload materials with the permission of the creators. To protect the privacy of the fanwork creators and avoid 'outing' them, the project organisers eschewed the usual practice of databasing the works by author and title and confined themselves to zine title, genre and year of publication.

In spite of these precautions, the project ran into trouble almost immediately. One comment by db, a creator of fanfiction, opposed, on principle, preserving and making such works available:

> While I understand your desire to preserve fannish works, I don't agree with what you propose. I dislike the idea of fannish works being used for academic purposes in general, and to have a public, lending archive of zines... well I can't say as I'm even remotely enthused. I come from the old school, underground and wishing to remain out of the public eye...

She/he also had security concerns, fearing the public availability of the material would serve the interests of what s/he calls 'TPTB' [The Powers That Be] rather than the underground world for which the material was created (db 2009). One of the issues raised related explicitly to the difference between digitised and non-digitised formats:

> I know I have no control over what people do with my zines once they own them but there is such a thing as courtesy and respect for the intent of the work in question. Not everyone is excited about the idea of their writing being made public, even in an archive format. There

are authors who wrote long before anyone could have conceived of something like the Internet; how are their rights being considered? Now, most of my authors write for fanzines – rather than post online – because they don't want their work available to the public in general; they're writing for that particular, small fanzine fandom.

(Blacque 2009)

Here, very starkly, the legal protections of copyright are running up against the ethical claims of creators to control their own work – a control that is significantly undermined by the technology of digitisation.

Preserving the gay movement past

Investigation into the social movements in Australia in the period from the mid-1960s to the mid-1970s has shown that for activists such as feminists and women's liberationists, gay and lesbian people, workers, Indigenous Australians, environmentalists and others, the legacy of the past is an inherent part of present struggles. And yet for all their impact in other ways, social movements of the past fifty years have generally proved less successful in preserving their own records. On this front, the gay and lesbian movement has been an important exception to this rule. LGBT archives have, as it happens, been more systematic and enduring, as demonstrated recently at the 4th international LGBT ALMS Conference, held in Amsterdam in 2012, where a large number of archives, libraries, museums and special collections were represented (Barriault 2009; Fullwood 2009; Willett 2012).

It is in this context that we want to discuss our current pilot study of one of Australia's social movements in one particular year – namely, the gay and lesbian movement in Australia in 1973. Australia is well served in regard to the preservation of its gay movement past. Since its establishment at the National Homosexual Conference in 1978, in response to a fear that the history of the then ten year old movement was being lost, the Australian Lesbian and Gay Archives (originally the Australian Gay Archives) has been collecting, preserving and celebrating the lives and experiences of lesbians and gay men and the broader LGBTIQ community in Australia. The Archives is based in Melbourne (Australia's second biggest city), and is an independent community-based, volunteer-operated, non-profit organization. Currently the collection holds 40,000 periodicals (covering 1,300 titles); 45,000 newspaper clippings, 2,000 ephemera files, 1,500 posters, 800 badges, 4,000 photographs, 4,000 books and 130 oral history interviews, It also contains personal correspondence and diaries, scrap books, court records, banners, paintings, film scripts, plays, audio and video tapes (Australian Lesbian and Gay Archives, n.d.). There are other important holdings, too, in the public realm that directly impinge upon our understanding of gay and lesbian history in Australia: records of parliamentary debates; in state and national libraries; state and national archives; university libraries; alternative media (left activist and community-based press and radio); as well as in private hands (Davison 2006).

The events of 1973 were recorded in the mainstream press as well as in the nascent gay press and in the papers and records of the organisations involved and in leaflets produced for the movement's interventions. The diversity of documentary genres makes 1973 a particularly suitable subject for the investigation of how digitisation can collect and preserve the records of political activism, and make them accessible in new ways. Other, day-to-day activities – the meetings of groups, the discussions and debates that were being held among friends, the attempts to construct new ways of living (in dress, communal living, and language) – are less tangibly, but nonetheless really, available for collection, preservation and dissemination.

The implications of copyright law for an online archive

The existence of such materials is one thing – the ability to use them is quite another. Recent decades have seen considerable convergence of copyright regimes in various parts of the world, driven by the globalisation of trade and capital accumulation. For example, there was a marked lengthening of the period of time after an author's death (from fifty to seventy years) for which a work produced in Australia remained subject to copyright requirements, as a consequence of the Australia-United States Free Trade Agreement (AUSFTA) of 2005. There have also been changes in the assumptions concerning a work's legal status at the moment of its creation or publication. Previously in some countries, works had to be knowingly registered as copyrighted in order to enjoy the legal protection associated with that status; now it is common to find a situation where all works are treated as being born 'private property' unless explicitly deemed otherwise.

At the same time, there remain differences between national copyright frameworks, differences that have important implications for a project like ours. Thus in Australia, all printed materials such as journals and pamphlets (including their individual contents) must be treated as copyrighted unless they were published before 1955, and only then so long as each author 'whose identity can be ascertained died before 1955' (Australian Copyright Council 2012, 8). In the United States, on the other hand, the situation is both more constricting in certain respects, and more liberal in others. Thanks to the Copyright Term Extension Act of 1998, the term of copyright for materials produced in the US was increased to ninety years. At the moment of writing, in late 2012, therefore, 'Works published before 1923 are, by and large, in the public domain ... works published in 1923 and later may continue to be protected by copyright' (Hirtle 2012b). An additional, significant rider, however, pertains to 'works registered or first published' in the United States before 1 March 1989 without carrying a notice of copyright: nearly all of *these* materials are likely to fall instead within the 'public domain', and can so, in a legal sense, be freely reproduced without the permission of their creators or owners (Hirtle 2012a). In the light of this, the Internet Archive (www.archive.org), which is currently one of the biggest repositories of freely accessible digital documents, is able to reproduce materials from the social movements of the sixties and seventies accompanied by a rights statement to the effect that they have been 'Published in the US without copyright before 1989'. This is particularly important, and particularly convenient, in relation to the documents of social movements where, given the radically anti-hierarchic, anti-leadership and collectivist ethos of the time, individual claims to authorship – much less ownership – of a document were rare. Disdainful of many of the dominant conventions, the authors of these documents have often made no exclusive claim to their ownership and use.

One option is to ignore copyright rights; to publish and be damned – or not. David Thorstad, publishing a collection of documents relating to a 1970s debate within the US Socialist Workers Party on the issue of gay liberation, declares that he had attempted to get permission from the authors of the various documents that he reproduces, some of which were statements collectively produced (by Party governing bodies for example), some of which were motions put forward in the name of branches or other groupings, some of which were individual contributions to the discussion (Thorstad 1976, 1). But it is clear that where he failed to get permission he published anyway. It is likely he calculated that, given the ideology of the party members regarding property rights, freedom of expression and the importance of open debate, there would be no legal repercussions. This is an approach that may appeal to some, but contains within it the risk of reprisals via the courts.

Without legal protections, or in cases where a creator and copyright holder clearly exists – or must exist in some legal sense – but cannot be located, or fails to respond to approaches, the issues are more difficult to sort out. The digitisation of such 'orphan works' has been the subject of considerable controversy, as witnessed by the ongoing Google Books saga (Frosio 2011). In Australia, the Law Reform Commission (ALRC) has recently published an issues paper concerning 'Copyright and the Digital Economy'. The section of the paper devoted to orphan works asserts that 'significant risks' await those who seek to reproduce such works, noting that 'In particular, orphan works represent a recognised problem in mass digitisation projects undertaken by public and cultural institutions' (ALRC 2012, 44). In advancing a number of possible solutions drawn from experiences elsewhere, the ALRC (45) makes clear that its guiding principle remains one of property rights, wherein the 'important public benefit' that may stem from 'access to these works ... must be balanced with ensuring that copyright holders are properly compensated for their work'.

But there is some scope within the existing law for dealing with the problem of untraceable owners. In Australia, at least, if it has been impossible to locate a copyright holder, and the efforts to do so are properly documented, publication 'in good faith' is a mechanism by which the claims of history to be freed from the claims of ownership may be asserted. According to the Australian Copyright Council (2012b, 7), any decision on this front must nonetheless be treated as a calculated gamble on the part of those seeking to reproduce orphan works.

How other movement archival projects have addressed copyright

One version of this approach is spelled out by the creators of the Reason in Revolt website, a project which offers an extensive representation of Australian leftwing texts of the past one hundred and fifty years. As Booth and associates (2005) explain,

> the bulk of material processed for the project has been from the nineteenth century and in the public domain, but in moving forward to the twentieth century the process of seeking copyright permission will become more demanding. It can be very difficult to track down copyright holders who were members of small radical organisations or marginalised social groups. Also, in some cases it is unclear who would hold the copyright, as for example in flyers or pamphlets issued around particular campaigns or issues, or material published under pseudonyms. As the project expands its cultural content there will also be additional copyright hurdles. Unpublished literary, dramatic and musical works, as well as unpublished anonymous material never come out of copyright into the public domain, and it is often impossible to find copyright holders for this material.

The approach undertaken here has been to seek the permission of authors where known. Where the author could not be contacted or identified, and the material was already in the public domain, the document in question was placed online, with the stipulation that it would be withdrawn should the author(s) subsequently contact the curators and request this (Booth at al. 2005). Such practices appear consistent in certain respects with the position advocated in 2012 by two Australian scholars, which seeks to authorise the 'non-commercial use' of orphan works following a 'diligent search' – but in this version, the whole process would need to be overseen by a collection agency (Brennan and Fraser 2011; see also ALRC 2012, 47). Finally, there is the matter of unpublished material, which we are still exploring – although for now we can note that, at least in the Australian case, this could be even more complex, given that copyright on such works may endure indefinitely.

This is similar to the approach adopted in Europe by the Open Up! Project, which is collecting and digitising the records of lesbian, gay, bisexual and transgender organisations from central, eastern and south eastern Europe [discussed elsewhere in this volume]. Open Up! was forced to grapple with copyright issues to an extent that the original developers of the project had not expected. But copyright is not the only legal and ethical issue that arises in the Open Up! Project or, indeed, in our own Australian gay liberation digitisation pilot.

Beyond copyright: the ethical dimensions

The project coordinator for Open Up! speaks of two other important issues – privacy and criminality. The project's terms of reference explicitly excluded from its collecting policy (or at least from the online provision of) 'extremely offensive or repulsive material (e.g. pornography, paedophilia)', but it recognised that, even beyond this, the circumstances of east, central and south-eastern Europe presented certain risks that might not apply in other parts of Europe. The fact is that until relatively recently, homosexual acts between men were illegal in much of Eastern Europe, and even today discrimination by the state and within civil society remains a serious problem (IHLIA 2012).

The problem of criminality is less of an issue in Australia (except insofar as the representation of children in sexual contexts is strongly sanctioned). It is inconceivable that police forces would revisit criminal behaviour such as homosexuality based on material from 1973. Even so, some people would very much prefer that past behaviour, writings, activities, political stances not be in the public realm. Now, it is true that if the details are in newspapers, flyers, oral histories or the like they are already in the public realm – but very much more easily accessed when online than if in hard copy alone. The legal protections afforded to privacy are of less importance here than the ethical claims. In a society in which homophobic discrimination still exists (if very much less virulently than in the past), it might not be unreasonable to protect people from the much more public exposure that online accessibility provides. But how to do this, and where to draw the line? The Australian Lesbian and Gay Archives, for example, has a published version of its ephemera file list that excludes files relating to still-living individuals who are not public figures (Australian Lesbian and Gay Archives, n.d. b). There is no suggestion in these cases of criminal behaviour, or even of views that they might no longer endorse – it is entirely a matter of protecting them from the level of scrutiny that the electronic age provides and which they could not have envisioned.

Similarly, in *Secret Histories of Queer Melbourne* (Willett, Murdoch, and Marshall 2011, 77), the editors made a decision to excise the name of a man when reproducing a 1950 newspaper report. The information is available in a library or online, but the editors felt a responsibility not to make this potentially embarrassing information any more easily available than it was. But publishing newspaper articles from 1973 (gay press or mainstream) or photographs, or signed leaflets and so on, is the very purpose of the 1973 digital archive. So, sorting out the legal issues surrounding copyright still leaves these ethical issues to be dealt with.

Some specific challenges for our pilot study

Here we focus upon three episodes from 1973 which we would like to include in our digitial archive, each of which touches upon the ethical considerations raised thus far. The first of these episodes concerns efforts, in the words of the *Camp Ink* magazine (1973, 6), 'to organise the homosexuals of Tamworth', a rural town in northern New South Wales best known then and today for its country music festival. If the Tamworth of the seventies was hardly an obvious site for gay political activity, the establishment of a local CAMP/Gay Liberation branch there was an important indication of how far the tides of change had begun to extend beyond the big urban centres on the country's eastern seaboard. An account by the group's central figure of his efforts to organise a post office box for Tamworth CAMP/Gay Liberation, provided in the pages of *Camp Ink* (1973), offers a farcical insight into the petty mindset of various local dignitaries – the postmaster, newspaper staff, a police detective – all determined to maintain public decency as they saw it. The chief documentary legacy of the Tamworth group, however, remains a newsletter that we also intend to reproduce within the 1973 archive. *Coming-Out* contains short informative articles that introduce readers to events such as Stonewall, others that address common misconceptions and prejudices ('Do homosexuals kiss each other?'). But the contributions that really stand out are the ones written in the first person, conveying what it is like to be queer in a small country town, and seeking to let those individuals too afraid 'to even give us his or her name and address' that 'there are gay brothers and sisters who fight for them'.

The question of how most appropriately to reproduce such materials intersects with a number of the issues discussed earlier. The main mover and shaker in the Tamworth group, who had already written on a number of occasions for *Camp Ink* under a pseudonym, used his real name in telling the story of how 'Police Intimidate New CAMP Group'. He also used his name in the Tamworth group newsletter. In the forty years since, however, he seems to have dropped from sight; indeed, given the distance of time, he might not still be alive. Is it appropriate to reproduce his name today? Should efforts be made to seek his permission to use his name? And what of other individuals who had provided their names in the pages of the newsletter?

It is true that by using his real name in the newsletter in 1973 he was making it available to the public. For some institutions that is the end of the matter. The National Library of Australia is currently digitising newspapers going back to the nineteenth century and has no qualms about what it is bringing to light in the new digital world. But for those of us who have a concern for the lives and reputations of members of marginalised and vilified communities, this is not so straightforward.

But nor is deleting such information necessarily the right choice – there is a cost to protecting privacy in this way. Recently, searching some federal public service files in the National Archives, one of the authors of this paper came across this same individual, writing to a minister in 1973. It was only by having had access to his name, that his efforts were recognised and given their wider context. If such information is withheld, then our history work is, in some small way, impoverished.

A second example. In September 1973, Australia's first nationally coordinated gay rights event, Gay Pride Week, was staged in a number of cities (Willett 2000, 108-10). The Archives holds a great deal of the ephemera produced for the week's activities, as well as newspaper clippings from both mainstream and alternative press. Recently a major cache of photographs surfaced in Melbourne, as the estate of a professional photographer, Rennie Ellis, was acquired and started to be digitised by the State Library of Victoria. A number of these showed events staged during Gay Pride Week in Melbourne. These photographs are invaluable artefacts which give us an insight into the activities that written documents do not. They are readily available for inspection and research purposes in the

Library's online catalogue in low resolution form. Copyright is retained by the Rennie Ellis Photographic Archive and permission is needed from them for any reproduction (Ritale 2013). The legalities are perfectly clear and uncontroversial and the material is publicly available – but a radical critique (not necessarily of the Archive or of the Library) might want to query whether images of activists in action ought to be private property, to be made available (or not) irrespective of their wishes.

A final episode concerns the expulsion of a student from a residential college at a Sydney university, and the campaign that unfolded in his defence. In Jeremy Fisher's (2006) own words, 'I was thrown out of Robert Menzies College at Macquarie University in 1973 when the dean discovered I was gay'. As well as demonstrations by students and protests from the university staff union, industrial action was taken by the militant Builders' Labourers Federation (BLF), whose members not only refused to continue work at the college, but promised to do the same across the university as a whole. Jeremy has written and spoken about the events of 1973 on a number of occasions in the years since (see, for example Fisher 2008), and the story has also been retold from a range of perspectives in accounts of the social movements of the period, from Jordan Humphrey's (n.d.) online *Radical History of Macquarie University*, to the voluminous analysis of the BLF's experiences penned by Meredith and Verity Burgmann (1998). To date, however, there has been no compilation of primary sources from the time, of which there are plenty, from campus and leftwing newspaper articles, to reportage in *Camp Ink* and other gay publications, as well as by mainstream media outlets. Like the other cases we have recounted, this episode also intersects with a number of the ethical concerns raised in this chapter, but here the chief protagonist has been happy to talk and write about the episode, including in his narrative quite personal details regarding his health at the time. Our efforts to clarify Fisher's attitude to the retelling of his story by others has had an unexpected consequence – he has agreed to an interview about the episode, which will, of course, enhance the value of the collections of materials about this event considerably.

SOME IMPLICATIONS FOR FUTURE PRACTICE

In this paper, we have tried to explore some of the questions that arise in doing digital history. Our concern has been less about the technical problems – though these are well worth addressing – than with the legal and ethical issues involved in reproducing material from one period in another. And while the gay and lesbian movement has profoundly transformed laws, public and professional attitudes and social behaviours – overwhelmingly in the direction of greater openness and acceptance – this does not on its own resolve the issues that arise. The fact that something can or can't be published legally matters. But so too do questions such as how might a person who was named – and happy to be named – in 1973 feels about being named forty years later. Amongst other things, is 'public' in a small renowned newsletter really public in the same way as it is on the web? There are no easy answers here, but the questions cannot be avoided.

REFERENCES

Australian Copyright Council (2012a). *Duration of copyright*. Information Sheet G023v16. [Fact sheet]. Retrieved from http://www.copyright.org.au/

Australian Copyright Council (2012b). *Permission: How to get it*. Information Sheet G051v13. [Fact sheet]. Retrieved from http://www.copyright.org.au/

Australian Law Reform Commission (2012). *Copyright and the digital economy*. Issues Paper 42, August. Retrieved from http://www.alrc.gov.au/publications/copyright-ip42

Australian Lesbian and Gay Archives (n.d.a)., *Australian Lesbian and Gay Archives*. Retrieved from www.alga.org.au

Australian Lesbian and Gay Archives (n.d.b) *Australian Lesbian and Gay Archives ephemera files: Subject listing*. Retrieved from www.alga.org.au/files/ephemera.pdf

Barriault, M. (2009). Archiving the queer and queering the archives: a case study of the Canadian Lesbian and Gay Archives (CLGA). In J. Bastian & B. Alexander (Eds.). *Community archives: The shaping of memory*. (pp. 97-108). London, Facet Publishing.

Blacque, D. (2009). Fanzine archive [online forum comment]. Retrieved from http://transformativeworks.org/comment/544#comment-544

Booth, S., Burgmann, V., Macintyre, S., Milner, A. & Ryan, M. (2005). 'Vanguards and Avant-Gardes: The "Reason in Revolt" online project on political and cultural radicalism'. *The Past is before us; Proceedings of the Ninth National Labour History Conference*. Sydney: Australian Society for the Study of Labour History.

Brennan, D. & Fraser, M. (2011). *The Uses of subject matter with missing owners – Australian Copyright policy options*. Retrieved from http://www.law.uts.edu.au/comslaw/Researchreports/MissingOwnersDiscussionPaperAugust11.pdf

Burgmann, M. & Burgmann, V. (1998). *Green bans, red union: Environmental activism and the New South Wales Builders Labourers' Federation*. Sydney: University of New South Wales Press.

Camp Ink (1973). Police intimidate new CAMP group. *Camp Ink* 3(2): 6.

Davison, K. (2006). *Lesbian Bisexual Gay Transgender Material Survey Project Report*. Melbourne: Museum Victoria.

db. (2009). Not a fan [Online forum comment]. Retrieved from http://transformativeworks.org/announcing-fan-culture-preservation-project#comment-51512pm.

Fisher, J. (2006). *Dr Jeremy Allan Fisher*. Retrieved from http://www.pridehistorygroup.org.au/home/71.html.

Fisher, J. (2008). Into the light: The early days of gay liberation. *Overland* 191, 52-56.

Frosio, G. (2011). Google Books rejected: Taking the orphans to the Digital Public Library of Alexandria. *Santa Clara Computer & High Technology Law Journal, 28(1),* 81-141.

Fullwood, A. (2009). Always queer, always here: creating the Black Gay and Lesbian Archive in the Schomburg Center for Research in Black Culture. In J. Bastian & B. Alexander (Eds.). *Community archives: The shaping of memory.* (pp.235-250). London, Facet Publishing.

McKemmish, S., Gilliland-Swetland, A. & Ketelaar, E. (2005). 'Communities of memory': Pluralising archival research and education. *Archives and Manuscripts 33,* 146-174.

Hartland, R., McKemmish, S. & Upward, F. (2005). Documents. In S. McKemmish, M. Piggott, B. Reed and F. Upward (Eds.). *Archives: Recordkeeping in Society.* (pp. 75-100). Wagga Wagga: Centre for Information Studies, Charles Sturt University.

Hirtle, P. (2012a). *Copyright term and the public domain in the United States 1 January 2012*, Cornell Copyright Information Center. Retrieved from http://copyright.cornell.edu/resources/publicdomain.cfm

Hirtle, P. (2012b). When Is 1923 Going to arrive and other complications of the U.S. Public Domain. *Searcher: The Magazine for Database Professionals, 20*(6), September. Retrieved from http://www.infotoday.com/searcher/sep12/Hirtle—When-Is-1923-Going-to-Arrive-and-Other-Complications-of-the-U.S.-Public-Domain.shtml

Humphrey, J. (n.d.). *Gay liberation at Macquarie*. Retrieved from http://radicalhistoryofmacquarieuniversity.wordpress.com/gay-liberation-at-macquarie/.

IHLIA (2012). *Open up! LGBTI history coming out of the closet: Interim report, 01 August 2011 – 18 May 2012*, Amsterdam: IHLIA.

Organization for Transformative Works (2009). *Announcing: The Fan culture preservation project!* Retrieved from http://transformativeworks.org/announcing-fan-culture-preservation-project-5152

Thorstad, D. (1976). *Gay liberation and socialism: Documents from the discussions on gay liberation inside the Socialist Workers Party* (1970-1973). New York: Author.

Willett, G. (2000). *Living out loud: A history of gay and lesbian activism in Australia*. St Leonards: Allen & Unwin.

Willett, G. (2012). 'How small collections can make a big difference'. Paper presented to the LGBTI ALMS Conference, Amsterdam. Retrieved from http://lgbtialms2012.blogspot.com.au/

Willett, G., Murdoch, W. & Marshall, D. (2011). *Secret histories of queer Melbourne*. Melbourne: Australian Lesbian and Gay Archives.

Section Three

Nuts and Bolts of Queer Digitization Projects

Introduction to Section Three: Nuts and Bolts of Queer Digitization Projects

How do people actually execute, complete, and assess a digitization project? What are the special concerns that people should have when digitizing queer artifacts, as well as creating online space for them? How should these digital collections be promoted, and is our audience the one we think it is? Last but not least, what is the statement that we make about an individual, different cultures, history, or political climates with these digitized collections?

Sally Johnson and Michael Otten of IHLIA (Internationaal Homo/Lesbisch Informatiecentrum en Archief) in Amsterdam unveil the "Open Up!" Project—a database of LGBTIQ periodicals from central and eastern Europe, and explain how IHLIA staff gathered the materials, constructed the database and search terms, and their plans for promotion of this resource. Laura Uglean Jackson from the University of Wyoming opens the doors to the Matthew Shepard Web Archive. Finally, the Lesbian Gay Bisexual Transgender Religious Archives Network explains how they meet the needs of their patrons—LGBT religious organizations—through digitization of their records, as well as highlighting the diversity of LGBT religious organizations.

Each of the institutions in this chapter have provided access to resources not only of interest to LGBTIQ Studies researchers, but to people in many different fields of study. They also provide their expertise in strategic planning, selection of tools for digitization, and how to make such resources sustainable. Forever more, these online resources will confirm the existence of LGBT history in countries where people have gone underground, will shed light on a young man whose death prompted a second LGBT civil rights movement, and will show another perspective of the relationship between LGBTIQ people and faith.

Open Up! LGBT History Coming Out of the Closet

Sally Johnson Project leader Open Up!
Michel Otten Communications officer Open Up!

Introduction

IHLIA LGBT heritage (International gay and lesbian Information Centre and Archive), is an international LGBT library, archive, information and documentation centre about homosexuality and sexual diversity. Currently IHLIA boasts the largest LGBT library collection in the Netherlands and Europe. The Open Up! Project is an IHLIA initiative to reveal the history of LGBT emancipation and development of LGBT movements in primarily Central, Eastern and Southeastern (CESE) Europe. In this chapter we will explore the process of Open Up!: how it started, the issues concerning digitization and copyright, and also the constraints and lessons. So, let's start to "Open Up"!

Significance of the Open Up Project

IHLIA's ambition is to advocate the importance of preserving and disclosing LGBT cultural heritage. The collection and the position in society of IHLIA are unique – in the Netherlands and the world; the archives and archive donations to IHLIA traditionally have an international character. Due to a lack of financial resources, however, IHLIA has made some clear but hard choices in the past concerning international activities and the digitization of archives. The latter resulted in a delay in the digital disclosure of the international part of the archive, although IHLIA considers this as their core business and priority.

With financial support of the Dutch Ministry of Education, Culture and Science IHLIA conceived the Open Up! Project in August 2011. The intent of the project was to create and share globally an interactive historical framework of lesbian, gay, bisexual, transgender and intersex (LGBT) emancipation movements in Europe. Open Up! offers LGBT movements a unique opportunity to document their own history. Open Up! is the first project to concentrate, digitize, and publish online historically relevant material like LGBT magazines, posters, and grey literature on this large of a scale. Open Up! will not only provide information for LGBT organizations and other non-profit organizations, researchers, journalists, governments and policy makers, but will also provide inspiration to newer, less established LGBT movements and activists and demonstrate that social emancipation is an on-going process.

Open Up! first focused on gathering materials from the countries in CESE Europe, because across this region, LGBT rights lag behind those in other parts of Europe. After the fall of the Iron Curtain, and the subsequent rush of countries to become members of (Pan)European organizations, this led gradually to reforms in law and society. The archives and documents of these LGBT organizations contain unique documents that help us understand how this change happened.

To achieve these goals, the project team digitized a collection of existing LGBT archives held by IHLIA, then collected and digitized new archive materials from LGBT movements and individuals from across Europe. These resources would form a new digital collection called 'Open Up!', searchable by the public, and accessible via a new and purpose-built web interface. Last but not least, 'Open Up' would also provide online opportunities for social interaction.

Development of a Project Plan for the Open Up Project

Normally, digitization initiatives operate according to one of two objectives:

- Preservation of documents and data through digitization;
- Sharing and providing users access to documents that have been digitized.

While the technical standards and process are practically the same for both sets of objectives, the volume of material and the time required for preparing archives and metadata are very different.

The original timeframe for project implementation was four months, with an initial digitization target of over 18 metres (over 145,000 pages). Within the first two months, it became apparent that certain aspects of the project design were unrealistic, like the expected time required for preparing archives and the copyright issues. The deliverables and results could not be achieved within this short timeframe.

There are also different implications regarding Intellectual Property (IP) rights. Since the focus of the Open Up! Project was 'access', IHLIA and the project team decided to reduce the volume of material selected for digitization, while increasing the number of hours for archivists to prepare the archives and metadata descriptions. The archivists also needed to develop a robust copyright and privacy policy and a process to acquire permissions. A copyright lawyer specialising in the non-commercial sector started researching the legal considerations the project would need to address concerning IP, privacy and its countries of focus.

As a result:

- The project timeframe was extended until August 2012 (to coincide with IHLIA's leading role in the International Archives, Libraries, Museums and Special Collections (ALMS) Conference 2012 on the Future of LGBTI Histories, 1-3 August 2012, Amsterdam);

- The geographical focus was confined to pan-Europe and CESE Europe (European Union (EU) enlargement states of 2004 and 2007, EU candidate and potential candidates countries, Council of Europe member countries in Eastern Europe);

- The project pursued a dual strategy of 'preservation' and 'access' – preserve as much as possible through digitization and publish what is possible in accordance with copyright and creative solutions. Consequently, the digitization target was reduced to just over 12 metres (approx. 95, 700 pages);

- Two archivists were recruited to work full-time for four months and one archivist to continue for a further 2.5 months; and

- A copyright legal specialist was engaged to advise and prepare policies and legal texts related to copyright and privacy. In addition, the project adopted the policy of requesting permission from traceable copyright holders prior to publishing.

Technical preparations

Consultations with organizations who have considerable experience in digitizing and publishing archives, such as the *Internationaal Instituut voor Sociale Geschiedenis* (*IISG*; International Institute of Social History) and *Aletta E-Quality* (Institute for Women's History) in the Netherlands, combined with advice from a short-term digitization consultant, helped define the standards and formats for digitization according to international standards:

Purpose	Specification/Standard
Digitization – master files	TIFF (Tagged Image File Format). Appears as .tif or .tiff Scan resolution: colour, minimum 300 dpi (dots per inch)
Content delivery – access files for users	JPEG-10 (Joint Photographic Experts Group)
Metadata – storing information about layout of a document and recognising text of printed documents	ALTO (Analysed Layout and Text Object) XML

Metadata was slightly more complex to develop. Fields had to be named according to the specific type of archive, and archivists deliberated upon standard lists of field descriptions such as 'record types', 'languages', and 'key subjects'. This work was described in a digitization manual. The Dutch company *MicroFormat B.V.* scanned the Open Up! materials and produced the digital items.

Selection of Materials

Selection of relevant materials in IHLIA Archives on LGBT movements and organizations

Identification, selection and digitization of published works in IHLIA's archive

Archivists first determined selection criteria for the project. They took into account the need to balance preservation and access, geographical focus, and potential user groups (e.g. researchers, LGBT activists and organizations, journalists, and policy-makers). Selection criteria for the Open Up Project is as follows:

- "Item meets the general objectives and purpose of the project, including:
  a. country/location of interest
  b. LGBT rights/issues/awareness/activism/organization/initiatives
- There is existing or potential user interest in the item

- Digitization of the item will significantly enhance access by at least one of the project's target user groups
- Rights and permissions for electronic use and either public or semi-restricted access are likely to be granted
- The item can easily be digitized (e.g. it is not oversized, fragile)
- The item does not contain extremely offensive or repulsive material (e.g. pornography, paedophilia)
- The item is not confidential, likely to endanger a person or expose a person's privacy"

Published works here refers to periodicals (e.g. newsletters, magazines, newspapers), grey literature (self-published materials such as books, reports, leaflets) and posters. They were prepared and sent for digitization in three batches. The approximate material counts are as follows:

Archive Type	No. Records	No. Pages	Period Covered
Periodicals	968	29,000	1978-2008
Grey Literature	58	5,200	1984-2011
Posters	4,358	4,300	1987-2002
Total	5,384	38,500	

Besides the periodicals, grey literature, and posters, IHLIA also has organizational archives in its collections. Organizational archives collect press clippings, conference papers and reports, annual reports, correspondence with policy or issue-based content that relates to target countries, project reports, and petitions. Normally organized in folders, they may contain as little as one page to as much as hundreds of pages. Because folders in organizational archives tend to contain a mix of different types of documents, some of which may be internal or confidential in nature, entire records may not be published and opened up. Since the project takes privacy and confidentiality very seriously, a folder may not be released for publishing if one document was declared confidential, even if the bulk of it contains publishable material. The archivists adopted this approach because of the project timeframe that did not allow for sufficient time to thoroughly prepare these archives for access purposes.

Organizational archives held by IHLIA contained materials associated with Open Up!'s target countries. They included International Lesbian Information Service (ILIS), Lesbian ConneXions, a series of leaflets and pamphlets, the Douglas Conrad archive, and the European Forum of LGBT Christian Groups. The entire lot covers the period 1979-2007.

How relevant materials on ILGA, ILGA-Europe and IGLYO were digitized and disclosed

Cooperation with the organizations *International Lesbian, Gay, Bisexual, Trans and Intersex Association (ILGA)*, *ILGA-Europe* and *International Lesbian, Gay, Bisexual, Transgender, Queer Youth and Student Organization (IGLYO)* started early in the project. IHLIA visited their offices in Brussels to discuss the Open Up! project, their organizational archives, and their potential involvement. Both *ILGA* and *IGLYO* endorsed digitization of the archives the project team had identified for inclusion. While *IGLYO* gave its permission for publishing its archives, *ILGA* has still to review and give its formal response.

When IHLIA and the project leader designed the Open Up! Project, they anticipated that *ILGA-Europe* would play a substantial and hands-on role with the Open Up! website. Unfortunately, this did not transpire due to capacity constraints ILGA faced. Nevertheless, *ILGA-Europe* facilitated some communication with their member organizations in CESE Europe and allowed us to place some informational material on their website.

How relevant archive materials of European LGBT organizations were acquired after gaps and missing links had been identified

Identification and digitization of new archive materials and support to local LGBT contributing organizations

In response to the Open Up! Project's call for interest at *ILGA-Europe*'s conference in Turin in October 2011, via the Open Up! web pages and also direct emails sent to local LGBT organizations in the Open Up! target countries, a handful of organizations offered their support. With two organizations– *Lesbian Section ŠKUC-LL / Lesbian Library & Archive (ŠKUC-LL)* in Slovenia and *Kaos GL* in Turkey – IHLIA entered into agreements to provide new archive materials to the Open Up! collection and describe the metadata according to the project's standards. These two organisations were able to fully commit to these agreements within the timeframe of December 2011 to April 2012.

The project provided a purposefully designed digitization manual to assist them with this task, and reimbursed costs including postage, depending on the quantity of materials prepared. The arrangement was a positive one; both organizations not only fulfilled their responsibilities, but also volunteered their knowledge and opinions concerning other aspects of the Open Up! Project. A third organization, *Hatter Support Society for Gays and Lesbians in Hungary (Háttér Társaság a Melegekért)*, was also a tremendous resource; they provided some new Hungarian leaflets and brochures with corresponding basic metadata.

In December 2011, at the invitation of *Homosexuelle Initiative Wien (HOSI Wien)* in Austria, the project team discovered a 'gold mine'. Folders and boxes containing almost 7,000 pages of documents related to the Eastern European Information Pool (EEIP), which *HOSI Wien* had managed on behalf of *ILGA*, and some 88 periodicals, were rescued and brought to Amsterdam for digitizing. These materials were stored in a damp basement and about to be discarded! They cover the period 1982-2010 and consist of a rich array of annual reports, conference reports, forms, letters, magazines, minutes, newspaper clippings, personal papers, petitions and reports. The *HOSI Wien* contribution constitutes the largest archive contributed to the Open Up! collection. Furthermore, since some of these materials can be opened up and published, this is a fine example of preservation and access in action!

Below is a summary of newly acquired and found archive materials added to the Open Up! collection. The periodicals among these new archives brought the final quantity of periodicals to 1,081; almost double the quantity originally foreseen.

Archive/Contributing Organization	No. Records/Folders	No. Pages	Period Covered
HOSI Wien	173	8,700	1982-2010
Hatter Support Society–Hungary	32	1,837	1996-2011
ŠKUC-LL–Slovenia	15	528	1984-2007
Kaos GL–Turkey	9	410	1994-2008
Total	229	11,475	

Note: Kaos GL provided metadata descriptions for its entire collection of magazines, most of which IHLIA already had in its archive.

Copyright, access and disclosure

Understanding the implications of copyright and privacy, and translating them into a robust, workable policy and guidelines, has been the most challenging aspect of the Open Up! Project. The collection is composed of works from a substantial number of countries, languages, publishers, and copyright holders that today are difficult to identify, as well as different types of archived materials, including content that some may regard as indecent or criminal. This variety of factors makes the task of seeking permissions to digitize and publish these materials an ambitious and lengthy one. In addition, comprehension of the legal frameworks that apply to different works, and the level of potential risks involved, required research and discussions with other experts.

As a result, it took six months to complete a set of copyright and privacy guidelines for the Open Up! Project, and to determine a copyright clearance process for both previously published materials and unpublished organizational archives. This process was informed by a specialist in copyright law who worked 80 hours for the project (10 of which were pro bono), experiences of *Aletta E-Quality* and the *IISG*, research on the Data Archive and Networked Services (DANS) initiative, and recent papers from the European Commission and the University of Amsterdam about access to information and 'Fair Use' in Europe. The project produced guidelines that sought to comply with copyright and privacy laws while providing flexibility to open up the archive collection as far as possible.

The guidelines inform IHLIA of the need to:

- obtain prior consent to publish or republish from all traceable right holders;
- create the different licence agreements to offer copyright holders;
- provide opportunities for opting out from obtaining prior consent without compromising the organization;
- identify documents that are not suitable for publishing due to breaches of privacy;
- establish the processes to follow for maintaining a log of all efforts to trace and request consent from right holders, and a complaints log for any complaints the organisation receives and action taken.

To date, from a total of 119 different publishers and right holders in 24 countries, 45 have been traced and received letters requesting permission for use of their works, 36 are in the process of being traced with the help of local LGBT organizations, and 37 are no longer active or cannot be traced. One can assume that of the 36 that are still being traced, the majority of those no longer exist and are consequently untraceable.

In addition to the guidelines, four important legal instruments will be made available on the Open Up! website. These are:

- *Terms of use*. These inform users about how to register and terminate an account and access and use the Open Up! digital collection.

- *Copyright policy.* This refers to IHLIA's respect of IP rights and how right holders can report an infringement.
- *Privacy policy.* This explains how IHLIA will handle and manage any personal data collected as a result of user account registration, and how IHLIA will manage personal data within the collection and the purpose of the restricted tier.
- *Disclaimer.* This serves to inform the public and right holders of the ownership of the website and its contents and emphasises the personal and non-commercial use of the Open Up! collection. As with the copyright policy, it invites right holders to report any copyright violation.

Web based interface

Three Tiers of Access

To open up the archives as far as possible while respecting copyright and privacy conditions, the project will introduce a creative mode of access to its web interface. This will offer rights holders the opportunity to decide how far they wish to open up their materials: to the public, to the LGBT community only, or not at all. The Open Up! Project will put in place three tiers of publishing or user access:

Tier 1–Open Access:

Publications are made available to the public via the Open Up! website through registration and the creation of a user account. The public will be able to browse and search these items but will not be able to copy, save or print.

Tier 2–Exchange and Share:

Publications are made available on a restricted basis only to members of LGBT organizations/movements and professional researchers. Users will have to apply for an account online and be authorised by IHLIA to access materials. They will be able to browse and search these items and those in Tier 1, as well as copy, save and print pages in limited quantities.

Tier 3–Restricted:

Publications are only made available at IHLIA's premises in Amsterdam, open only for professional researchers. Users will have to apply for permission and be authorised by IHLIA to access materials. They will be able to browse and search, but will not be able to copy, save or print.

Web strategy and concept

The Open Up! Project commissioned an external web consultant to develop a web strategy that would articulate the project's options and needs regarding browsing, viewing and searching the Open Up! digital collection, security related to the tiers of access and data, and hosting and maintenance. Broadly, it was agreed that the focus should be on search functionality and user access rather than fancy design. Finally, to keep costs down, Open Up! would adapt open source software as often as possible.

Web building and design

After a tender process for finding a good web building company the vendor *De Ontwikkelfabriek B.V.* in Groningen (The Netherlands) was awarded the contract. They have considerable expertise in digital archives, viewing software and adapting open source software. The main elements of their work included:

- design, look and feel of the Open Up! website;
- an open source content management system (Drupal) and search platform (Apache SOLR);
- search methods to accommodate free text search (akin to a 'Google' type search) and faceted search (via filters such as country or keyword);
- discovery features to browse and explore the digital archive
- identification of appropriate open source viewing software for viewing or 'reading' the digitized materials online
- user account creation and access control;
- multi-language support;
- site system maintenance with periodic backups;
- user acceptance test for feedback and final improvements.

Web testing and content

The ALMS Conference (International Archives, Libraries, Museums and Special Collections Conference 2012 on the Future of LGBTI Histories, 1-3 August 2012, Amsterdam) marked the end of most Open Up! project activities. During this conference Lonneke van den Hoonaard, managing director of IHLA, presented a prototype of the website in order to obtain some first impressions and feedback from participants, who are also among Open Up!'s targeted users. This feedback was collected by *De Ontwikkelfabriek* and used for final revisions of the site. Many positive responses were heard during the breakout session afterward.

www.openup-lgbtcollections.org

On 2nd August 2012, when the prototype of the website was presented, the site also went officially online. At that time the site wasn't completely finalized, and up to now IHLIA is still making revisions of this new resource. However, everyone can already discover the Open Up! collection. Please visit our site at www.openup-lgbtcollections.org. There you will have the ability to see which archives have been opened up and which posters and periodical covers the project has digitized. IHLIA is still actively seeking feedback and ideas from those people interested in heritage and archives to give their opinion about the site; feel free to contact us at openup@ihlia.nl to give your feedback.

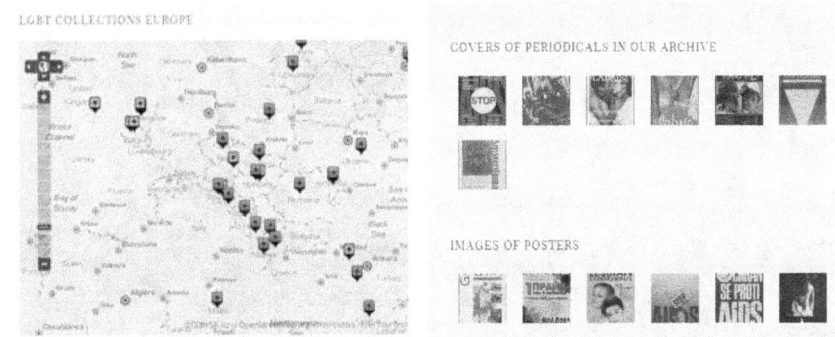

Left: screenshot of the homepage with a map of Europe where people can click on a red pin to find out what Open Up! has in the collection about that specific country and on the blue pins which are linked to the organisational archives Open Up! has digitized

Right: screenshot of covers of periodicals and images of posters.

The site offers a search feature akin to a Google search; the obtained results can be filtered by country, archive type, and period. When people actually would like see the content of the documents, they must register for an account. At this moment, it is possible to search in English and the Slavic languages, unfortunately not using the Cyrillic script. There are no plans right now to provide any sort of transcripts (e.g. English) for materials in Slavic languages.

Up to this moment Open Up! hasn't promote this new resource on a large scale. We are thinking right now about the possibilities to promote this site for researchers, LGBT organizations worldwide and the general public etc.

Queers Online

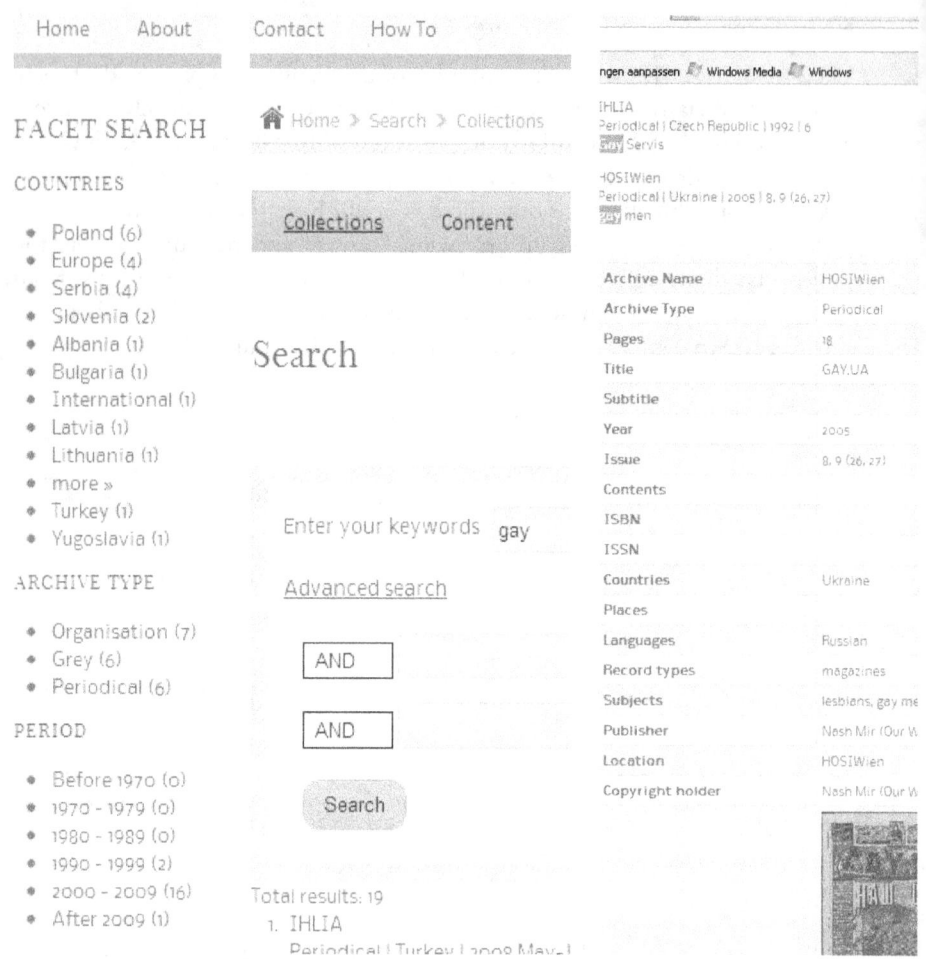

Screenshots of the search feature on the website

CHALLENGES AND LESSONS

As mentioned before, the greatest challenge to the project was the timeframe. With the expectation of opening up archives, i.e. access, a timeframe of at least 12 months, if not 18 months, would have been more realistic. An extension was granted which allowed the project to speed up the digitization activities, but it still underestimated the time and investment required for copyright clearances and web interface construction. As a whole, the timeframe compromised the ability to raise awareness about the project and mobilise substantial interest among local LGBT audiences in Central, Eastern, and Southeastern Europe. In addition, it meant that many organizational archives were not in an immediate condition for opening up.

Lessons learned from the project planning experience included:

- Critically appraise the timeframe, as well as the personnel and hours for archive and metadata preparation and processing copyright clearance from publishers/rights holders, if planning to focus on 'access' with a digital archive project.
- Ensure sufficient investment of time and resources for website development.
- Review and perform feasibility checks of project designs thoroughly before endorsing them.
- Build in a period for reaching out and engaging local stakeholders through field trips, small roundtables, project wiki pages, etc. (if time allows) in order to get greater buy-in and support.

Copyright hardly featured in the original project design, but it is a highly complex matter. Any organization seeking to use or publish a third party's work must take on the task of seeking permissions seriously and judiciously, even if there appears to be some scope for flexibility and creativity. While the project has produced a framework for copyright clearance for IHLIA to implement, it took some six months to develop and refine, even with the continued advice of an IP lawyer. This framework is not set in stone; it will need to be updated following changes in the copyright and privacy legal environment, and also after implementing the clearance process. Unfortunately, the project exhausted its funds for legal advice during the course of developing the legal texts for the website. IHLIA will need to finalise these texts. Lessons learned on copyright include:

- Ensure sufficient budget for legal advice on copyright. Not only are experts expensive, but researching, preparing documents and legal texts take time since they have to be precise.
- Copyright and privacy can be the biggest bottlenecks for digitization projects that aim to publish and give access to a new digital archive. Make sure ample time is available for high level discussions on these complex matters, and for sorting through archives to separate the 'publishable' from 'unpublishable'.

Local LGBT organizations are often eager to get involved with a new initiative, but they often have low capacity, are run by part-time albeit hardworking volunteers. As a result, local organizations will require more time to fulfil responsibilities. The main lesson here is:

- Arrange visits to the offices or regional hubs of local LGBT organizations to explain the project. Discuss opportunities for working together on the project, and determine a common work plan if seeking to partner or engage these organizations. That way, the project will be more tailored to the needs of the organization and their ways of working.

More to Open Up!

For IHLIA, Open Up! has been an intense project. We hope this initiative becomes a significant contribution to the archival record of an intriguing period in Europe's history and transition. But this is only the beginning. In the near future, IHLIA hopes to extend the website, and to expand and continue the gathering and opening up of LGBT histories by collaboration with existing and new partners. We share one goal: when together we acquire collections and make all of them findable, visible, and retrievable, our European (and worldwide) community, straight and gay, knows that we play a major role in telling the story of our place. Collecting the past and present informs and inspires the future. Such work helps us understand how change happened, and gives names and faces to our unsung heroes.

Appendix

Project information:
Project Title: Open Up! European LGBT History Out Of The Closet!
Project Period September 2011 – April 2012
Funder: Dutch Ministry of Education, Culture and Science
Budget: €299,275.00 The budget was revised three times to take into account the change in project strategy and reflect altered costs, such as the website, scanning contract, copyright advice and personnel.

The Open Up! Project collaborates with a number of international and national LGBT organizations, including:

- Háttér Társaság a Melegekért (Hungary);
- HOSI Wien (Austria);
- International Institute of Social History (IISH) (The Netherlands);

- International Lesbian, Gay, Bisexual, Trans and Intersex Association (ILGA) (Belgium);
- International Lesbian, Gay, Bisexual, Trans and Intersex Association – Europe (ILGA-Europe) (Belgium);
- International Lesbian, Gay, Bisexual, Transgender, Queer Youth and Student Organization (IGLYO) (Belgium);
- Kaos GL (Turkey);
- Okvir (Bosnia and Herzegovina);
- One World Platform for Southeast Europe (Bosnia and Herzegovina); and
- ŠKUC-LL (Slovenia).

Acronyms

Below is a list of acronyms used in this chapter.

ALMS	Archives, Libraries, Museums and Special Collections
CESE Europe	Central, Eastern and Southeastern Europe
DANS	Data Archive and Networked Services
EU	European Union
HOSI Wien	Homosexuelle Initiative Wien
IGLYO	International Lesbian, Gay, Bisexual, Transgender, Queer Youth and Student Organization
IHLIA LGBT heritage	International gay and lesbian Information Centre and Archive
IISG	Internationaal Instituut voor Sociale Geschiedenis (International Institute of Social History)
ILGA	International Lesbian, Gay, Bisexual, Trans and Intersex Association
ILIS	International Lesbian Information Service
IP	Intellectual Property

LGBT   Lesbian, Gay, Bisexual, Transgender
LGBTI   Lesbian, Gay, Bisexual, Transgender, Intersex
ŠKUC-LL   Lesbian Section SKUC-LL / Lesbian Library & Archive

IHLIA, February 2013

Documenting an Aftermath:
The Matthew Shepard Web Archive

Laura E. Uglean Jackson
American Heritage Center, University of Wyoming

Introduction

The American Heritage Center (AHC) is the University of Wyoming's (UW) repository for manuscript collections, rare books, and university archives. As home to the University's archives, it is part of the AHC's responsibility to acquire historical materials documenting university history, including issues and events related to UW students. While murders had previously taken place in Laramie, and occasional controversies at the University made national headlines, nothing like the murder of UW student Matthew Shepard, the media frenzy that followed, and the impact it had on communities and individuals throughout the world had ever before occurred in Laramie or to a member of the university community. For these reasons, the AHC began documenting the murder and aftermath in a physical collection immediately after news broke of it. Ten years later, the AHC created a collection of websites related to Matthew Shepard.

In addition to describing the website collection, this chapter analyzes the web archive to determine if it includes a variety of perspectives and voices. It takes into account previous studies which observe that the prevailing public memory of Shepard's murder as created by television shows and the news media portrayed gays and lesbians "as either villain or victim and constructed their identity as a 'problem' that is easily solved by heterosexuals" (Lynch 2007, 225). Additionally, the story told by the national news media and television networks had a strong disconnect from the perspectives and memories of those within or strongly connected to the LGBT community and, to an extent, the local

Laramie population (Dunn 2010; Loffreda 2000; Lynch 2007; Ott and Aoki 2002). By assessing the contents of the web archive and reflecting on the effects of the murder, one can assess if it documents an alternative public memory that portrays Matthew Shepard in a more accurate light and that documents actual effects on individuals – both those who knew Shepard and did not–in Laramie and throughout the world.

Matthew Shepard's Murder and Aftermath

Matthew Shepard, a gay UW student, grew up in Casper, Wyoming. He attended his last two years of high school in Switzerland and when he was twenty one he decided to enroll at the University of Wyoming. He ultimately wanted a career in international relations and to advocate for human rights (Shepard 2009, 41). Within three months of living in Laramie, Shepard had easily made friends and joined the Lesbian, Gay, Bisexual and Transgendered Alliance (LGBTA, UW's only LGBT student organization at the time). In the evening of October 6, 1998, after joining a group at the College Inn for coffee after the weekly LGBTA meeting, Shepard went to a bar by himself and ended up leaving with two men, Aaron McKinney and Russell Henderson. Henderson drove them to a deserted area on the outskirts of town. There, McKinney and Henderson tied Shepard to a fence, severely beat him with the butt of a pistol, and left him unconscious in the cold and windy Wyoming night (Loffreda 2000, 3, 9). Never to regain consciousness, Shepard died four days later in a hospital in Fort Collins, Colorado.

While Matthew Shepard still lay in a coma, media from around the nation descended upon Laramie to cover the story of a young gay man found nearly beaten to death. As news of Matthew Shepard's attack, then death, spread, individuals and communities around the world responded. Across the globe people held candlelight vigils and rallies; friends and strangers created memorial websites. People expressed their responses to Matthew Shepard's death through books and songs and a production titled *The Laramie Project*. Television movies were made. In December 1998, the Matthew Shepard Foundation was created by Shepard's parents, Judy and Dennis Shepard. UW renamed an annual conference dedicated to social justice issues to the Shepard Symposium on Social Justice. On a deeper level, Matthew Shepard became a political symbol to advocate for equal rights for gay, lesbian, bisexual, and transgender persons. His murder "turned equal rights and protections for gays and lesbians into topics of national debate" (Neff 1999, 40). Shepard's death reinvigorated the push for federal and state hate crimes law to include LGBT individuals. On a more personal level, a mother lost a son, and friends of Matthew Shepard mourned his death. Fourteen years later, vigils are still held before performances of *The Laramie Project*, and concerts to commemorate Matthew Shepard continue.

These events, actions, thoughts, and memories surrounding Shepard's brutal beating and death were recorded in various ways. Newspapers and magazines recount the events, beginning on October 9, 1998 with a bicyclist finding Shepard comatose in a barren field, covered in blood except for where "part of his face was cleaned by tears" (Edwards 1998, 14). They then cover the first vigils and rallies held while Shepard was still in the hospital, and include interviews with Laramie residents and national political figures about his death and its significance. UW correspondence and other official records document the university's reaction and response. Material from the UW LGBT student organization includes documentation of the response from the LGBT community in Laramie and from schools around the country. As time went on, many of the emotions, opinions, and reflections about Shepard's murder were recorded on the World Wide Web.

The Matthew Shepard Collection

Only days after news broke of the brutal beating, archivists at the AHC voluntarily began acquiring documentation by clipping newspaper articles from local papers. This collection became the Matthew Shepard Collection. Today it contains approximately three and a half cubic feet of materials such as correspondence from the university president's office, records and ephemera collected by the LGBT student organization, media coverage, and websites printed on paper.

The Matthew Shepard Collection largely documents the university's reaction and the story told in local newspapers and national magazines. The hundreds of articles from national newspapers such as *USA Today* or gay magazines such as *The Advocate* are not represented, most likely because of lack of ready access to them during the time following Shepard's death, when clippings were most heavily acquired. However, snippets of various opinions and perspectives appear in the collection. For example, there are at least two articles from *Out* magazine portraying a very different perspective than that of the national, and even local, news organizations. There are also a number of unique primary sources in this collection, such as a letter from McKinney's grandmother to then-UW President, Phil Dubois. In the letter she blames Shepard for enraging her grandson to beat him because of his "very aggressive sexual advances" and states, "Gays should not push their life style on others" (American Heritage Center 1983-2008, box 5, folder 7). In Dubois's response, also in this collection, he expresses sympathy for what she had recently gone through (as her daughter had passed away recently) but stated, "Violence and murder cannot be excused by attempting to blame the victim." Additionally there is a cassette tape containing the recording from a panel at the "Wyoming Conference on English," in which local journalists express criticism towards the national media coverage of Shepard's murder (box 4, folder 3). Although these two items in particular document varying viewpoints, the Matthew Shepard Collection documents a small piece of the murder and aftermath, largely through a local media and university administration lens. Although these histories are important, there were (and still are) gaps to fill.

Matthew Shepard Web Archive

Rationale for the Archive

October 12, 2008 marked the tenth anniversary of Shepard's death. It was in commemoration of this significant anniversary that in spring of 2008 the AHC applied for, and received in May, a UW President's Advisory Council on Minority's and Women's Affairs (PACMWA) grant to assist with the costs of a web archiving service. Archivists at the AHC thought that a web archive would help fill the gaps in the printed web pages within the physical Matthew Shepard collection. "Of the [physical] collection's seven boxes, three contain hardcopy printouts of approximately thirty web sites from 1998-1999. The sites are mostly memorials to Shepard and guest book commentaries; UW Web sites were not captured, such as the *Matthew Shepard Resource Site* with audio and video clips of statements, and photographs of the Peter, Paul and Mary concert of October 1999"(American Heritage Center 2008, 2). In 2008, a Google search for "Matthew Shepard" resulted in more than 435,000 hits (2). Ultimately, this web archive would provide more primary material for researchers "and in so doing raise awareness on campus and beyond of the historical significance of his tragic death" (5). Although the grant proposal does not mention that a web archive would likely include voices from friends, family, strangers, and LGBT individuals, the democratic nature of the web lends itself to include a variety of perspectives.

Creation of the Web Archive

According to Wikipedia (2012), web archiving is "the process of collecting portions of the World Wide Web and ensuring the collection is preserved in an archive, such as an archive site, for future researchers, historians, and the public. Due to the massive size of the Web, web archivists typically employ web crawlers for automated collection." The Free Dictionary (n.d.) defines web archiving as "Saving the pages from Web sites as they change over time for historical purposes. Using spiders similar to the ones search engines routinely deploy, there are services that archive the pages of a company's own Web site or pages from selected Web sites across the Internet."

With the grant money, the AHC purchased a one-month subscription to Archive-It, an offshoot of the Internet Archive that crawls, harvests, hosts, and provides an access interface for website collections. The PACMWA Grant Proposal (2008) explains why Archive-It was preferred: "The functionality offered by the Archive-It subscription will ensure scholars and researchers can use these sites to trace changes and retrieve information that is no longer currently available on the Web." Archive-It staff provided an over-the-phone training session on how to use the Archive-It interface to crawl sites. Essentially, the archivist selects websites to include in the collection and adds seeds, which are "starting point URLs where the crawler begins harvesting" websites into the system (Donovan 2011). For example, to collect the Matthew Shepard Foundation website the starting seed would be www.matthewshepard.org. The crawler would harvest all pages linked to the main page if the link's primary URL is matthewshepard.org. Links to external sites, such as stophate.org, would not be harvested. The archivist selects how often the crawl will take place (daily, weekly, monthly, yearly, etc.) and how long the crawl will last (anywhere from twelve hours to seven days). The Archive-It web crawler (Heretrix) captures the main URL page, including embedded content, and any other webpages that are part of the main website. The archivist can adjust the scope settings of any particular seed to limit how many pages (also called documents) are harvested. The terms of the contract allowed the AHC to collect up to one hundred and fifty websites and 2.5 million documents within the month of October 2008.[1] We conducted weekly crawls that often took a couple of days.

All of the websites were captured without having to ask for permission. At least two websites could not be captured because they had a robot blocker programmed into them. The site administrators did not reply to email requests asking them to remove the .txt files so that they could be captured. By the end of October, we had captured less than half the number of websites allowed in the Archive-It contract. Archive-It readily offered to extend the time period into November so that we could capture as much as possible. In the end, we captured seventy websites and 1.9 million documents rather than the allotted one hundred and fifty websites and 2.5 million documents. Four years after the capture, thirty percent of the websites found in the collection are no longer on the World Wide Web.

---

1   A document can be an entire web page or a component of a web page, such as a tiff or pdf file.

Harvesting and providing electronic access to websites preserves the *experience* of using a website and captures web content that cannot be printed, such as audio and video. Furthermore, capturing websites helps document the murder as it was felt around the world. Preserving and providing access to these websites would help keep Shepard's memory alive and help to tell a more complete story for researchers studying Shepard's murder and, ultimately, LGBT history.

Description of the Matthew Shepard Web Archive

The Matthew Shepard Web Archive collection contains web pages, videos, PDFs, and other distinct electronic files (see: http://www.archive-it.org/collections/1176). It includes websites from organizations affected by, present during the aftermath, and established because of Shepard's murder (e.g. the Matthew Shepard Foundation). Other organizational sites include Matthew's Place, which is part of the Matthew Shepard Foundation. This site contains resources for coming out and talking to friends and family about sexual identity. Unfortunately the archived site is not fully functional. Several of the images and pull-down menus do not appear correctly, and the guest book is inaccessible. Despite the problems with functionality, it documents one way that the Shepard Foundation provided free resources to people struggling to come to terms with their sexuality.

There are blogs, blog entries, and forums specifically about Matthew Shepard and the ten year anniversary of his death. There are also blogs or forums with tangentially related subject matter, such as posts for and by LGBT youth. It has websites of films, books, and music created in response to Shepard's murder and in memorial of Shepard's life. For example, the website for Randi Driscoll's song, "What Matters", which was directly inspired by Shepard's murder, and the website for the HBO production of *The Laramie Project* are in this category. There are a number of memorial and commemorative websites that were created by friends and strangers to Matt. As promised in the PACMWA grant application, we captured University of Wyoming sites. These include the Matthew Shepard Resource site which contained statements from University President Phillip Dubois, student body president Jesus Rios, and the LGBTA chair. We also captured the websites of Spectrum (formerly LGBTA) and the UW Rainbow Resource Center. The archive also contains a handful of articles on the web. There is an article from *WEHONEWS.com* about a memorial in West Hollywood commemorating Matthew Shepard. There is also an article written in 2007 about "The Campaign to Kill the Matthew Shepard Act." These articles, and others, were captured and included in the web collection because they did not exist in the physical collection, they were easy to capture, and we were unlikely to receive clippings of them.

Significance of Content

Since Shepard's murder and the aftermath that followed, scholars and Shepard's friends and family members have written about him and the effects of his murder. Much of the scholarship and study into the aftermath offers critical perspectives on national media portrayal of the event, television movies about the murder and aftermath, and the reaction from state and federal legislators, national equality organizations, and UW administration. According to Ott and Aoki, the mainstream media described the murder and effects in a way that "reaffirm a dominant set of discourses that socially stigmatizes gay, lesbian, bisexual, and transgendered (GLBT) persons; and to hamper efforts to create and enact a progressive GLBT social policy" (484-85). Information contained in mainstream newspapers and magazines is a main source of information about Shepard's murder and serves as a large part of the historical record. The Matthew Shepard Web Archive documents the after effects of Matthew Shepard's murder through websites created by various individuals and organizations and offers a variety of perspectives for researchers that did not appear in the mainstream media or public narrative. Because the web archive largely consists of primary sources (rather than secondary, such as newspaper articles), it offers first-hand accounts of individual and group reactions and testimony. By providing worldwide access to these sources, a more complete and accurate portrayal of Shepard's murder and aftermath can be preserved and made accessible.

Interestingly, one website supports the theory and argument that the media's portrayal of the murder and after effects was inaccurate. The Gay and Lesbian Alliance Against Defamation (GLAAD) website includes a resource kit for media covering hate crimes, which was created to commemorate the ten year anniversary of Shepard's murder. The mainstream media received criticism for its negative portrayals of Laramie and Wyoming, inaccurately reporting that Shepard was crucified on a fence post, and publishing stories to add to the sensationalistic nature of the media frenzy in general. This resource kit supports the notion that journalists need some guidance in covering hate crimes. Rather than criticizing their work, GLAAD created a kit for journalists containing valuable guidelines for the respectful, ethical coverage of a hate crime. This is included in the archive.

Blogs, forums, and other web pages containing comments and posts may best document individual voices and perspectives not found elsewhere, including perspectives or effects on family and friends. For example, "Big Gay Jim's Bigger,

Gayer Blog," was written by one of Shepard's friends, former president of the UW LGBTA. "Big Gay Jim" wrote about the ten year anniversary:

> I do know it still hurts. I do know I still have questions. I do know there are amazing people here in Laramie and abroad doing incredible work. They have opened their hearts and minds. They have looked around them, rolled up their sleeves, and jumped in...working to make their corner of the world a safer, more welcoming place for EVERYone. It might be one person at a time, or in a way that reaches thousands, but they do whatever they can.
>
> Tonight I think of Matt, alone on the prairie on a cold and windy October night...just like tonight.
>
> Today's lesson: Do whatever you can, whenever you can. Never underestimate your power to affect the world around you.

Also captured was "Logan's Voice", a blog by Matt's brother, Logan Shepard. In the "About Me" section, he wrote, "I haven't had a public persona in the years past, but it has been ten years and now I am ready share what life has been like in recent years." Although the blog contains only a handful of entries, and most are not about Matthew Shepard or LGBT issues, it provides readers with some sense of Logan's perspective and experience.

Another website captured is a discussion forum initiated by Matt's friend Romaine Patterson, author of *The Whole World Was Watching: Living in the Light of Matthew Shepard*. The forum contains the experiences of individuals acting, producing, or watching *The Laramie Project* from around the country. Moises Kaufman of The Tectonic Theater Project wrote *The Laramie Project* based on over two hundred interviews with Laramie residents. First staged in Denver in 2000, it has since been produced dozens of times by major and local theater companies, schools, and made into an HBO film in 2002. Unlike other television movies, *The Laramie Project* "represents an attempt to create a more progressive public memory" (Lynch 2007, 230). The testaments from people involved with the play provide context to the production which, because it is based on interviews, provides a more accurate representation of the murder and aftermath and serves as part of the historical record in and of itself.

Another group of sites that captures various and individual perspectives are web memorials. These appeared almost immediately after Shepard's brutal beating and eventual death. We captured memorial sites such as one created by an individual known only as "Texas Dude". The hit counter implies that it has existed since October 12, 1998. The site's creator wrote, "I didn't know Matthew

Shepard, but as soon as I heard about the vicious way he had been attacked I felt a bond with him, because I was beaten in a similar way on June 3, 1993." The site plays an instrumental of "Stairway to Heaven" and the viewer scrolls down one long page to view images of Matt and see quotes and links to other websites. Other memorial websites include information about a community poem being written about Matthew Shepard, photos from Flickr of a memorial that took place in Australia, and another Flickr photo of a license plate that reads "End H8," which was created in commemoration of Shepard. Web sites such as these document actions by strangers around the world to memorialize Shepard's life.

A handful of memorial-type sites could be found on Facebook but unfortunately they could not be captured.[2] At the time, the Archive-It web crawler, Heretrix, could not properly capture many social media pages. This has since changed and there are procedures for capturing Facebook, Twitter, and other social media successfully.

Archive-It was able to supply use statistics from January 2010 to September 2012. On average, the website collection received eighty-four viewers a month. The total number of pages, images, and other files viewed during this time span was 39,421.

What the Matthew Shepard Web Archive Is Not

While the Matthew Shepard Web Archive sounds extensive, it does not contain anything and everything on the web related to Matthew Shepard. Unlike many fan sites or sites about a particular person or topic, it does not attempt to be a comprehensive web resource. For example, it does not include many of the news articles that exist on the web. Although many news articles contemporary to the event remained accessible online during the crawl period, these were not captured because many newspaper articles already existed in the Matthew Shepard collection in physical form. Web content that was at the most risk of being lost (unpublished material) was made a priority.

It also does not contain many of the sentiments voiced by GLBT individuals and Laramie residents in books and documentaries. In Beth Loffreda's book *Losing Matt Shepard*, several Laramie residents offer their perspectives about the aftermath and provide different viewpoints than those found within the narrative suggested by the mainstream media. One example of a divergent viewpoint is the resentment felt by Jim Osborne, the former president of

---

2 Although the Facebook pages could not be captured, their presence showed that people continued to memorialize Shepard's life more than six years after his death (Facebook wasn't launched until 2004).

UW's LGBT student organization, toward the Human Rights Campaign (HRC), which used the symbol of Matthew Shepard to raise money for their organization. At the time, the HRC did not filter money back to Wyoming, where it could have been used for resources such as education, counseling, and legislation (Loffreda 2000, 97). While the web archive contains pages from the HRC website, they do not contain information to corroborate or support the claims made by Loffreda and interviewees. The reason that the HRC site appears at all in the collection is to capture a page containing information about the Matthew Shepard Act, federal legislation originally presented in 2001, and eventually passed in October 2009.

Another example of differing perspectives is the Peter, Paul and Mary concert that took place in Laramie on October 12, 1999, to commemorate the one-year anniversary of Shepard's murder. Photos of this concert were one of the pieces of information that the grant proposal specifically aimed to include in the web archive. The physical collection contains accounts of the band members' reactions in newspaper articles. For example, this one from the *Laramie Boomerang* (1999): "Peter Yarrow, who seems to be the spokesman for the group, went to the infamous fence where Matthew Shepard, a gay man, was killed. He kneeled down and kissed the rock cross that someone erected after the murder. He cried. 'Now I am one with Matthew Shepard', he said. Afterward, he wrote new lyrics for a Phil Ochs song called, 'There but for Fortune' for the concert. The emotions are genuine." On the surface, this seemed like a fine gesture, but many Laramie residents questioned the band's motives for playing and why the university spent $250,000 for them to perform rather than to bolster LGBT resources and programs at the university (Loffreda 2000, 96). People also expressed the opinion that the band members did not seem sincere, perhaps because of the large amount of money they received to perform, but also because they did not attend the President's reception after the concert. Unfortunately, the website collection does not document these sentiments. If anything, the little documentation about the concert portrays the band and their performance in a positive light.

Unlike many website collections, the Matthew Shepard Web Archive is not an active collection. Our subscription to Archive-It was only for the month of October 2008. Only websites available during the crawl period (October 1 – November 15, 2008) are included. The crawl did not continue for a couple of reasons. First, we were documenting an event that occurred ten years ago. The amount of new material created about or in response to Shepard's murder would, it was assumed, escalate during the ten year anniversary month, and then most likely decline. Further, the costs of continuing to subscribe to the Archive-It service were prohibitive. The AHC was only able to do this project with the assistance of a grant from the PACMWA. At the time, it was not financially feasible to continue a lengthier subscription through Archive-It especially with a predicted decline in new websites and online materials. This has its disadvantages. For example, Logan Shepard continued contributing to his blog through 2009 and in December 2008 reflected on his brother's death in a poignant entry about what would have been Matt's thirty second birthday. Other important content, such as the passing of the Matthew Shepard Act in 2009, would have helped tell the complete story by including an important effect of Shepard's murder.

One of a Kind

Unlike LGBT repositories and other website collections containing a broad scope of LGBT histories, the Matthew Shepard Web Archive aims to document one event, one individual, and the many effects that this individual's murder had on communities, friends, and family. There really is no other website collection like this, although there are several LGBT website collections accessible through Archive-It. The U.S. LGBT Web Collection includes national LGBT organization websites, and websites related to LGBT issues such as "Don't Ask, Don't Tell" and marriage equality, representing both sides for and against (2011-2012). This national website collection is managed and funded by the University of Texas at San Antonio, which also manages three other collections documenting Texas-based LGBT organizations and individuals.[3] The "San Antonio Area Gay, Lesbian, Transgender and Queer Related Web Collection" contains websites of LGBTQ organizations and individuals in the San Antonio area while the "General Texas Gay, Lesbian, Bisexual, Transgender and Queer Related Web Collection" contains websites from organizations and individuals throughout Texas with a focus on Austin, and the "Rio Grande Valley Area Gay, Lesbian, Bisexual, Transgender and Queer Related Web Collection" focuses on the Rio Grande Valley area. The "Human Rights Commission-Lesbian Gay Bisexual Transgender Advisory Committee" collection contains meeting minutes and reports documenting the committee and is managed by the San Francisco Public Library. Like the Matthew Shepard Web Archive, all of these collections are accessible on Archive-It. Unlike the Matthew Shepard website collection, these collections appear to still be active and are captured once annually.

---

3   Not coincidentally, Mark Shelstad, university archivist at UT-San Antonio from 2008-2013, was also the former university archivist at UW and drafted the PACMWA grant.

The Matthew Shepard Web Archive is also unique because it documents an event that occurred ten years prior to the collection being created. Today website harvesting and website collections are useful tools for documenting current events, and most website collections initiate the first crawl during the event or immediately prior to its occurrence. Examples of this include the Occupy Movement, the Arab Spring, and the earthquake in Haiti. Had we been able to create a web archive from the time of the murder, it would probably contain a lot more information and document years' worth of online information related to Matthew Shepard, including events during the one-year and subsequent year anniversaries. Furthermore, documenting websites from the beginning would have helped meet the objective of trying to tell another story other than the one found in the national media. Major newspapers were quick to include quotes such as, "Openly gay behavior is not only discouraged, it's dangerous" and "Wyoming is not really gay friendly" (Brooke 1998, A9). The web archive contains websites such as Wyoming Equality, Spectrum, and the UW Rainbow Resource Center, GLBT organizations that, from their existence alone, might help to dispel the myth perpetuated by the media that gays and lesbians were unwelcome in Wyoming. But, these websites were from 2008- not 1998. Because they were not captured at the time of Shepard's murder, it is impossible to use the archived websites to show that LGBT groups existed in Wyoming, even if Wyoming Equality and Spectrum were both in existence in 1998 under different names.

That said, in 1998 the Web was only four years old and was a comparatively small, albeit growing, space. Sites such as Facebook, YouTube, and Flickr did not exist. Website harvesting technology was not yet readily accessible. The only practical way for most archivists to preserve a website was to print it (and there are printed websites in the physical Matthew Shepard Collection). At present, repositories have multiple options to begin website collections when an event happens. Archive-It and the California Digital Library provide this service at a cost. Tech-savvy archives can use open-source software such as HTTrack to crawl and harvest websites on their own, for free.

While there are websites devoted to now-deceased individuals or events that occurred decades ago, these differ from a web archive in a number of ways. First, these websites typically contain links to other web content, not snapshots of websites or web content captured by a web crawler and then saved offline or in a digital library. If the host site or any of the sites linked to it change, there is no way to access the previous version. A web archive preserves a collection of websites in a place other than where the websites live so that they can be saved and preserved should the websites change or cease to exist.

Second, these types of websites often contain digital surrogates of physical content (e.g. magazine articles published pre-Internet or photographs). This material exists elsewhere in physical form. A web archive's content is solely websites. The websites may contain digital surrogates, but the web archive collection itself is comprised of born-digital content. A web archive is a collection of websites, whereas a website *about* an event or individual is a collection of information and resources about a particular individual or topic.

Finally, with fan pages and the like, one notices an inherent bias or one-sided viewpoint on the individual or event represented in the website. The websites do not contain material that is controversial or negative about the event/subject. For example, one potentially controversial website in the Matthew Shepard Web Archive is the Westboro Baptist Church website. This group, which regularly demonstrates at funerals of soldiers and AIDS victims, protested at Shepard's funeral and during Aaron McKinney's trial by holding signs reading, "Matthew Shepard in Hell" and "God Hates Fags." Fan sites or sites dedicated to a person's memory are created for a different purpose and are usually intended to recognize the individual and remember them. Although the Westboro Church played a part in the aftermath and they used (and continue to use) Shepard's image on picket signs, it would simply not be appropriate or even desired to include links to or information about the Westboro Church in, say, a memorial page about Matthew Shepard. However, preserving the Westboro Baptist Church websites holds them accountable for their protests and hate-filled messages, should they ever cease to promote their "values" or claim a different opinion. By remaining neutral and documenting all sides and perspectives of an issue, one can further the efforts of social justice. It holds those "in the wrong" or committing the injustices accountable, it preserves the memory of it so that it cannot someday be denied or forgotten.

Despite these great differences, fan pages are similar to web archives in that both provide one place to look for information from many sources about a particular subject or individual. Fan sites of musicians seem to parallel a web archive to a certain extent, but these sites are still at a much greater risk of disappearing due to link rot or the creator taking it down. For example, the Harvey Milk Foundation maintains a list of links to online articles and other websites related to Harvey Milk, but some links have disappeared because they are merely links to once active sites. Unlike the websites found in a web archive collection, the pages were not harvested and preserved in a different location than where they were originally found.

Conclusion

The web archive contains much more than links to information on Matthew Shepard. It contains perspectives, viewpoints, and memories from a variety of individuals and groups. In part it does contribute to an alternative memory, one that includes reactions, reflections, and statements about Shepard's murder from family, friends, strangers, and organizations. A website archive is a useful tool for achieving primary source documentation from various entities about a person or event. However, it is a piece of documentation within a greater whole. The entirety of the effects and aftermath cannot be documented in the website collection because much of the information does not exist in web form. It lives in the papers of Beth Loffreda; in the administrative records of the Matthew Shepard Foundation; in the interviews and raw footage from Bev Seckinger's documentary *Laramie Inside Out*; in the photos of the Angel Network (a group of students dressed in giant angel wings to visually block the Westboro Baptist Church protest), and in a myriad of other unknown personal papers, institutional records, and individual memories. The AHC has made efforts to acquire many of these records and plans to work to continuously acquire documentation on Shepard's murder and the after effects. These materials, together with the more mainstream historical record from newspapers and television movies, make up the public memory of Shepard's murder and the aftermath.

REFERENCES

American Heritage Center, University of Wyoming. (1983-2008) Matthew Shepard collection, #300014.

American Heritage Center. (2008). Archiving Matthew Shepard: 10 years and 300,000 websites later. For *PACMWA Grant Proposal*. Laramie, WY: Mark Shelstad.

Boles, F. (1994). Just a bunch of bigots. *Archival Issues, 19*, 53-66.

Donovan, D. (2011). Create a collection – Archive-It help. Retrieved from: https://webarchive.jira.com/wiki/display/ARIH/Create+a+Collection

Dunn, T.R. (2010). Remembering Matthew Shepard: Violence, identity, and queer counterpublic memories. *Rhetoric & Public Affairs, 13*, 611-652.

Edwards, T. (1998 November 20). McKinney to face trial in Shepard murder. *Laramie Boomerang*, pp. 1, 14.

Loffreda, B. (2000). *Losing Matt Shepard: Life and politics in the aftermath of anti-gay murder*. New York, NY: Columbia University Press.

Lynch, J. (2007). Memory and Matthew Shepard: Opposing expressions of public memory in television movies. *Journal of Communication Inquiry, 31*, 222-238.

Ott, B. L., & Aoki, E. (2002). The politics of negotiating public tragedy: Media framing of the Matthew Shepard murder. *Rhetoric & Public Affairs, 5*, 483-505.

San Francisco Public Library. (June 2010) Human Rights Commission-Lesbian Gay Bisexual Transgender Advisory Committee. A collection in Archive-It. Retrieved from: http://www.archive-it.org/collections/1954

Shepard, J. (2009). *The meaning of Matthew: My son's murder in Laramie, and a world transformed*. New York, NY: Hudson Street Press.

University of Texas, San Antonio. (June 2010-2012). General Texas Gay, Lesbian, Bisexual, Transgender, and Queer Related Web Collection. A collection in Archive-It. Retrieved from: http://archive-it.org/collections/1752

University of Texas, San Antonio. (Jan 2010-2012). Rio Grande Valley Area Gay, Lesbian, Bisexual, Transgender, and Queer Related Web

Collection. A collection in Archive-It. Retrieved from: http://archive-it.org/collections/1751.

University of Texas, San Antonio. (June 2010-2012). San Antonio Area Gay, Lesbian, Bisexual, Transgender and Queer Related Web Collection. A collection in Archive-It. Retrieved from: http://archive-it.org/collections/1750

University of Texas, San Antonio. (July 2011-2012). U.S. LGBT Web Collection. A collection in *Archive-It*. Retrieved from: http://archive-it.org/collections/2778.

University of Wyoming. (2008). Matthew Shepard Web Archive. A collection in Archive-It. Retrieved from http://www.archive-it.org/collections/1176.

Web Archiving. (n.d.) In *The Free Dictionary*. Retrieved from http://encyclopedia2.thefreedictionary.com/Web+Archive.

Web Archiving. (2012). In *Wikipedia*. Retrieved from http://en.wikipedia.org/wiki/Web_Archive. http://www.archive-it.org/collections/1750, http://www.archive-it.org/collections/1752, http://www.archive-it.org/collections/1751

Lesbian Gay Bisexual Transgender Religious Archives Network

Overview

The LGBT Religious Archives Network (LGBT-RAN) is a recent, innovative venture launched to encourage organizations and activists to preserve their histories and thereby to support and encourage scholarly study of lesbian, gay, bisexual and transgender (LGBT) religious movements around the world.

LGBT-RAN can best be understood as a "virtual" archive. It is not a physical repository that collects and preserves papers and records. Instead LGBT-RAN is an online resource center that encourages the preservation of history and makes historical information easily accessible through its web site.

Recognizing that history is written from the perspective of those who preserve their records, LGBT-RAN's overarching purpose is to ensure the preservation and accessibility of the voices and experiences of a great diversity of LGBT religious leaders and groups.

LGBT-RAN's development has been possible only because of the information technology revolution of recent decades that provides widespread and easy access to a large volume of data at a low cost. While LGBT-RAN was an early provider of digital historical information, now virtually every library, archive and museum makes extensive information available online.

LGBT-RAN primarily assists LGBT religious leaders and groups in determining how to preserve their records and papers in appropriate repositories. Secondly, LGBT-RAN provides a digital online information clearinghouse for these archival collections, and other LGBT religious history resources for historians, researchers and other interested persons.

LGBT-RAN has rather narrowly defined audience and user bases. On the one hand, LGBT-RAN reaches out to LGBT religious groups across all faiths and the activists involved in these movements around the world. A second user group is scholars researching and writing about the development and impact of LGBT religious groups and activists. This group tends to be quite internet/web savvy and they find LGBT-RAN quickly and easily through their research. A third, more diffused user group is casually interested laypeople who find LGBT-RAN via online searches, Facebook, and links from other historical databases. In recent months LGBT-RAN has received referrals from twenty-nine related websites.

Some Historical Background

The seeds of this project were planted in conversations between long-time gay religious activist Mark Bowman and the administration of Chicago Theological Seminary in 2000. LGBT religious movements have had and continue to have a profound impact upon religious and social institutions in the U.S. and around the world in recent decades, for example:

- Challenging heterosexism and sexism implicit in much theology and religious practice;
- Redefining traditional understandings of sexual ethics;
- Questioning religious participation in the legal contract of marriage; and
- Exposing hypocrisy and incongruency between personal behavior and public image that undermines the integrity of religious leaders;

Yet there was little scholarly research and writing being done on LGBT religious history in order to document these profound changes in religion and society. So the original concept for the project was to gather papers and records of LGBT religious leaders and organizations into a physical repository that would provide valuable original source materials for historical research.

A planning grant from the E. Rhodes and Leona B. Carpenter Foundation was secured to spend a year surveying LGBT historians, archivists, and religious activists on how to best shape this project. The collective response was a strong affirmation for the need to move posthaste to preserve and present the history of LGBT religious movements. It was also reported that LGBT religious leaders and groups were already taking initial steps to donate their records to repositories — some to LGBT archives, some university libraries, and some to denominational archives — so that a plan for creating a central physical repository was not needed.

What was needed, however, was support for grassroots efforts in historical preservation:

1. to encourage LGBT religious leaders and groups to save and donate their records to archives;
2. to provide professional guidance and assistance in the process of identifying which records should be preserved and where; and
3. to develop an information clearinghouse that would be a portal to the collections and historical data existing in archives and libraries, thereby spurring scholarly research and writing.

The confluence of this concept of a grassroots historical preservation venture with the explosion of digital technology and the Internet provided a unique opportunity to develop a broadly-based, low-cost, widely-accessible electronic portal into LGBT religious history — the LGBT-RAN web site. Through the regular input of an Advisory Committee — comprised of a dozen LGBT religious historians, archivists and activists — and other LGBT-RAN constituents, this web site has evolved over the past ten-plus years into a model of how social movements can help define their place in the historical record.

To reiterate: another archive to collect and preserve historical records from LGBT religious movements, such as the correspondence, membership records, financial records, photographs, videos, publications, and memoirs that characterize the life of a movement, was unnecessary. Such repositories already existed around the United States and in other countries. What was needed instead was a means to highlight the major importance of preserving historical records to folks active in LGBT religious movements who are not archivists themselves—and to help them find the appropriate repositories for their collections of records. This became the initial, primary goal of the LGBT Religious Archives Network—to serve as a portal to guide leaders and activists to find homes for their historical documents.

Thus LGBT-RAN was initiated in 2001 as a project of the Chicago Theological Seminary (CTS). As the project grew in the ensuing years it required more administrative support and oversight than CTS was able to provide. After a nationwide search for another sponsor, LGBT-RAN became part of the Center for Lesbian & Gay Studies in Religion and Ministry at the Pacific School of Religion in Berkeley, California in 2008.

LGBT-RAN's primary clientele comes to locate appropriate repositories, either for documents of every type that they wish to preserve or to find original sources for research. However, LGBT-RAN also stimulates interest and research in LGBT religious history. To this end LGBT-RAN has introduced a large "profiles gallery" with short biographies of leaders, a collection of oral histories, and digital exhibitions of important records. Now many users come to explore this ever-growing amount of historical data, even though the primary purpose is to guide users to archives that house the primary records of our history.

Mission Statement

The Lesbian, Gay, Bisexual and Transgender Religious Archives Network (LGBT-RAN) coordinates and supports the identification, collection and preservation of personal papers and organizational records from lesbian, gay, bisexual and transgender religious movements. To encourage scholarly research and historical study of these important movements for social change, LGBT-RAN disseminates information about these records and provides and facilitates access to them, using digital technology when possible.

Four Components

The website has four main components, displayed on the website home page (www.lgbtran.org). See figure 1 for a screen shot of the home page as of July 2012. The core component of LGBT-RAN's database is the Collections Catalog, identifying and listing existent collections along with the repository in which they are preserved. The other components—Profiles Gallery, Oral History Project, and Exhibitions—are designed to help with advocating for the preservation of records. In order to encourage these groups and leaders to preserve their papers, LGBT-RAN features their biographical profiles, selected oral histories, and online exhibitions.

Figure 1: a screen shot of our opening website page (www.lgbtran.org) listing our main components.

1. Profiles Gallery

Figure 2: a screen shot from our Profiles Gallery.

The Profiles Gallery presents biographical sketches of persons who have been leaders or prominent initiators in LGBT religious movements around the world. The stories of these persons are a rich repository of wisdom and encouragement for emerging activists and leaders, for today's students and for historians of the future. LGBT-RAN is constantly adding new biographical sketches. As of June 2012, there were 330 profiles, including such notable figures as Faisal Alam, founder of LGBT Muslims; Rev. Ellen Barrett, an Episcopal priest and monastic, the first openly gay person and one of the earliest women to be ordained priest in the Episcopal Church; Dr. John Boswell, one of the most significant scholars in gay and lesbian studies; Rev. Peter Gomes, African American Harvard chaplain and professor and a leading voice against religious intolerance; Harry Hay, best known as the founder of the U.S. gay movement (and the Mattachine Society) but is increasingly known as a pioneer of gay spirituality; Christopher Isherwood, who helped create new English translations of Hindu texts, including the popular *Bhagavad Gita: Song of God* while the Vedanta Society continued to serve as the spiritual foundation for his social beliefs and his sexual identity; Father Mychal Judge, who accompanied firefighters to the World Trade Center towers on the morning of September 11, 2001 and died comforting them; Rabbi Sharon Kleinbaum, Senior Rabbi of New York City's Congregation Beth Simchat Torah (CBST) since 1992; and Rev. Elder Troy Perry, founder of Metropolitan Community Churches.

LGBT-RAN is making a concerted effort to include a more diverse collection of leaders. Among the latest 75 new profiles, 16 are from outside the U.S., 11 are persons of color, 6 are transgender, and 6 are from traditions other than Christianity.

In January 2012, LGBT-RAN introduced a new, more interactive feature to the Profiles Gallery. Readers are invited to submit their own "remembrances" relating to any person posted in the Profiles Gallery, especially any significant experience with or knowledge of the person. The LGBT-RAN Coordinator serves as the moderator of these remembrances—receiving them and editing and posting as appropriate. For example, these remembrances were posted for profile of the Rev. Sylvia Pennington:

As Remembered by Bill Garnett

In 1986 I was in the eighth year of a hiatus I had taken during which I did not affiliate with any organized church body. I met a pastor who just moved to Kansas City, Missouri, to start a new church for the gay community that would be apart from the MCC "franchise." To kick the church off, Pastor Allen had an ordination ceremony at which Rev. Sylvia presided. I can still remember her sermon, which used the Gospel story of the Prodigal Son for its basis; I felt like Rev. Pennington was preaching that sermon specifically for me. After the ceremony I talked with Rev. Pennington for twenty/thirty minutes. At the end of our discussion, Rev. Sylvia took a copy of *But Lord They're Gay* and *Good*

News for Modern Gays, wrote a dedication to me in each and signed each. I promptly read both books and when her third book came out, I got it and read it also. Because of Rev. Pennington I got back active, first with this new church, a liberal RLDS community church, and finally a local Episcopalian church, all as an openly gay man. As of a year and a half ago, I joined a United Church of Christ/Disciples of Christ church. As a result of my meeting with Rev. Pennington, my church and spiritual life has grown and my involvement has also increased. She really turned my life around and I will be forever grateful to her.

— February 7, 2012

As Remembered by Dave:

Sylvia saved my life. I was married with a young family living in rural Montana. I didn't know a good person could be genetically gay. I thought I had a mental illness or demons. No one could help me, and I was worn out, exhausted from the struggle. Sylvia came to Billings, about 80 miles away. I don't remember the exact year, but it was in the last years of her life. She somehow rounded up names of people who had attended gay events. I was so broke and financially broken that I had to hitchhike to see her, sometimes in rainstorms. I met with her several times. She told me that God loved me and saved my life. I had no money when others ordered catered sandwiches. I could not get the owner of the house to respond to my request for even a heel off a loaf of bread. I had nothing to eat all day. Sylvia shared her sandwich with me. My story is too long to tell tonight. I am amazed that anyone would travel around Montana where there was no one to affirm us, and stand up to all the religious opposition, and spend her own money to reach someone like me. I am still a coward about showing my identity in my small redneck town, but she did not care how many people condemned her. She challenges me to be the same. I never believed in the concept of saints, but I truly think Sylvia is a saint. Sometimes I talk to her in heaven and thank her for rescuing me, just in case she can hear. I have had a happy productive life. I have gone on to save tens of thousands of lives with my agricultural programs, so God had a reason for designing me. All those people would be dead if Sylvia hadn't saved me.

— April 2, 2012

2. Oral Histories.

Figure 3: a screen shot from our Oral Histories Collection.

The Oral History Collection provides in-depth interviews with a diverse group of early and/or important LGBT religious leaders. LGBT-RAN's Oral History Collection is unique in that users can either read or listen to each interview. The posting for each person includes the audio interview, a written transcript, photographs and biographical notes. In July 2012, this collection was comprised of 25 interviews, including: Daayiee Abdullah, an imam in progressive Islam; Allen Bennett, first openly gay rabbi in the U.S.; Karen Doherty, co-founder of Conference for Catholic Lesbians; and Virginia Mollenkott, evangelical feminist theologian.

LGBT-RAN contracted with Dr. Monique Moultrie to implement an African-American Oral History Project, funded by a small grant from the Riverside Church (New York) Sharing Fund. Dr. Moultrie conducted interviews with Bishop Zachary Jones, Rev. Darlene Garner, Imam Daayiee Abdullah, Rev. Cedric Harmon, Dr. Sylvia Rhue, and Rev. Dr. Yvette Flunder. Other recent additions to the Oral History Collection include: Bishop Melvin Wheatley, early advocate for LGBT justice in the United Methodist Church; Randi Solberg, Norwegian leader of the European Forum of Lesbian & Gay Christian Groups; Patrick McArron, early leader of Dignity, the LGBT Catholic group; and Lynn Jordan, historian and one of the founders of the Metropolitan Community Church San Francisco.

3. Online Exhibitions.

These exhibitions present artifacts from LGBT religious collections in digital format organized as you might see them in a museum or library. Each exhibition explores a particular subject of LGBT religious history and includes diverse artifacts, such as photos, articles, correspondence, documents and audio or video clips, that have been found in archives. In its ongoing efforts to make original source materials on LGBT religious history widely accessible to students, researchers and other interested persons, LGBT-RAN invites collaboration with other groups to create additional exhibitions.

As of July 2012, exhibits include:

Council on Religion and the Homosexual: Portrays the formative years (1964-68) of this ground-breaking coalition of clergy and lesbian & gay activists in San Francisco. Created in collaboration with the LGBT Historical Society.

The Ordination of William R. Johnson: Presents the first ordination of an openly gay person in mainline Protestant Christianity in the U.S. William R. Johnson was ordained by the Golden Gate Association of the United Church of Christ on June 25, 1972.

Maranatha: Riversiders for LGBT Concerns: Explores the history and life of one of the first LGBT ministries within a church in the United States.

Congregation Beth Simchat Torah: Explores the early history of the world's largest LGBT synagogue located in New York City. Created in collaboration with the congregation.

Queers Online

Figure 4: a screen shot from our Online Exhibitions.

Shower of Stoles: Presents pictures and stories of over 1,000 stoles and other liturgical items that comprise the Shower of Stoles Project, which depicts the ministries of LGBT persons. Created in collaboration with the Institute of Welcoming Resources.

Sampler of Early Documents: Shows a dozen early (1964-81) newsletters or articles that document the formation of a diversity of LGBT religious groups or movements.

Another opportunity for interactivity was provided in the newest exhibition, The Ordination of William R. Johnson. In this case, readers/viewers have been invited to contribute an artifact, memory or reflection to this exhibition.

We have several potential exhibits "in the works," to appear in the near future:

New LGBT Quaker History Project

Mitchell Santine Gould, noted Walt Whitman scholar, has made a generous gift to LGBT-RAN to underwrite the development of a LGBT Quaker History project. LGBT-RAN is using these funds to facilitate a working group of historians, archivists and activists who will research and compile information on significant LGBT movements and leaders within the Society of Friends. The working group has decided to focus on the 50th anniversary of the publication of *Toward a Quaker View of Sex*, a ground-breaking study published by Quakers in the U.K. in 1963. As one of the first studies published by a Christian group with a positive perspective on homosexuality, it had widespread impact in the U.S. as well as the U.K. It is expected that the result of this project will be some form of digital presentation of LGBT Quaker history.

LGBTQ and Faith Exhibit

This is a project of the Stonewall National Museum and Archives (http://www.stonewallnationalmuseum.org/). Its vision/goals are to provide historical context for understanding the past, present and future of the role of religious/spiritual faith in the lives of people who are lesbian, gay, bisexual and transgender, to educate about institutionalized religious policies and practices related to LGBT people and issues, and to highlight the contributions of 10-15 pivotal figures and events to attitudes about the intersection of being LGBT and a person of faith. Based on our discussions with the Stonewall National Museum and Archives, we expect to be able to display their exhibit on our site.

4. Collections Catalog.

The Collections Catalog identifies research collections of original sources from or about LGBT religious organizations and activists. Most, but not all, collections listed in this catalog are held in public archives and are open for research to everyone. Each catalog entry includes a link to the holding repository and, whenever available, a link to the online finding aid created by or for the repository.

This catalog is fully indexed by names, faith traditions, LGBT organizations, geography, and subject headings. Clicking on any index term will generate an alphabetical list of all relevant entries. The free-text search box can be used to

Queers Online

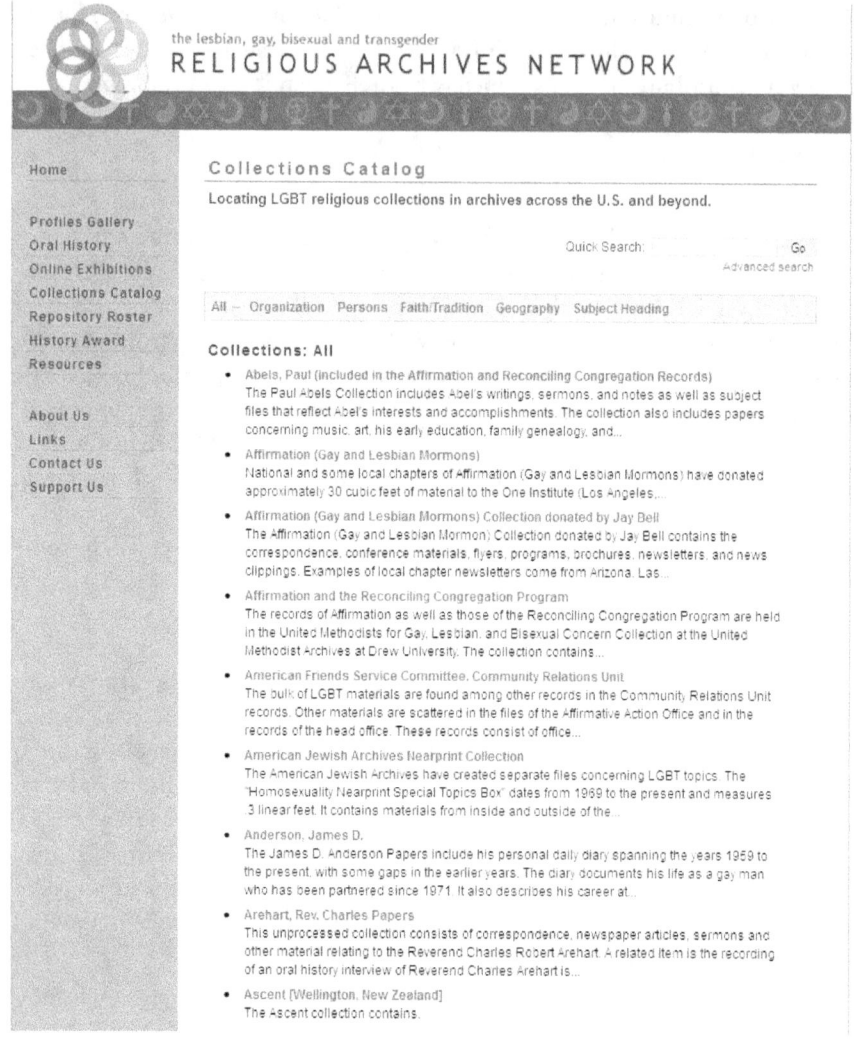

Figure 5: a screen shot from our Collections Catalog.

search across all fields in the catalog record. As of June 2012, 205 collections were listed and indexed. Newest additions include the Dr. Virginia Ramey Mollenkott Collection, the Rev. Tommie Lee Watkins Jr. Papers, Anita Hill Papers, John V. Moore Papers, Harry Hay Papers 1967-2002, the Jim Kepner Collection, the John V. Moore Collection, Diane Weddington Papers, Robert Wheatly Papers 1919-2001, the Robert P. Wheatly Collection, Robert M. Clement Papers, Roy Eddy (Motive) Papers, Insight Magazine, and the Chris Glaser Collection.

Additional Features

1. Repository Roster.

Figure 6: a screen shot from our Repository Roster.

This listing of established archives is provided as a resource for individuals and organizations seeking an appropriate archival "home" for personal papers and organizational records of LGBT religious movements. The list is by no means exhaustive, but includes selected archives that have a strong track record and demonstrated interest in acquiring LGBT religious collections. Prospective donors are welcome to contact any of these archives directly through the Web links provided; additional information on listed repositories is also available from the LGBT-RAN staff.

If anyone works for, or knows of, an archive that should be included in this listing, they can send this to LGBT-RAN. As of July 2012, 25 recommended repositories are listed.

2. LGBT Religious History Award.

In order to promote scholarship in LGBT religious history, the LGBT Religious Archives Network invites submissions for its annual LGBT Religious History Award. To be eligible, papers must demonstrate original research using generally accepted historical methods and must focus on a topic relevant to the study of LGBT religious history. Up to two submissions per author will be accepted in any given year. Both unpublished and published papers are eligible, provided the latter have been published since the previous year.

Papers are welcome from all scholars in the field, including established and junior scholars, independent scholars (those without academic affiliation), and graduate and undergraduate students. All papers will be evaluated according to the same criteria, but if the number of student submissions is sufficient, the jury may consider awarding a separate Student Award for that year's competition.

Recent honorees have included:

2011-12 Co-Honorees. Rebecca L. Davis for her paper, "'My Homosexuality Is Getting Worse Every Day': Norman Vincent Peale, Psychiatry, and the Liberal Protestant Response to Same-Sex Desires in Mid-Twentieth-Century America," and Anthony Petro for his paper, "Protest Religion! ACT UP, Religious Freedom and the Ethics of Sex."

2009-10 Honoree. Shaun Jacob Halper for his paper, "Fashioning a Gay Jewish Identity in Interwar Prague: The Case of Jiří Langer (1894-1944)."

2007-08 Honoree. Dr. Heather Rachelle White for her paper, "From Sin to Sickness: Pastoral Counseling and the Sex Variant, 1946-1963."

2006-07 Honoree. Dr. Kathryn Lofton for her paper, "Queering Fundamentalism: The Case of John Balcom Shaw (1860-1935)."

A record number of papers—fifteen—have been submitted for the 2012-13 LGBT Religious History Award.

Figure 7: a screen shot from our History Award page.

3. Resources.

This page lists information about publications, videos, awards and honors, presentations, and our newsletters by date that may be of interest to LGBT-RAN users.

Queers Online

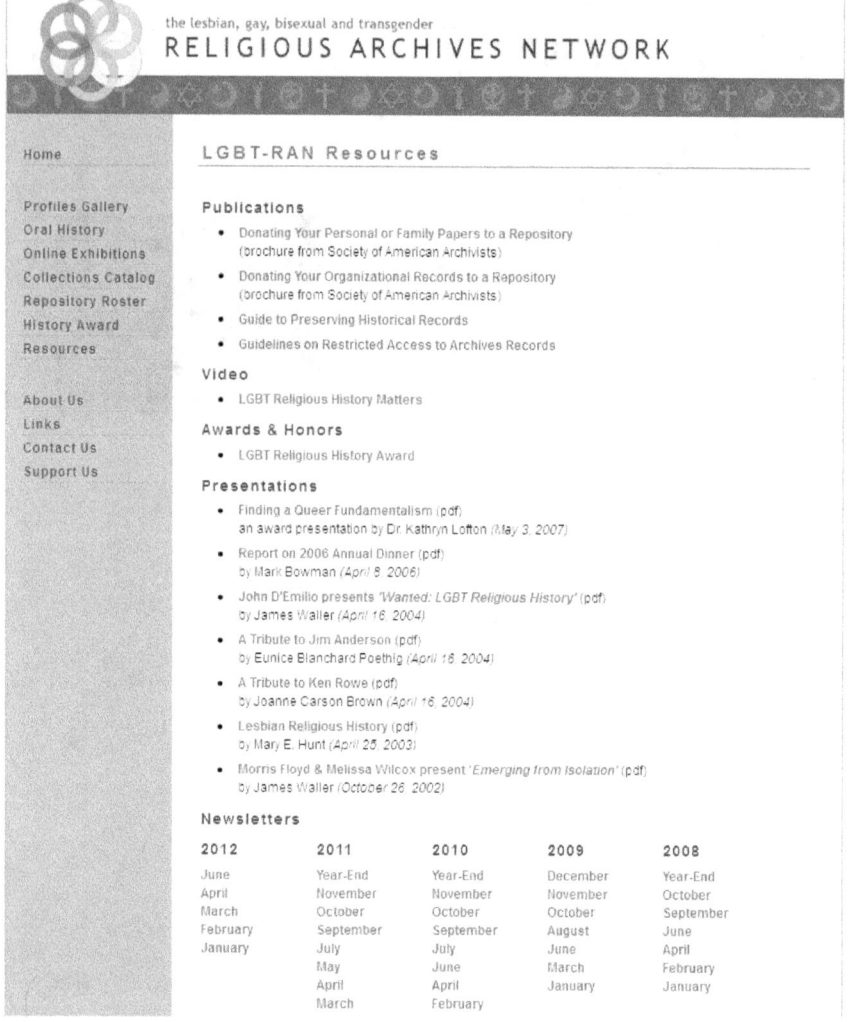

Figure 8: a screen shot from our Resources page.

Marketing

MARK BOWMAN, OUR FOUNDER AND COORDINATOR: Our constituency is miniscule — LGBT, religious & historical. However, since it's small, it's also identifiable — we know who the groups and key leaders are. I have appeared and led workshops at the national gatherings of most of the large LGBT religious groups in the U.S. and even to the European Forum of

LGBT Christian Groups. We have initiated contact with leaders of every LGBT religious group that we have found around the world. We also have been invited to speak to the handful of related professional associations: theological school librarians; LGBT historians; LGBT archivists; and LGBT religious scholars. We are well-known within our very small constituency.

CARL FOOTE, OUR WEB DESIGNER/PROGRAMMER: Our target audience is people who are interested in the very narrow intersection of LGBT, religious and archival issues. Outside of that combination, the subjects are so broad that we generally do not appear near the top of search results. For example, there is such a large and diverse discussion of gays and religion on the internet that a Google search for "gay priests" will not list LGBT-RAN on the first page of search results. A search for "gay religious archive", however, will put LGBT-RAN at the top of the list.

Given limited funds, our online attempts to promote gay religious archives beyond our target audience have been organic in nature. The Profiles Gallery and Exhibitions sections of the website have a significant outreach component. A majority of new visitors to the site (around 60%) arrive because of an interest in a particular activist, and LGBT-RAN ranks high when searching on activist names. A Google search for Janie Spahr, for example, currently lists her profile on the LGBT-RAN website in seventh place.

The online Exhibitions are of interest to those who teach. An exhibit's digitized artifacts have been collected around an LGBT-religious organization or event, with little commentary provided. This makes the exhibitions a valuable resource in the gender, sexuality, religion, history (etc.) classroom — a place where students can go to see the originals, draw their own conclusions, create their own narratives. An ongoing project is to create teaching resources based on the contents of the LGBT-RAN website.

In general, activists (and to a lesser extent organizations) draw more people to the LGBT-RAN website than topics of interest. The most likely reason for this is competition with the ongoing social/political conversation online. The one exception to the rule has been "lesbian nuns" — outside of an erotic context, there has been little information on the web to compete with LGBT-RAN.

Challenges

MARK BOWMAN, OUR FOUNDER AND COORDINATOR: We will always be limited in financial resources so the key to establishing a somewhat comprehensive and accurate historical resources network and website is getting volunteers to assist us in providing historical data. Our challenge is how to invite and motivate people to participate in this historical preservation venture when so much time and energy is still going into combatting injustices that LGBT persons face.

A new initiative was launched in the summer of 2012 to help solidify LGBT-RAN's financial base. Recognizing that the basic cost of growing and maintaining the website is around $50 per day, LGBT-RAN constituents have been invited to provide a gift of that amount and "host" the website for one day. The donor chooses the date on which s/he will host the web site and may designate person(s) to honor or memorialize on that date. This information is posted prominently on the web site (see Figure 1 above).

Some Final Thoughts

We believe that LGBT-RAN is a ground-breaking, unique model of a grassroots historical preservation effort: how a small population was able to use digital technology to spur the preservation of its history. We were among the first, if not the very first, to shape an initiative like this. We always expected that other groups would spring up, taking advantage of our model, such as, say, labor organizers, environmental activists, or Southern fiddlers. There are a large number of small constituent groups that could use this digital resource and information clearinghouse model to preserve their history. Unfortunately we do not know of comparable ventures, outside of oral history projects in some constituencies.

Also, just as the early LGBT political movements were largely anti-religious so the early LGBT historians tended to be anti-religious as well, both discounting the importance and value of LGBT religious activity. We believe this has changed dramatically over the past decade. National LGBT political groups are courting religious groups and individuals to be part of their coalitions. Also LGBT historians and scholars are recognizing that LGBT religious groups and allies played critical roles in initiating and supporting actions for justice for LGBT persons in many locales as well as nationally.

We believe that there is something characteristic of the LGBT movement that lends itself to the LGBT-RAN type of endeavor, a "New York" model in the 1970's (for lack of better words) where a small, interrelated group of activists after Stonewall was able to push a fringe (but culturally important) issue into the national media conversation. With that strong foundation, the AIDS crisis forced the issue of LGBT liberation, as well as AIDS, onto the mainstream's plate.

We have looked around the web for projects similar to LGBT-RAN. The closest we have found so far is Occupy NYC, which has a subgroup concerned about documenting their protests and making their movement's narrative available to academics and historians: again, a small number of people, a national stage and issue.

We continue to hope that other groups will adopt our model and get to work preserving their histories. We are ready and willing to help!

AUTHORS STATEMENT:

James Doig Anderson is professor emeritus of library and information science, Rutgers University; he has served on the LGBT Ran International Advisory Committee since the beginning. **Mark Bowman** is our Coordinator since the beginning in 2001 and is largely responsible for launching this project. **Carl Foote** is our Web Designer/Programmer since the beginning in 2001. He is the one who created our web presence and continues to maintain it.

Section Four

Still Not Totally Out:
Continuing Obstacles to Queer Resource Access

Introduction to Section Four: Still Not Totally Out: Continuing Obstacles to Queer Resource Access

In the twenty first century, people believe that they can find all information through Google or their social media channels. As E-Reading gains popularity, libraries acquire a wide variety of EBook choices for their patrons, including the option for readers to select EBooks themselves from particular platforms. Due to the low cost of popular fiction EBooks, some readers bypass the library completely and help themselves to Amazon Kindle store offerings. Unfortunately, twenty first century readers still ask "Where are the queer books?" or, more precisely, "Where are the *good* queer books?" Twenty first century K-12 students still cannot do effective online research on LGBTIQ topics due to filtering software. Even more insidious are well-meaning library colleagues and publishers who inadvertently sabotage access to LGBTIQ materials in quiet but lethal ways.

In the chapter "Censorship of Online LGBTIQ Content in Libraries", I discuss library practices and laws that affect access to digital LGBTIQ materials for those most in need of those resources. Self-censorship, inappropriate cataloging, failure to promote LGBTIQ materials on library webpages—as well as Internet filtering software—all play a role in turning LGBTIQ information seekers away from the library. At the end of that chapter, I provide recommendations to reverse some of those practices, or to work around them.

In the chapter "The Quest for LGBTIQ EBooks", I address the challenges of LGBTIQ EBook acquisitions, the need for quality LGBTIQ EBooks, and challenges to global LGBTIQ EBook access. While more publishers are providing EBook versions of classic LGBTIQ titles, and authors are giving permission to digitize "classic" LGBTIQ works, these EBooks are not always available in library collections, and LGBTIQ readers often need guidance in how to search for LGBTIQ EBooks. Public, academic, and school librarians have been slow to assess the user needs and format preferences of LGBTIQ patrons, and continue to focus on the acquisition of print LGBTIQ books and access to these materials.

These obstacles to queer resource access remain a global issue. Governments, schools, and libraries restrict access to LGBTIQ content to "protect" their populations, while corporations restrict access to LGBTIQ content to those who can afford to pay for it. Online EBook providers such as Amazon have algorithms that retrieve results which do not reflect LGBTIQ readers' desires, as mainstream publishers do not always promote classic books with LGBTIQ content as LGBTIQ fiction. I bring these issues to the attention of as many librarians and LGBT publishing organizations as I can. I hope that, after reading these chapters, you will join me in my fight.

Censorship of Online LGBTIQ Content in Libraries

Rachel Wexelbaum

Introduction

Historically, librarians in the United States have addressed censorship of LGBTIQ print materials. Most of the time, school and public libraries have chosen to "self-censor". In other words, librarians will either choose not to select LGBT materials, shelve LGBT materials in hidden locations, fail to promote LGBTIQ materials, "hide" LGBT materials during processing and cataloging, or remove LGBTIQ materials from their collections completely. The American Libraries Association does not condone these practices, as they go against the American Libraries Association Bill of Rights.

Unfortunately, librarians working in public libraries and K-12 school media centers in the United States may be more likely to restrict access to LGBTIQ online content. Whether through filtering, inappropriate cataloging practices, failure to promote LGBTIQ resources through the library website, or not selecting particular LGBTIQ EBooks for patron-driven acquisitions systems, people seeking out LGBTIQ information online at their public libraries or school media centers might be denied access. Children and teenagers, people with disabilities, the homeless, and the transgender community are populations most frequently affected by such intentional or accidental online censorship.

While Americans often criticize other countries for implementing laws that restrict all citizens' access to online content addressing LGBTIQ subjects or other content deemed illegal by their governments, Americans feel the need to "protect" children and teens from content they perceive as "inappropriate". Librarians, pressured by the Children's Internet Protection Act (CIPA) and the Children's Online Privacy Protection Rule (COPPA), as well as the desires of concerned parents, are reconsidering "freedom of access" to anything that the community would consider pornographic or sacreligious. At the same time, use of filters to restrict non-pornographic online LGBTIQ content in American libraries is now leading to lawsuits. Librarians who must comply with CIPA and COPPA need more training on how to employ filters without restricting content or online spaces appropriate for minors.

"The Dirty Little Secret"—Most Librarians Are Censors

While library associations around the world express their support for freedom of information, diversity, and social justice issues, public and school librarians still choose not to provide certain materials to their users. In the first national survey of school media specialists, *School Library Journal* discovered that 70% of the librarians surveyed would not buy titles considered controversial out of fear of attacks from parents (Whelan 2009). According to the same survey, the most frequently cited reasons school librarians gave for not purchasing materials for their collections included sexual content (87%), objectionable language (61%), violence (51%), and homosexual themes (47%) (2009). As LGBTIQ books often contain (or are perceived to contain) sexual content and homosexual themes, they are most at risk for librarian censorship (Downey 2013; Whelan 2009). The fear of parental and community censure even causes some librarians not to acquire books that receive awards from American Libraries Association, just because the book may have one objectionable word (Downey 2013; Whelan 2009). This attitude extends to pre-selection of EBook titles for patron-driven acquisitions systems such as Overdrive. A small rural library may have no LGBTIQ content in their Overdrive collection, while the San Francisco Public Library Overdrive collection will have over 1,000 LGBTIQ EBooks in theirs.

It is possible that the way women are raised to conform to particular heteronormative values may influence their attitudes toward freedom of information. An international survey conducted by the Georgia Institute of Technology's College of Computing determined that married women with children under sixteen years old are most likely to support Internet censorship (Depken 2006). While a mother's instinct is to protect their children from harmful influences, which does affect female librarian attitudes toward censorship (Barbakoff and Ferrari 2011), the driving forces behind most female librarian self-censorship are often obedience to authority and fear of how others may perceive them (Downey 2013). These attitudes, sadly, are causing many people to abandon libraries and look elsewhere for LGBTIQ information and support.

Internet Monitoring and Censorship

According to the Global Internet Survey of 2012, only 28% of respondents from the United States strongly agreed with the statement "The Internet should be governed in some form to protect the community from harm", compared with 50% of all respondents from the twenty countries surveyed (Internet Society 2012). In the same survey, only 22% of respondents from the United States strongly agreed with the statement "Censorship should exist in some form on the Internet", compared with 35% of all respondents (2012). While Americans may be less likely than people from other countries to support online monitoring and censorship, the United States federal government passed legislation that threatens freedom of access to any information or online resources perceived as dangerous to our society.

First, Congress passed the Children's Online Privacy Protection Act of 1998 (COPPA) to regulate the ability of children 13 years of age or younger to visit particular websites or provide their personal information on those sites without permission from a parent or guardian (Federal Trade Commission, n.d.). Next, Congress enacted the Children's Internet Protection Act (CIPA) in 2000 in response to concerns regarding children's access to online content perceived as obscene or harmful (Federal Communications Commission 2014). CIPA mandates that all schools and libraries receiving federal funding for Internet access through the E-rate program must block or filter any online content considered "(a) obscene; (b) child pornography; or (c) harmful to minors (for computers that are accessed by minors)" (2014). CIPA also requires that school "Internet safety policies must include monitoring the online activities of minors" (2014). Schools applying for E-rate funding for the first time must demonstrate compliance with CIPA. While the Federal Communications Commission states that "CIPA does not require the tracking of Internet use by minors or adults", in 2001 the federal government passed the USA PATRIOT Act, which empowers the federal government to monitor the online activities of any individuals believed to be a threat to domestic security, or to request that people who observe any suspicious online behavior to contact the authorities.

Net Nanny is the most popular filtering software in the United States (10TopTenReviews, n.d.). It allows administrators to monitor the online activities of anyone logged into a "Net Nanny protected" computer, as well as restrict or deny access to social media sites, blogs, or websites that contain particular keywords or images. Net Nanny can restrict or deny access to websites located through Google searches or visits to specific URLs typed into the browser. The administrator can choose the level of restriction, keywords, and URLs that he or she does not want computer users to see. Net Nanny produces a filtering software for schools and libraries called ContentWatch for Education which has the same features as Net Nanny but is licensed for use in public computer labs, classrooms, or on mobile devices owned by the institution (ContentWatch 2014).

Children and teens who visit libraries to use the computer labs are restricted to using those computers set up with Internet filtering software. This is especially the case for public libraries that serve as the de facto libraries for their local school districts (Barbakoff and Ferrari 2011). Patrons must log into the public access computers with their library barcode and unique password; once logged in the computer will begin to time and record their activity. Adults who use the computer labs in public libraries also have their activity timed and recorded. While public libraries are not required to provide information about the online activities of their patrons to outside authorities, they may keep track of the online activity of patrons accused of viewing pornography on public access computers, or patrons attempting to hack into particular sites. Computer users may or may not know that their computer activity is being monitored, or that filtering software is denying them access to information, unless they have learned about that information from another source. In effect, filtering creates an information and digital divide between students in underserved and affluent school districts, as well as poor individuals without their own devices and wealthy ones with access to their own personal filter-free devices (or the technical skills to hack the filter) (Batch 2014). Filtering may also pose a barrier to those with visual, auditory, and learning disabilities, as filtering software may impact captioning, website layout, availability of images, or speech to text / text to speech functionalities in word processing programs and dictation software (van de Bunt-Kokhuis, Hansson, and Toska 2005).

Public and school libraries without LGBTIQ print collections that program their Internet filters to restrict access to websites and social media sites that include neutral and positive LGBTIQ-related URLs, keywords, images, and social media sites violate the American Libraries Association's Library Bill of Rights, as well as the individual's freedom to read and freedom to seek information. In certain situations, LGBTIQ youth and their parents can sue libraries for blocking educational websites that support LGBTIQ youth. In Tennessee, high school student Andrew Emitt discovered that he could not search for LGBT scholarships in his school computer lab, or websites from well-known LGBT organizations, but he could retrieve websites promoting "reparative therapy" by "ex-gay" ministries. This discovery led Andrew and the high school librarian (who chose to remain anonymous) to contact the American Civil Liberties Union and file a lawsuit against their school district. As all Tennessee public schools use the same filtering software with the same restrictions, the court's decision in favor of Emitt forced all of the school districts in Tennessee to lift the restrictions on all LGBTIQ websites (American Civil Liberties Union of Tennessee 2009). In 2012, Parents and Friends of Lesbians and Gays (PFLAG) filed a lawsuit against the Camdenton R-III School District in western Missouri, where the court declared use of the filter to block out positive LGBTIQ websites as discriminatory and unconstitutional (Volokh 2012).

Students brave enough to speak to librarians and school administrators about their LGBTIQ information needs had support from peers, teachers, and other adults in their communities. In most cases, however, people are still afraid to approach librarians and ask them for help locating LGBTIQ content. Imagine a homeless youth searching online for an LGBTIQ-friendly shelter or community center at their public library and not being able to find such information—would they be willing to out themselves as homeless or LGBTIQ to potentially judgmental library staff? Imagine a transperson trying to locate appropriate medical information or support services at a filtered public library computer terminal—would they feel safe asking library staff for assistance?

The OPAC and Library Website—Censoring LGBTIQ Existence?

Historically, Dewey Decimal and Library of Congress classification systems have frequently ignored, mislabeled, or "misidentified" individuals of diverse sexual orientations and gender identities (Johnson 2010; Roberto 2011). While librarians think that call numbers and subject headings make physical materials easier to find, they prove extremely intimidating for the average person. The online catalog could lead someone inadvertently to "the LGBT section" of the library, simply because the LGBTIQ titles may be in the same call number range. Depending on circumstance, the LGBTIQ titles owned by the library honestly fall in the same subject area, and would naturally receive the same classification, or an administrator may wish to place all materials containing LGBTIQ content—whether fiction or non-fiction, social sciences or biology, drama or law—in one section of the library based on curricular needs or perceived user preferences (CannCasciato 2011). Grouping all LGBTIQ materials together under one call number or one subject heading de-queers the rest of the catalog, and thus the library collection. It is no wonder that some people searching for LGBTIQ information will not browse the stacks or use the OPAC. They would like to use the library, but they may want a page on the library website where they can go anonymously for recommended books or online resources. Sadly, not every school or public library decides to promote recommended LGBTIQ resources through their websites, even if those resources sit on their shelves waiting for readers. This is especially true for young adult LGBTIQ resources. To this day, regardless of whether or not a library has access to LGBTIQ materials, most school and public library websites will rarely make public mention of new LGBTIQ acquisitions or online resources. Sometimes the filtering software will even deny people access to the American Libraries Association's GLBT Round Table webpage and blogs, even though the GLBT Round Table does not review erotica or pornography.

Recommendations

While some librarians will support filtering if that is what they perceive serves the community best (Barbakoff and Ferrari 2011), other librarians see filtering and censorship driving away patrons (Rodriguez 2014). In the case of libraries that censor online LGBTIQ content, this causes people to look elsewhere for LGBTIQ information. By restricting access to online LGBTIQ content, libraries are delivering the insidious message to young people that LGBTIQ people, their histories, their cultures, and their causes are *dangerous and a threat to society that shall not be named.* As more states include sexual orientation and gender identity in their non-discrimination laws, school and public libraries will need to revisit their filtering policies and how they promote LGBTIQ resources through their websites.

Before moving forward with such an endeavor, the librarian should reflect upon their self-censorship practices, and come up with strategies to change those thought processes and behaviors—particularly if these self-censorship habits do not match their personal attitudes toward diversity and social justice (Downey 2013). Next, the librarian should form a committee of library staff, parents, teachers, teens, and community members to assess the existing filtering software. The committee should test their Internet filtering software and record what websites get restricted. If the filter goes so far as to restrict access to interactive, collaborative resources such as Google Drive or online encyclopedia entries about LGBTIQ issues, the committee will need to discuss if the filter is really effective and clearly identify what they want restricted. With community support, the librarian can bring these recommendations to the individual or group in charge of programming the filter. After they make the changes, the committee should test the filtering software again, this time on a computer programmed with software and features for those with disabilities. If the filtering software has an impact on those programs and features, it could violate the Americans with Disabilities Act, and will need to be uninstalled from that computer. Last but not least, the librarian should check their online catalog, EBook collections, and streaming audiovisual collections for LGBTIQ content.

If the content exists, the librarian should investigate how it is being promoted through the library webpages. If there is no mention of these resources as they are acquired, no subject guide, or no mention of such resources during LGBT History Month or Pride Month, the librarian should investigate why that is. If no one on staff has time to develop those online resources, and if the library has a volunteer program, the librarian should ask potentially interested teens or library school students if they would like to help. The librarian and volunteers may want to review the webpages of those libraries that do promote LGBTIQ content to determine whether or not that approach would be appropriate for them. If the community is unreceptive to promotion of LGBTIQ content on the library webpage, create a moderated Facebook, Tumblr, or GoodReads account and provide a link on the appropriate webpage or library social media account. Interested library patrons can join, learn about LGBTIQ library resources, and connect with new friends in the community.

REFERENCES

American Civil Liberties Union of Tennessee. (2009, Jun 4). Tennessee schools end censorship of gay educational web sites after ACLU lawsuit. [Press release]. Retrieved from http://www.aclu-tn.org/release060409.htm

Barbakoff, A. & Ferrari, A. (2011, Mar 25). Filter this. *In the Library with a Lead Pipe.* Retrieved from http://www.inthelibrarywiththeleadpipe.org/2011/filter-this/

Batch, K.R. (2014). *Fencing out knowledge: impacts of the Children's Internet Protection Act 10 years later.* Policy Brief No. 5. Chicago, Illinois: American Libraries Association.

CannCasciato, D. (2011). Ethical considerations in classification practice: a case study using creationism and intelligent design. *Cataloging & Classification Quarterly, 49* (5), 408-427.

ContentWatch. (2014). School web filter—prevent cyberbullying—leading Internet content filter—ContentWatch. Retrieved from https://www.contentwatch.com/solutions/industry/education

Depken, C.A., II. (2006, Sept 4). Who supports Internet censorship? *First Monday, 11* (9). Retrieved from http://firstmonday.org/ojs/index.php/fm/article/view/1390/1308

Downey, J. (2013). Self-censorship in selection of LGBT-themed materials. *Reference & User Services Quarterly, 53* (2), 104-107.

Federal Communications Commission. (2014, Jul 16). Children's Internet Protection Act. Retrieved from http://www.fcc.gov/guides/childrens-internet-protection-act

Federal Trade Commission. (n.d.) Children's Online Privacy Protection Rule ("COPPA"). Retrieved from http://www.ftc.gov/enforcement/rules/rulemaking-regulatory-reform-proceedings/childrens-online-privacy-protection-rule

Johnson, M. (2010). Transgender subject access: history and current practice. *Cataloging & Classification Quarterly, 48* (8), 661-683.

McCarthy, M. (2005). The continuing saga of Internet censorship: the Child Online Protection Act. *Brigham Young University Education and Law Journal, 83*, 83-101.

Moyle, K. (2012). Filtering children's access to the Internet at school. *ICICTE 2012 Proceedings*. Retrieved from http://www.icicte.org/Proceedings2012/Papers/10-3-Moyle.pdf

Roberto, K.R. (2011). Inflexible bodies: metadata for transgender identities. *Journal of Information Ethics, 20* (2), 56-64.

Rodriguez, J. (2014, May 16). San Jose revisits library filtering. *Mercury News*. Retrieved from http://www.mercurynews.com/bay-area-news/ci_25771701/

10TopTenReviews. (2014) Net Nanny parental controls review 2014. Retrieved from http://internet-filter-review.toptenreviews.com/netnanny-review.html

van de Bunt-Kokhuis, S., Hansson, H. & Toska, J.A. (2005). The filter project: about economic and cultural filtering of online content. Paper presented at the EDEN 2005 Annual Conference, Helsinki, Finland. Retrieved from http://www.eurodl.org/materials/contrib/2005/Sylvia_van_de_Bunt_Kokhuis.htm

Volokh, E. (2012, Feb 16). Viewpoint discrimination in K-12 school library filtering. *The Volokh Conspiracy*. [Web log]. Retrieved from http://www.volokh.com/2012/02/16/viewpoint-discrimination-in-k-12-school-library-filtering/

Whelan, D.L. (2009). A dirty little secret. *School Library Journal, 55* (2). 27-30.

The Quest for LGBTIQ EBooks

Rachel Wexelbaum

Introduction

An increasing percentage of LGBTIQ information seekers desire online resources over print. The rise of EBooks—cheap, convenient, and available online—have led a significant number of LGBTIQ readers to abandon libraries and bookstores for Amazon and other online EBook providers. Meanwhile, public, academic, and school librarians have been slow to assess the user needs and format preferences of LGBTIQ patrons, and continue to focus on the acquisition of print LGBTIQ books and access to these materials. While more publishers are providing EBook versions of LGBTIQ titles, and authors are giving permission to digitize "classic" LGBTIQ works, public library EBook collections such as Overdrive, as well as academic EBook collections made available through EBSCOHost, Electronic Book Library (EBL), JSTOR, Project MUSE, and ProQuest ebrary do not include the number of critical LGBTIQ titles that they should. This chapter will address the challenges of LGBTIQ EBook acquisitions, the dire need for quality LGBTIQ EBooks, and challenges to global LGBTIQ EBook access.

Definition of an LGBTIQ Book

In this book chapter, the author defines an LGBTIQ book as one that addresses LGBTIQ populations and issues. An LGBTIQ author most likely writes LGBTIQ books, but this is not always the case. LGBTIQ fiction will have at least one main character that identifies as lesbian, gay, bisexual, transgender, intersex, queer, questioning, gender-nonconforming, gender variant, or gender queer. Most LGBTIQ books, even those published by "mainstream" publishers, are advertised to an LGBTIQ audience. An LGBTIQ book may be print or electronic; the author will specify the book format as needed throughout the chapter.

LGBTIQ Readers in the Age of EBooks

In the 21st century, librarians continue to write about library patrons seeking LGBTIQ information in the stacks to promote LGBTIQ collection development (Garnar 2000; Fikar 2004; Downey 2005; Mathson and Hancks 2006; Lupien 2007; Adler 2010; Schaller 2011; Campbell Naidoo 2013; Chapman 2013; Hughes-Hassell, Overberg, and Harris 2013; GLBT Youth 2014; Yilmaz 2014). Since the Internet and EBooks have become ubiquitous, however, libraries are seeing a decrease in print book circulation (Martell 2008). Younger generations of LGBTIQ readers may be contributing to this statistic, even though national studies have shown that Millennials and Generation Z are the most likely generations to read for leisure, and actually read more books than those of older generations (Pew Internet & American Life Project 2012; Pew Research Center 2013).

Almost no studies exist of LGBTIQ readers or LGBTIQ reading habits in the age of EBooks. In 2011, Michigan LGBT romance writer Jessica Freely conducted an informal Survey Monkey survey of gay romance readers through the Goodreads M/M [male/male] Romance group to determine how and where they look for books (Freely 2013). While she received over 1,500 responses from the group, more than half of these readers identified as heterosexual. This survey, while of interest to writers and publishers of gay romance, does not include any questions about gay romance readers seeking out books from their libraries, nor does it include any questions about where these readers acquire print books. Freely made the assumption that these readers only purchase EBooks from online sources. Freely also did not provide data specific to the LGBTIQ gay romance readers who responded to the survey.

In 2012, librarian Rachel Wexelbaum, with the support of Lambda Literary Foundation (LLF), wanted to find out what type of books today's LGBTIQ readers were reading, how they found out about books, and where they would go to acquire books (Abrams 2013). She created a Survey Monkey survey, which LLF posted on their website and online magazine. Wexelbaum also sent the link to those Facebook groups and listservs for LGBTIQ readers and librarians that she could identify. From these sources, Wexelbaum received 1,213 responses from people ages 18-65+. In response to their sexual orientation and gender identity, 96% chose to identify as lesbian, gay, bisexual, transgender, asexual, or "other"; 1.4% identified as straight, and 2.5% preferred not to answer. As the number of LGBTIQ responses is statistically significant, Wexelbaum will call her survey "the LGBTIQ Reading Habit Survey" in this chapter.

Book Format Preferences of LGBTIQ Readers

Of 1,213 LGBTIQ Reading Habit Survey respondents, 51% stated that they read EBooks for pleasure. Less than four per cent of EBook readers in this survey, however, read EBooks exclusively. The top two reasons given for liking EBooks were "They are inexpensive" and "They are easy to find". Readers were much less likely to respond "They are easy to read" for EBooks, which was their top reason for print book preference. Older generations of readers are more likely to have tablets or EReaders than younger generations (Pew Research Center 2014). This also proved to be the case in the LGBTIQ Reading Habit Survey. Those who owned tablets or EReaders were more likely to read EBooks, but did not necessarily prefer them to print books. Readers of EBooks were also heavy readers of print books.

Genre Preferences of LGBTIQ Readers

When asked how many EBooks they read are LGBT related, 41% responded "less than half" and 28% responded "more than half". Those who indicated that half or less of their EBook leisure reading consisted of LGBT EBooks were prompted to provide reasons for not reading LGBT EBooks. Readers most frequently responded "Quality of LGBT EBooks is not good" (65%) and "I can't find any" (40%). Surprisingly, 60% of the LGBT EBook readers surveyed stated that, when it came to LGBT-specific leisure reading, format availability was not important. For leisure reading in general, nearly 90% of LGBTIQ readers stated that content was more important to them than format.

LGBTIQ readers identified "fiction", "sci-fi and fantasy", and "non-fiction" for their top three choices of leisure reading in both formats. At the same time, LGBTIQ readers identified a wider range of genres that they enjoyed in EBook format over print. LGBTIQ readers were more likely to read mystery, romance, erotica, and porn in EBook format than print.

How LGBTIQ Readers Find Out About Books and EBooks

LGBTIQ readers find out about books and EBooks from different sources. LGBTIQ readers are more likely to find out about print books for leisure readings from friends, either through face to face conversation or social media, while they are more likely to find out about EBooks through websites and online retailers than from people they know. Librarians were more likely to recommend print books for leisure reading (23%) than EBooks (12%).

Where LGBTIQ Readers Acquire Books and EBooks

LGBTIQ EBook readers were most likely to acquire books in both formats from Amazon. The fact that nearly 50% of respondents owned an Amazon Kindle to read EBooks might have influenced readers' EBook purchasing choices. LGBTIQ EBook readers were more likely to visit the library to acquire print books than EBooks, though, especially those in the younger age groups.

Demand for LGBTIQ EBooks

As more readers purchase tablets, EReaders, or SmartPhones, the demand for EBooks in any subject will increase. As youth are coming out and transitioning at earlier ages, and often have mobile devices or access to a laptop or personal computer, they or their parents would appreciate easily accessible LGBTIQ materials. As advances in LGBTIQ civil rights result in changes to our existing legal, educational, health, law enforcement, and religious systems, students and practitioners would also appreciate easily accessible LGBTIQ materials. More colleges and universities are offering LGBTIQ-themed classes or programs; instructors are becoming more sensitive to the financial needs and format preferences of their students, and search for affordable course materials available in electronic format.

The highest demand for LGBTIQ EBooks comes from populations that do not have access to LGBTIQ print materials. People living in places where print books cost more than EBooks, or far away from book stores and libraries, appreciate any online provider of LGBTIQ EBooks. Readers of LGBTIQ EBooks perceive that reading on a device provides a level of safety and privacy which they might not have if they were reading an LGBTIQ print book in public. Even those readers of LGBTIQ content who do not enjoy reading EBooks will fight for the rights of those without safe spaces to have access to LGBTIQ EBooks.

While most LGBTIQ reading habit survey participants indicated that they were not likely to read romance, erotica or porn for pleasure, they were more likely to read these genres in EBook format (Rosman 2012). As of September 2014, more than 90% of the top 100 paid Amazon Kindle gay and lesbian bestsellers fall in the romance or erotica category. The #1 title on the list—*Double Full* by Kindle Alexander—is ranked #158 in the Amazon Best Sellers Rank for Paid Kindle Store EBooks; quite an accomplishment when nearly 2.3 million EBook titles exist in the Kindle store at the time of this writing. *Fingersmith* by Sarah Waters, the only non-genre award-winning fiction title in the top 100 paid Amazon Kindle gay and lesbian bestsellers, ranked at #33 on that list, but #3,566 in the Amazon Best Sellers Rank for Paid Kindle Store EBooks.

LGBTIQ Books, EBooks and Libraries

While an increasing percentage of librarians have embraced EBooks for leisure reading and share them through LibraryThing, GoodReads, and other forms of social media, they continue to write scholarly and professional journal articles about the availability of LGBTIQ *print* books. The number of LGBTIQ fiction and non-fiction titles published annually has steadily increased. LGBTIQ organizations such as the American Libraries Association GLBT Round Table, Lambda Literary Foundation, Polari, and the Publishing Triangle review and promote LGBTIQ fiction and non-fiction, and give annual awards to the best in each genre. These organizations each have Facebook pages and Twitter feeds for librarians to follow. LGBTIQ books are also reviewed in mainstream library review sources such as *Choice, Publishers Weekly,* and *Library Journal.* No self-respecting librarian can feign ignorance as to where to locate LGBTIQ readers' advisories or recommended LGBTIQ titles in any genre. The underrepresentation of LGBTIQ titles in public, academic, and K-12 EBook collections, however, may lead patrons searching for LGBTIQ EBooks to search elsewhere.

Challenges to LGBTIQ EBook acquisitions for libraries

Cost

EBook titles licensed for libraries often cost more than print titles (Besen and Kirby 2012). Libraries with small budgets may not invest as heavily in expensive EBook titles, especially academic libraries whose mission is to develop collections that support general undergraduate curricula and not specialized research. Libraries that have invested in patron-driven or demand-driven acquisitions systems will sometimes put stop-gaps in place to prohibit the automatic purchase of EBooks that cost more than a prescribed amount, or do not meet the collection development criteria of the library.

In non-English speaking countries, libraries will subscribe to EBook collections where translations of titles are provided in that country's language. If the language of that country is spoken only in that nation, the cost of that subscription will increase. For countries that do not have significant native language LGBTIQ publications, the acquisition of translated versions of LGBTIQ EBooks could take a huge bite out of dwindling acquisitions budgets.

Lack of coverage in subscription-based EBook collections

American public libraries often subscribe to the Overdrive EBook collection. As of September 2014, Overdrive includes titles from over 10,000 publishers worldwide (Overdrive, n.d.). In 2012 Overdrive introduced a patron-driven acquisitions service so that patrons could select EBook titles to read which were not included in the original Overdrive collection. Because of this, each public library across the United States will vary widely in their LGBTIQ EBook holdings. Public libraries slow to adopt the patron-driven acquisitions service for their Overdrive collection may turn LGBTIQ EBook readers away, as the original Overdrive EBook collection included no LGBTIQ materials.

Academic library EBook collections may be more likely to have LGBTIQ EBooks than the public library. EBSCOHost, ProQuest ebrary, Electronic Book Library, JSTOR and Project MUSE are slowly improving their LGBTIQ EBook holdings. As of September 2014, EBooks compose more than half of the items in EBSCOHost's LGBT Life with Full Text Database; they are academic non-fiction titles primarily in humanities, social sciences, education, social work, and law. Only twenty five percent of these LGBTIQ EBooks provided in LGBT Life were published in the 21st century, which means that librarians would still need to supplement this collection with other titles. While there are some classic LGBT Studies titles included among the older EBooks, and LGBT Life has focused on diversity, most of the EBooks in this collection are not necessarily considered core resources or examples of great scholarship. Most colleges and universities do not include LGBT Life in their EBSCOHost databases at all as they may not be sure if usage would justify the additional cost.

K-12 school media centers are beginning to invest in EBooks. As of September 2014, EBSCOHost has not added LGBTIQ content to their K-12 EBook collections. The new K-12 EBook-on-demand service, BrainHive, includes only two LGBTIQ EBooks in their selection. This forces children and young adults either to search the stacks of their school libraries for LGBTIQ content (which could put them at risk for bullying) or to abandon their school library to search elsewhere for content that they can read in a private space. Filtering software may also affect K-12 student access to LGBT EBooks.

LGBTIQ authors often seek out independent or self-publishing options for their books (Boyd 2002; Pilkington 2011; Vinjamuri 2012). Historically, LGBTIQ titles from small presses or those that are self-published are less likely to be ordered by libraries than those from large mainstream publishers. Self-published LGBTIQ EBooks, while wildly popular through the Amazon Kindle store, will not appear in EBook collections or patron-driven acquisitions systems designed for libraries.

Lack of electronic version of the title

When new book titles are published, not all authors and publishers put out a print and electronic version at the same time. Older titles also do not always come in an EBook version that libraries could add to their EBook platforms. At one point, these titles were not even available as EBooks through Amazon. In a 2010 study of award winning LGBTIQ fiction and non-fiction titles available in Kindle EBook format, Rachel Wexelbaum (2011) discovered that less than 33% of award-winning LGBTIQ titles were available as Kindle EBooks, and the likelihood of EBook availability decreased with age of the book. Wexelbaum informed the Lambda Literary Foundation about this issue, who communicated with Amazon, publishers, and writers about this problem. Over time, more authors and publishers are working together to re-release Kindle EBook versions of LGBTIQ classics for current and future generations. While some of these EBook titles may also be made available for Overdrive, almost none of them are available for academic EBook platforms.

Access challenges for patrons

Where is the library?

The older someone is, the less likely they are to go to the library to borrow books (Pew Research Center 2013). At the same time, the younger someone is, the less likely they are to know that their library has EBooks (Pew Research Center 2012). This means that older people interested in LGBTIQ books will seek out other sources for such materials, and younger people may consider their library to look for LGBTIQ materials but will not know where to start.

Ignorance of library catalog / discovery tools / search strategies

According to the LGBTIQ reading habit survey, most LGBTIQ readers do not read as many LGBTIQ EBooks as they may like because they either cannot find them or do not perceive them as good quality. If they assume that their library may not have LGBTIQ materials in the first place or are afraid to ask, they will either have to try searching for these EBooks through the library's online catalog or through the search engines of online booksellers. As of September 2014, if someone searching for LGBTIQ books does not know an exact title or author, a keyword search for "gay" in a library catalog may retrieve a multitude of results but will also include books with authors by the name "Gay". An Amazon Kindle store search for "gay" will retrieve gay romance and erotica titles which might not even appear on their gay and lesbian bestseller list. For this reason, it is no wonder that LGBTIQ readers perceive that LGBTIQ books are not as good as "mainstream" books.

Technical challenges

People who wish to read EBooks from their library may face some frustrations in doing so. First, procedures to access and download EBooks from library platforms involve several steps, and differ from device to device (ebrary, n.d.; EBSCO 2014; Farkas 2011; "Transferring an EBSCOhost e-book to an Apple iOS or Google Android device", n.d.). Often people must upload several apps on their tablet or SmartPhone in order to read EBooks from different sources.

To this day, Amazon Kindles will not support EBooks copy-protected using Adobe Digital Editions. Amazon Kindle owners still cannot access academic titles from EBSCOHost, ebrary, EBL, Project MUSE or JSTOR. Kindle Fire tablet owners, however, can upload Blue Fire Reader and access EBook content from those academic library platforms (EBSCO 2014; ebrary, n.d.; Ebook Library 2013).

Last but not least, libraries and EBook aggregators have made little headway in negotiating interlibrary loans for EBooks (Farkas 2011; Vaccaro 2014). Even if libraries within a consortium all subscribe to the same EBook platform, each library has its own contract with the vendor, as well as its own circulation system. In order to access an EBook from an academic library catalog from off campus, a patron must log into the system using their unique user ID and password issued to them by the academic institution. Those not affiliated with the institution will not have access to another library's EBooks.

Even if libraries have patron-driven acquisitions set up to enhance their EBook collections, academic librarians may pre-select content for their patrons to review based on collection development criteria, cost, and curricular needs. In the case of LGBT materials, librarians often self-censor their selections and may select very few LGBT titles or none at all (Downey 2013). Not all academic librarians will select the same range of content in their subject areas, and each library within a consortium will have different EBook holdings. This proves most frustrating for patrons using the all-powerful general discovery tools on their library websites. The discovery tools will retrieve all print books and EBooks within a consortium or library system, but the patron will only be able to access EBooks that their library owns or has permission to access. In the case of LGBTIQ EBooks, this means that patrons may have far less access to LGBTIQ materials through their library systems than they did before the age of EBooks.

Future Research and Recommendations

Public, academic, and school libraries must conduct more user studies of their LGBTIQA patrons in order to determine their LGBTIQ print and EBook needs. It is quite possible that these readers are locating LGBTIQ books elsewhere and not often finding "the good ones". If this is the case, and if libraries put in the effort to select award-winning and well-reviewed LGBTIQ titles, then librarians must promote their LGBTIQ collections as well as patron-driven acquisitions systems through multiple face-to-face and online fora to improve connections with their users. At the same time, librarians, publishers, and writers should meet with Amazon representatives to discuss their algorithms for LGBTIQ book searches, and how they affect reader perceptions of LGBTIQ books as a whole. Last but not least, LGBTIQ readers still want to read print books; conduct careful circulation analyses of these titles and compare to your library's LGBTIQ EBook holdings before weeding!

REFERENCES

Abrams, D. (2013, Feb. 14). Survey underway on LGBT reading habits and book discovery. *Publishing Perspectives*. Retrieved from http://publishingperspectives.com/2013/02/survey-underway-on-lgbt-reading-habits-and-book-discovery/

Adler, M. (2010). Meeting the needs of LGBTIQ library users and their librarians: a study of user satisfaction and LGBTIQ collection development in academic libraries. *Serving LGBTIQ library and archives users: essays on outreach, service, collections and access*. Ed. Ellen Greenblatt. Jefferson, North Carolina: McFarland.

Besen, S.M. & Kirby, S.N. (2012). E-books and libraries: an economic perspective. [PDF file]. A report prepared for the American Library Association. Retrieved from http://www.ala.org/transforminglibraries/sites/ala.org.transforminglibraries/files/content/final%20economic%20report%20sept2012.pdf

Boyd, R. (2002). eBooks 101. *Lambda Book Report*.

Campbell Naidoo, J. (2013). Over the rainbow and under the radar. *Children & Libraries: The Journal of the Association for Library Service to Children, 11* (3), 34-40.

Chapman, E.L. (2013). No more controversial than a gardening display? Provision of LGBT- related fiction to children and young people in U.K. public libraries. *Library Trends, 61* (3), 54-568.

Downey, J. (2005). Public library collection development issues regarding the information needs of GLBT patrons. *Progressive Librarian, 25*, 86-95. Retrieved from http://www.progressivelibrariansguild.org/content/pdf/Braverman2005.pdf

Downey, J. (2013). Self-censorship in selection of LGBT-themed materials. *Reference & User Services Quarterly, 53* (2), 104-107.

ebrary. (n.d.). Downloaded ebrary books can be transferred to a Kindle Fire, then read offline using Bluefire. ebrary Support Center. [Web log]. Retrieved from http://support.ebrary.com/kb/ebrary-books-on-kindle-fire/

Ebook Library. (2013). EBL-News. Retrieved from http://www.eblib.com/?p=news&i=5923

EBSCO. (2014). Downloading eBooks. Retrieved from http://www.ebscohost.com/ebooks/user-experience/downloading-ebooks

Farkas, M. (2011, Jan 18). Ebooks and libraries: a stream of concerns. *Information Wants to be Free.* [Web log]. Retrieved from http://meredith.wolfwater.com/wordpress/2011/01/18/ebooks-and-libraries-a-stream-of-concerns/

Fikar, C.R. (2004). Information needs of gay, lesbian, bisexual, and transgendered health care professionals: results of an Internet survey. *Journal of the Medical Library Association, 92* (1), 56-65. Retrieved from http://www.ncbi.nlm.nih.gov/pmc/articles/PMC314103/

Freely, J. (2013, June 11). Gay romance readers survey: demographics and buying habits. *Friskbiskit.* [Web log]. Retrieved from http://www.friskbiskit.com/2013/06/gay-romance-readers-survey-demographics-and-buying-habits.html

Garnar, M. (2000). ISC 12. Changing times: information destinations of the lesbian, gay, bisexual, and transgender community in Denver, Colorado. *Information for Social Change.* Retrieved from http://www.libr.org/isc/articles/12-Garnar.html

GLBT youth. (2014). Retrieved from https://youthserviceslibrarianship.wikispaces.com/GLBTQ+Youth

Hughes-Hassell, S., Overberg, E. & Harris, S. (2013). Lesbian, gay, bisexual, transgender, and questioning (LGBTQ)-themed literature for teens: are school libraries providing adequate collections? *School Library Research, 16.* Retrieved from http://files.eric.ed.gov/fulltext/EJ1012828.pdf

Lupien, P. (2007). GLBT/Sexual diversity studies students and academic libraries: a study of user perceptions and satisfaction. *Canadian Journal of Information & Library Sciences, 31* (2), 131- 147.

Martell, C. (2008). The absent user: physical use of academic library collections and services continues to decline 1995-2006. *The Journal of Academic Librarianship, 34* (5), 400-407.

Mathson, S. & Hancks, J. (2006). Privacy please? A comparison between self-checkout and book checkout desk circulation rates for LGBT and other books. *Journal of Access Services, 4* (3), 27- 37.

Overdrive. (n.d.) Publisher index. Retrieved from https://www.overdrive.com/publishers

Pew Internet & American Life Project. (2012, Oct. 23). Younger American's reading and library habits. [PDF file.] Retrieved from http://libraries.pewinternet.org/files/legacy-pdf/PIP_YoungerLibraryPatrons.pdf

Pew Research Center. (2014, Jan. 16). E-Reading rises as device ownership jumps. [PDF file]. Retrieved from http://www.pewinternet.org/files/2014/01/PIP_E-reading_011614.pdf

Pew Research Center. (2013, Dec. 11). How Americans value public libraries in their communities. [PDF file]. Retrieved from http://libraries.pewinternet.org/files/legacy-pdf/PIP_Libraries%20in%20communities.pdf

Pew Research Center (2013, June 25). Americans' reading habits over time. Retrieved from http://www.pewresearch.org/2013/06/25/library-readers-book-type/

Pilkington, M. (2011, May 18). LGBT authors at home in digital publishing. Good E-Reader. Retrieved from http://goodereader.com/blog/electronic-readers/lgbt-authors-at-home-in-digital-publishing

Rosman, K. (2012, March 14). Books women read when no one can see the cover. *Wall Street Journal.*
Retrieved on June 18, 2012 from http://online.wsj.com/article/SB10001424052702304450004577279622389208292.html?KEYWORDS=covers

Schaller, S. (2011). Information needs of LGBTQ college students. *Libri: International Journal of Libraries & Information Services, 61* (2), 100-115.

"Transferring an EBSCOhost e-book to an Apple iOS or Google Android device." (n.d.) [PDF file]. Retrieved from http://www.ucumberlands.edu/library/instructiondocs/EBSCOAppleAndroid.pdf

Vaccaro, A. (2014, June 27). Why it's difficult for your library to lend Ebooks. Boston.com. Retrieved from http://www.boston.com/business/technology/2014/06/27/why-difficult-for-your-library-stock-ebooks/rrl464TPxDaYmDnJewOmzH/story.html

Vinjamuri, D. (2012, Aug. 15). Publishing is broken, and we're drowning in indie books—and that's a good thing. Forbes. Retrieved from http://www.forbes.com/sites/davidvinjamuri/2012/08/15/publishing-is-broken-were-drowning-in-indie-books-and-thats-a-good-thing/

Wexelbaum, R. (2011). Maintaining an LGBT studies collection in an academic library. [PowerPoint]. Presented at the 2011 Acquisitions

Institute at Timberline Lodge, Mount Hood, Oregon. Retrieved from http://www.acquisitionsinstitute.org/home/previous-conferences/2011acquisitionsinstitute

Yilmaz, M. (2014). Gay, lesbian, and bisexual themed materials in the public libraries in Turkey. *Libri, 64* (1), 11-27.

Zickuhr, K. & Rainie, L. (2014, Sept. 10). Younger Americans and public libraries. Pew Research Internet Project. Retrieved from http://www.pewinternet.org/2014/09/10/younger-americans-and-public-libraries/

Afterword

Since library school, I have read a lot of books about different aspects of LGBTIQ librarianship. Most were published anthologies of personal or scholarly essays about why queer people become librarians, or the challenges of providing LGBTIQ resources and services to people. I discovered these books on my own, on a mission to discover others like me in the career field I had chosen, who loved LGBTIQ books and history as much as I do.

As time went on, I noticed that LGBTIQ librarians continued to write and edit books about collection development and library services for LGBTIQ populations, but no one was writing books about how the Internet was changing the playing field for people specifically seeking LGBTIQ information. I knew from my own research that different people and institutions created websites, wikis, blogs, and social media fora to promote and exchange information, and that LGBTIQ people around the world were beginning to gain awareness of each other's' stories and histories. I wondered how libraries, archives, and museums were participating in this global conversation. I wondered what they were doing in the Internet age to invite people through their doors and share their treasures.

I wanted to collect book chapters from contributors who are regularly engaged in this work, so I submitted a call for chapter proposals to every LGBTIQ library, archive, museum, and publishing outlet of which I was aware. I also reached out to multiple individuals who I knew were doing work that would fit in this book. I would like to thank those people who took a chance, submitted a proposal, and completed the chapters that people may read for guidance or nostalgia. In *Queers Online*, I also touch on the challenges that libraries face in providing LGBTIQ digital content to their patrons.

Queers Online is my first edited book. All of the contributors to this volume are scholars and practitioners, passionate and incredibly knowledgeable in their fields, who want to share their expertise and experiences with the world. Some were graduate students at the time I put out the call for chapters, some were interns, some were seasoned archivists or academics. Some of the contributors to this volume are new to writing, and for others English is not their first language. In some cases, the contributors risked censure to share the information they did in this book—even if under a pseudonym. All of the contributors have achieved amazing things and I wanted my colleagues to know about them. I worked with all of the contributors to help them meet their goals as well as to answer questions that I know other people in the field would have. They rose to the challenges that I posed, and also shook me from multiple ignorant slumbers.

A traditionally published book, whether in print or electronic format, is neither complete nor current. At best, it will stand as a historical document for our descendants, and will inspire others to write more on new information formats, technologies, and online spaces that impact the entire enterprise of LGBTIQ information gathering and cultural dissemination. The topics covered in the following chapters deserve whole books, and perhaps that will happen one day. There are also topics that are not covered in this book, due to lack of contributions in that area, lack of knowledge, or perhaps because at the beginning of this enterprise those topics did not yet exist! Those topics missing from this volume also deserve whole books of their own, and perhaps that will happen one day. I personally would love to work on a publication specifically focusing on LGBTIQ individuals and social media—please contact me if you are interested in collaborating!

Perhaps you will be the writer or editor of that very next book, or go the next step and create an open online medium for such information. Not only will I wish you all the best in your endeavor, but I will be here for guidance should you need it. I will tell you up front that editing a book or managing a blog or a wiki is not what you think it is, and from beginning to end you will need courage and support.

The editor does not necessarily know everything, which is why he or she puts out a call for contributors for a book in the first place. All the editor has is a vision, the confidence to put it out there, and the courage to see it through to the end. Maybe I was not the most qualified person to edit this book as a first timer, but Library Juice Press Gender & Sexuality series editor Emily Drabinski believed in my vision. If you, dear reader, share my vision to promote LGBTIQ digital initiatives and scholarship, let's network and collaborate to make it happen.

Rachel Wexelbaum
@voxpopulare
Skype: skypelibrarian

Author Bios

James D. Anderson worked as a librarian, professor, and researcher primarily in academic libraries. He began his library career in a small college in Alaska, placed there by the Board of National Missions of the United Presbyterian Church as alternate service as a conscientious objector For much of his library career, he worked at Rutgers University with a focus on information retrieval (IR), design of IR databases, knowledge representation methods, browsable displayed indexes, and terminological thesauri for mapping and managing diverse vocabularies of information seekers. At Rutgers University he was a tireless advocate for lesbian and gay concerns, including equal benefits for domestic partners. In 1991, Rutgers president Francis L. Lawrence presented Anderson with a university public service award "in recognition for…more than a decade of work to educate and encourage your University and the General Assembly, Presbyterian Church (U.S.A.), to accord to Lesbian and Gay people the same rights and responsibilities enjoyed by all other citizens." He was named one of 400 leading activists in the gay and lesbian movement in the U.S. by *The Advocate* in 1984. From 1980 to 1998, he served as the national communications secretary and board member for Presbyterians for Lesbian & Gay Concerns (PLGC) and the editor and publisher of its journal *More Light Update* through 2003. In retirement Anderson continues to teach cataloging and classification online for Rutgers, and tutors 1st graders at a local inner-city elementary school.

Katie Herzog is an artist and Director of the Molesworth Institute in Los Angeles, California. She has worked for Monterey County Free Libraries, the Whittier Public Library, and the Kappe Library at the Southern

California Institute of Architecture, among others. Her most recent work, titled "Transtextuality: SB 48," was exhibited at Night Gallery in Los Angeles in July, 2013. Based on Gerhard Richter's "48 Portraits" (1972) of men of letters whose images were sourced from an encyclopedia, Herzog's painting installation consists of 48 portraits of transgender men and women of letters, painted from images found online.

Laura Uglean Jackson is an Associate Archivist at the American Heritage Center, University of Wyoming, and the University Archivist responsible for the University Archives and Records Management Program. She is also the acquisitions archivist for the AHC's under documented communities collecting area, which includes LGBTIQ organizations in Wyoming. In 2008 she oversaw the creation of the Matthew Shepard Web Archive. Her research interests include how social justice issues in academia are documented and made accessible for research.

Sally Johnson is a project manager and proposal writer specialising in peacebuilding, governance and civil society, with experience in 10 countries in Africa, Southeastern Europe and the Middle East. She accepted IHLIA's challenge of the Open Up! Project because of her affinity with Southeastern Europe, interest in grassroots movements and growth into regional networks, appreciation of LGBTIQ rights and activism, and the application of ICT to expand and amplify the voice. Sally is also a certified teacher of English and offers English language and proofreading services on demand.

Sine Nomine is an MALS student at Empire State College where her studies focus on the digitally preserved and presented public histories of underrepresented populations. She is active in the ALA GLBT-RT Roundtable, where her contributions include an index of the entire run of the newsletter, and reviewing books for the newsletter.

Michel Otten is a freelance communications officer for IHLIA and the Open Up! Project. Michel started his professional writing career with interviewing an elderly gay man about his life, culminating in a book with his life story, photos, and other memorabilia, in 2012.

Kevin Powell is a Texas native with a Bachelor's Degree in history from Texas Tech University and a Masters of Science and Information Studies from The University of Texas School of Information. He currently works in the field of Digital Asset Management.

Lane Rasberry has been a Wikipedian since 2008 (user:bluerasberry). He promotes access to health information—particularly related to HIV/AIDS and other LGBTIQ health concerns—through Wikipedia. He is the Wikipedian in Residence at Consumer Reports, a United States-based non-profit consumer advocacy organization. In addition to Wikipedia, his interests include clinical research, access to science information, public health, and consumer rights.

Rebecka Sheffield is a doctoral candidate in the Faculty of Information at the University of Toronto, and part of the collaborative program at the Mark S. Bohnam Centre for Sexual Diversity Studies. She holds an undergraduate degree in Women's and Gender Studies from the University of Saskatchewan, a post-graduate certificate in Book and Magazine Publishing from the Centre for Creative Communication at Centennial College, and a Master of Information Studies degree from the University of Toronto, where she specialized in archives and records management. Rebecka's research draws from social movement theory and archival studies to explore the development of queer archives as social movement organizations. She is particularly interested in the partnerships that have developed among queer archives, mainstream heritage organizations, and academic institutions, and the implications that these relationships have for queer, activist, and research communities. Rebecka served as guest editor of *Archivaria*'s special section on queer archives and has been published in *Museum Management & Curatorship* and *American Archivist*. She publishes a blog, www.archivalobjects.com, and is a volunteer archivist at the Canadian Lesbian and Gay Archives in Toronto, Ontario.

Jane Sandberg received her MLIS from the University of Illinois at Urbana-Champaign. She currently works at the Burlington Public Library in Burlington, Washington, and is also the webmaster of Trans Web Resources (http://transwebresources.com). She is interested in how marginalized groups transform and are affected by cataloging and IT practices.

Shawn(ta) D. Smith-Cruz is a lesbian separatist, writer, archivist and reference librarian. Her essays blend storytelling with documentation and archiving. She is currently editing a new chapbook series, *Her Saturn Returns: Queer Women of Color Life Transitions,* a compilation of narratives of queer women and color in their Saturn return. Shawn is moderator of Queer Housing Nacional, a queer housing listserv for queer women of color and our allies, and has been a collective member of the Lesbian

Herstory Archives since 2007, and the herstoric WOW Cafe Theater since 2005 where she co-produces Rivers of Honey, a monthly Cabaret highlighting the art of women of color. Shawn is pursuing her MFA in Fiction at Queens College while working as a reference & instruction faculty librarian at the Graduate Center of the City University of New York, where she is the LGBTQ Studies liaison. She is a former Archive Coordinator for StoryCorps and lives in Brooklyn, NY with her partner and co-producer, Jasmine Cruz.

Rachel Wexelbaum is Collection Management Librarian at Saint Cloud State University in Saint Cloud, Minnesota. Rachel is one of the founding members of MnnGAYS, the unofficial LGBT subunit of the Minnesota Library Association. She serves as referee of the GLBT Studies section of *Resources for College Libraries*, and reviews LGBT materials for the Lambda Literary Foundation's (LLF) online magazine: www.lambdaliterary.org. Currently she is conducting an international survey with LLF on 21st century book reading habits of LGBT populations. Her research interests include Wikipedia, LGBT information resources and services, LGBT information seeking behavior, and representation of minority literatures in digital collections.

Graham Willett is Honorary Fellow with the School of Historical and Philosophical Studies at the University of Melbourne in Australia. He is the author of *Living Out Loud*, a history of gay and lesbian activism in Australia, and many other articles and chapters on Australian GLQ history. He has a particular interest in sharing that history with wide audiences through writings, exhibitions, history walks and the like. He has served on the committee of the Australian Lesbian and Gay Archives for almost 20 years.

Steve Wright is a senior lecturer in the Caulfield School of Information Technology, Monash University in Australia. Together with Graham Willett, he is currently compiling an online archive concerning the Australian gay and lesbian movement of the early seventies. His research interests centre on the use and creation of documents in social movements of the twentieth century, and the possibilities and challenges involved in making such documents available to a wider audience through digital archives.

Kate Zieman holds Master's degrees in Information Studies (University of Toronto) and Communication and Culture (York/Ryerson Universities). She currently works as a Senior Media Librarian at the Canadian

Broadcasting Corporation in Toronto, where she conducts research for news, current affairs and arts programming. She became involved with the Canadian Lesbian and Gay Archives in 2006, and over the years she has served as a board member and as an outreach volunteer. She is interested in queer Canadian history and has published articles, interviews and reviews on this subject in *Queeries Magazine* and *Archivaria*.

Index

access
- censorship vs., 207-9
- challenges to, 48-51, 131-33
- classification systems, 209-10
- eBooks, 216-19, 223
- identity terms, 50-51
- obstacles, 46-51, 119-20, 131-32
- physical vs. digital, 1-2, 22-25, 83-84, 88, 132
- policies, 30, 89-90, 125-26
- preservation and, 94, 109, 133-34
- privacy and, 122-26, 132-33, 138-41, 153, 157
- Web 2.0 and, 23-26, 55

acquisition policies
- eBooks and, 220-23
- Lesbian Herstory Archives, 90-91
- Matthew Shepard Collection, 167-68, 175, 177
- Open Up! Project, 152-55

activism
- documenting early queer, 111-13, 128-29, 133-34
- off- and online gay activism, 9-11
- transition from offline to online, 86-89, 99
- Wikipedia and LGTBIQ, 65-67

American Library Association (ALA) Bill of Rights, 205, 208

anonymity
- coming out online, 9-13, 203-4
- copyright laws and, 135-37

digital repositories, 23-25
donors to Lesbian Herstory Archives, 89-90
online spaces, 43-44, 47-48
Second Life, 46

archival practices
- Archive-It (University of Texas San Antonio), 15, 169, 173-75
- Lesbian Herstory Archive, 88, 99-101

archives
- copyright and, 134-37, 151
- defined, 19-20, 168, 176-77
- digital, 22-23, 130-31
- educational purpose, 31-34
- European LGBT materials, 154-57
- marginalized groups in, 21-22
- physical vs. online, 22-25
- purpose, 13
- religious, 189-94
- of websites, 176-78

audio collections
- cataloguing, 102-3, 106-8
- digitization of, 105-9
- religious oral histories, 188-89

book format preferences, 217

cataloguing
- censorship, 205
- identity terms, 50-51
- RDA, 50

236

standards and Herstory Special Collections, 100-101
strategic plans, 102-3
types of materials, 96-98, 103-5

censorship
Children's Internet Protection Act (CIPA), 205
Children's Online Privacy Protection Rule (COPPA), 205, 207
classification systems and, 209-10
internet monitoring and, 207-9
librarians as censors, 206
Net Nanny, 207-8
strategies to end LGBTIQ censorship, 209-11

channels of communication
listservs, 67
queer, 9-10

classification systems
censorship in OPACS, 209-10
identity terms in, 50-51
Library of Congress Subject Headings (LCSH), 50, 100-101, 209

collection development. *See* acquisition policies

content management software, 93
ContentDM, 93-96

copyright
archival projects and, 134-37, 151
Australian Law Reform Commission (ALRC), 135-36
Canadian law, 117-20

digitization of photographs and, 94, 116-18, 121
ethics and, 119-20, 137-39, 155, 157
globalization and, 133-36
Google Books and, 135
international laws, 134-36, 155-57
moral rights and, 119-20

Daughteres of Bilitis, 86, 99

digital spaces. *See* online spaces

digitization
audio, 105-9
cataloguing for, 114-16
challenges of, 113-16, 147
defined, 113-14
intellectual property and, 116-17
ISO guidelines, 115
metadata for, 152
OPAC software, 102
preservation, 13-15, 94, 113-16
privacy and, 122-24
project plan development, 150-52, 158

eBooks
libraries and, 219-21
technical challenges of, 222-23

Gay & Lesbian Alliance Against Defamation (GLAAD), 10, 171

gender identities and information needs
transgender people, 44-46

237

IHLIA. *See* International Homo/Lesbisch Informatiecentrum en Archief

images. *See* photograph collections

information needs defined, 44

International Homo/Lesbisch Informatiecentrum en Archief (IHLIA; International Gay and Lesbian Information Centre and Archive)
  challenges, 160-62
  copyright, 155-57, 161
  digitization project, 150-52, 154-55
  materials selection, 152-54
  purpose, 149-50
  web access, 157-59

Internet Archive
  Archive-It (University of Texas San Antonio), 15, 169
  WayBack Machine, 14

LGBT Religious Archives Network (LGBT-RAN)
  four components, 184-92
  marketing, 196-99
  purpose, 181-84
  religious history award, 194

LGBTIQ
  acronym usage in book, 3
  books defined, 215-16
  information on Wikipedia, 68-70
  libraries' awareness, 229-30
  transition from physical to digital spaces, 10-12

mainstream news media
  gays' portrayal, 165-67, 171

Matthew Shepard Web Archive
  description of, 170-73

Net Nanny, 207-8

Online Public Access Catalogues (OPACs)
  cataloguing practices, 96-99
  censorship and, 209-11
  database management, 96-98
  search features, 191-92

online spaces
  anonymity. *See under* anonymity
  challenges of, 48-51
  coming out and, 11-13, 203-4
  evolution of, 7, 9-12
  importance of, 10-11, 26, 47-48
  marginalized groups and, 24-25
  naming practices in, 49-50
  physical lives and, 11
  preserving, 14-16
  redefining pornography, 25-26
  resource promotion in, 210-11
  transgender use of, 47-49
  transition from physical, 9-11

Outfest Film Festival, 13

Parents and Friends of Lesbians and Gays (PFLAG), 10

PFLAG. *See* Parents and Friends of Lesbians and Gays

photograph collections
    access to, 113-16, 120-22
    Canadian Lesbian and Gay Archives (CLGA), 111-13
    cataloguing, 120-22
    content management software for, 93-96
    copyright and, 117-19
    digitization of, 107, 116-17
    Lesbian Herstory Archive, 92-95
    moral rights, 119-20
    privacy and online, 122-25

physical spaces
    Lesbian Herstory Archive origin, 86-87
    limitations, 46-47
    museums and marginalized groups, 21-22
    online vs., 22-25

Pink Triangle Press, 111-12, 119-21

preservation. *See* digitization

privacy
    mainstream press vs. online archives, 132-33, 138-41
    online spaces and, 47, 157
    visibility vs., 124-26, 153

public histories
    educational purpose, 31-34

repositories. *See* archives

safe spaces
    digitizing archives and, 83-84
    eBooks and, 218-19

Europe and online archives, 149-50
Internet as, 10-12, 24-25
need for, 1

search engines
    limitations regarding LGBT terms, 48-49, 55-57, 221-22

social media
    coming out, 11-12, 203-4

Spanking Central case study, 26-31

Tom of Finland Foundation, 64-66

USA PATRIOT Act, 207

video collections
    digitization, 101, 103
    pornography and archival collections, 25-26
    Spanking Central, 26-30

WayBack Machine, 14. *See also* Internet Archive

Web 2.0
    community spaces, 25-26, 120-22
    creation and exchange of information, 23-25

web directories
    curation, 53-54
    defined, 51
    limitations, 54-55
    transgender, 51-53

websites
    preservation of, 168-70, 173-76

www.ingramcontent.com/pod-product-compliance
Lightning Source LLC
Chambersburg PA
CBHW051355290426
44108CB00015B/2018